T0163588

WAKING UP DEAD

WAKING UP DEAD

A True Story of Suicide, Divine Intervention
and a Life Transformed

EDDIE ANDERS

NASHVILLE

NEW YORK • MELBOURNE • VANCOUVER

companion product for:

WAKING UP
Dead

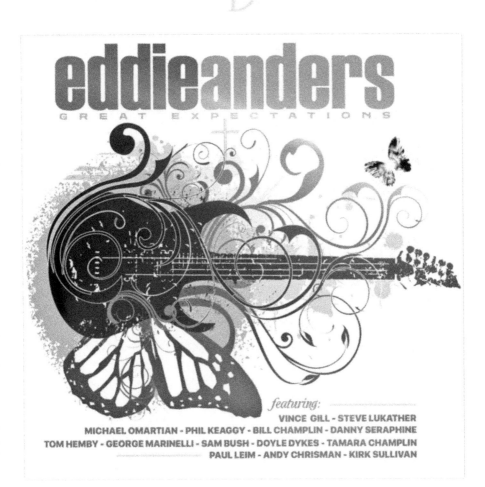

Available on

iTunes   Amazon

or at

www.eddieanders.net

Waking Up Dead

A True Story of Suicide, Divine Intervention and a Life Transformed

© 2017 Eddie Anders

All rights reserved. No portion of this book may be reproduced, stored in a retrieval system, or transmitted in any form or by any means—electronic, mechanical, photocopy, recording, scanning, or other,—except for brief quotations in critical reviews or articles, without the prior written permission of the publisher.

Published in New York, New York, by Morgan James Publishing. Morgan James is a trademark of Morgan James, LLC. www.MorganJamesPublishing.com

The Morgan James Speakers Group can bring authors to your live event. For more information or to book an event visit The Morgan James Speakers Group at www.TheMorganJamesSpeakersGroup.com.

ISBN 9781683501398 paperback
ISBN 9781683501411 eBook
ISBN 9781683501404 hardcover
Library of Congress Control Number: 2016910507

Cover Design by:
Megan Whitney
megan@creativeninjadesigns.com

Interior Design by:
Chris Treccani
www.3dogdesign.net

In an effort to support local communities, raise awareness and funds, Morgan James Publishing donates a percentage of all book sales for the life of each book to Habitat for Humanity Peninsula and Greater Williamsburg.

Get involved today! Visit
www.MorganJamesBuilds.com

CONTENTS

TO THE LOVING MEMORY OF MY PASTOR, MENTOR AND DEAR FRIEND

DON H. POLSTON

He was my father in the faith, yet selfishly, there was far more to our relationship beyond ministry, a fact only realized in full after his passing. As I compose this dedication, I am on a flight bound for home following his Memorial Service in Iowa, once again having the honor of leading worship in the Sanctuary and on the platform we shared together in ministry for years prior to his retirement. A couple of weeks ago, I did the same for his funeral held in Indianapolis.

In all honesty, my heart aches in a way I have never really known before.

Much of what you will read within the pages of this book has to do with my struggles in a lifelong search for somewhere to belong. In recent days an epiphany has transpired, forever altering life going forward. Pastor's precious wife, Ruth Ann, called only days prior to her husband's untimely yet inevitable passing requesting my presence in both services. I was to lead the music and more importantly, look after the *"flow"* of what we all knew would prove to be very powerful times. Her instruction was that I protect the anointing, to go before her, the family and those would attend in their support, and prayerfully set the stage for us remember, rejoice, celebrate, mourn and heal together. Most importantly, to be diligent in honoring our God who has given us the Eternal

Hope and peaceful comfort of knowing we will one day be reunited with Pastor and countless other friends and family.

We need not mourn as those who have no hope.

During these days, the entire Polston family has embraced me with an extraordinary love. Walking thru this precious and holy time together, they have 'shared just how strongly Pastor had expressed his love for me to them over the years. In most amazing ways, they affirmed me as part of their family, bringing a healing to my soul that is challenging to articulate. We had maintained a close relationship for a very long time, yet I presumed this to be normal with a vast array of other people scattered around the globe. One after another, various members of the family would share with me of how Pastor loved me, believed in me and prayed for me as his own. He told me that often enough, but to hear his grandchildren tell me has been more special than I could possibly be able to describe.

The knowledge gained by serving under the leadership of Pastor Polston, I use everyday of my life. He and Ruth Ann have been shining examples of people who are conduits for the anointing and Presence of God. When he prayed, things happened. Pastor not only taught about faith, he was faith personified. Yet, he was never arrogant about it. He loved on my kids, feeding them candy in his office. Ten minutes later he would be leading some prominent community businessman or an Iowa farmer into personal relationship with Jesus.

He always told me how he wished he had come along a bit later or that I had been born a few years sooner. His only regret concerning our relationship was that our lives had not intersected in such a way we could have been yoked together in ministry for a lifetime.

So yep, my heart hurts to know he is no longer at the other end of a phone call, but tonight something in me is complete for the first time, knowing there is a place, a Heritage to which I belong. The choice is not to live in the past or in regret of wishing what could have been, it is bringing that Heritage into the immediate present and distant future, to carry on a legacy entrusted to us.

When I went thru the darkest days of my life, Pastor stood with me. Not behind me or at a distance - right by my side. My failure caused him no embarrassment or apprehension. When others bailed on me by the church-full, he helped love me back to life.

SO THANK YOU DON H. POLSTON – forever my pastor and friend.

I dedicate this book to your memory. I pledge to God to live the balance of my life in a way that will honor the trust you placed in me and reflect the love and Grace of God you so genuinely exemplified over our many years of friendship.

To Ruth Ann and the entire Polston family - I love you dearly.

Thank you for allowing me a place in your circle.

Eddie

Our spiritual history with Eddie and Nancy Anders began many years ago. My husband, Sr. Pastor, Rev. Don H. Polston (now deceased) depended on Eddie to catch the soul of the service, play the right song, and continue in the flow of the Holy Spirit as hundreds came to Christ. We shared a mutual pursuit for God. In the greatest crisis of his life, we never doubted that he would that he would rise again with more zeal and purpose for the furtherance of the Gospel, which he has done.

His transparency revealed in this story is a comfort to us all. God is abundantly able to take us also from our greatest struggles to triumph through Him who has unspeakable love.

Ruth Ann Polston

THOUGHTS FROM THE GULF COAST

by DR. JOHN ROGER BRELAND

My library at home is filled with hundreds of very special and personal books, some signed by famous authors and several are signed by friends who have shared their life stories. I read the New York Times every Sunday and enjoy their bestseller list. The forewords are always interesting to read.

Eddie asked me to write a foreword for his book. While this is not my first foreword, it might be one of my most interesting and challenging, given the storyline contained within the chapters that follow.

Eddie and Nancy were members of TRUTH and traveled with me for several years. Eddie is a musical and people genius. He sings, writes, plays multiple instruments and knows everybody. His walls are lined with pictures of his musical heroes and friends. Since the '70's I have been trying to decide if there is anything he can't do. He's a teacher - servant and friend.

WAKING UP DEAD is a fascinating sequence of events that changed Eddie's life and what he has learned since his rescue and healing. I closely followed those events of his encounter with death. For a season, Eddie forgot who he was and Whose he was. The story you are about to experience will remind you that Jesus is the same yesterday, today and forever. My friend, Bill Gaither, wrote a song I recorded many years ago: *"I LOST IT ALL TO FIND EVERYTHING"*.

I am thankful Eddie at last realized his ALL, his everything, is in Jesus alone.

Enjoy Eddie's journey of WAKING UP DEAD. I'm thankful he has moved – FORWARD.

Eddie, 'glad you're awake.

Dr. John Roger Breland
VICE PRESIDENT / EXECUTIVE DEAN
CENTER FOR THE PERFORMING ARTS
THE UNIVERSITY OF MOBILE
MOBILE, ALABAMA
MAY 2016

THE PRELUDE

OBSERVATIONS FROM THE WEST COAST

by JASON ANDERS

One day, when I was in the eighth grade, my dad picked me up from school in our family van *(painted to look like a giant keyboard)* and casually asked if I would like to travel as a roadie for the summer tour with a band I'd never heard of, Newsong. My friend Andrew was with me, observing this exchange wide-eyed, as I replied without hesitation, *"Sure."* Cut to a few months later, a tour bus is picking me up on the side of the road in Knoxville, Tennessee and I found myself waving goodbye to my family preparing to spend the summer traveling the country with a group of guys I'd never met - and it was the time of my life.

This is the kind of magic my dad has made the norm for me my entire life. He has created countless experiences for our family out of thin air no one else is capable of. Whether it was opening up a puppet shop in the middle of Dollywood or creating a highly successful dinner theater on a hill in Pigeon Forge, he has always possessed a supernatural ability to make the impossible a reality. Nothing has inspired me more than the life of my father. The way he's lived has informed me how to live my life. He's taken so many wonderful creative risks when he could have just settled for the mundane. He taught me the meaning of *"you only live once."*

Well, sort of...
Technically, he's lived twice.

Years ago I was working at Walt Disney World when I received the call from my manager that there was an emergency. My mom was on the phone telling me that my dad was missing. The next couple of days were the longest of my life as the mysterious disappearance of my father led me to believe with each passing minute that he was indeed dead. For all intents and purposes, he was. He had attempted to take his own life by downing a bottle of pills. It wasn't the first time that something like this had happened with him, but it was definitely the grimmest. His absence was palpable.

That my dad survived this suicide attempt, an outcome baffling even his doctors, is a gift he truly deserved. He was given a second chance - much like the one Ebenezer Scrooge received in A Christmas Carol, a role my dad actually played on stage, casting me alongside him as one of the ghosts. It's the kind of happy ending you see in the movies but rarely in real life. I don't know what I would have done had I lost him. Seeing him conscious in the hospital room after his stomach had been pumped was just about the happiest moment of my life. I had already started grieving him and there he was, alive and well. If I didn't believe in miracles before, I did now.

Reading this book has been as much a journey for me as it has for him in writing it. It's a little like watching a behind-the-scenes documentary on your life that's filled with surprises you knew nothing about. Little did I know the struggles that he was enduring when I was a kid, all while begging him to take me to see Batman Returns for the fifth time. I'm so glad that he is still here, still willing to take yet another creative risk in telling his story. It's an important one, because no one reading this is exempt from being beaten down by the cruel nature of this world, a dark jungle filled with real storybook villains who will confiscate your soul if you allow them the access to do so. He knows this better than anyone, and he's here to help navigate you out of the darkness and into the Light.

I believe this book will do what my dad's work has always done; inspire, uplift and challenge people in ways that they never realized they needed. I've spent my whole life witnessing people express their gratitude towards my dad over what he's done for them, through not only his work but in his personal relationships with them. That's his genuine heart and soul. He is a man who loves God, loves his family and loves others. I don't think I've ever known anyone in my life with a bigger heart of gold, stronger love or more passion.

When I grow up, I want to be just like him.

Jason Anders
LOS ANGELES, CALIFORNIA / MAY 2016

CHAPTER 1

6 JULY 2006

FLYING INTO THE GROUND

It had become perfectly routine and predictable for me to be awake at three a.m. No reason for Nancy to be alarmed. I had been on this schedule for years. Since the days of building the Cafe, I rarely slept more than four hours a night, even on a double prescription of Ambien. Day after day I would arrive at my office between four and five a.m., discovering so much more could be achieved in the pre-dawn hours prior to the arrival of the other staff and before the phones began to make intrusive demands on my day.

I loved to be alone and this was the perfect time for solitude. Interruptions were non-existent and appropriate performance for the benefit of others was never required on my part.

Normally I would spend this time in conversation with God, writing lyrics, answering email or listening to and rehearsing new music. It would be sessions of planning worship services and arranging music for the praise team. In spite of the fact my devotional life had remained intact, with time in prayer and reading the Word still a priority, I felt more and more isolated spiritually. Although I believed God had never once abandoned me, there was a strong sense the anointing had lifted from me, that empowering presence of the Holy Spirit. Without question, there was anger and rage boiling deep inside, however, it was well disguised and directed toward myself. Self-accusation became the theme of my daily internal discourse. I continued to compose praise songs, lead worship, and teach hundreds of people the Word of God and it's power to transform lives and provide strength through the darkest of times. For myself, it was as though I had become sealed in a glass tube with the things of God swirling all around me, yet unable to touch any of it for myself. There had developed a significant self-inflicted immunity from grace and healing.

I had desperately prayed for a breakthrough with my emotional detachment and isolation right up until this very morning. And yet, today would be the day I would finally step across the line.

About 4:15 am, I arrived at the office and turned off the security system as usual. Weeks before, I had packed all the items needed for my departure and stored them in the back of my Geo. Books, photos, and various mementos I wanted with me in my last hours were under wraps - needing only to write the last good-bye notes to my family and several staff members who were on my mind.

The notes to those staff members were fairly blunt and to some, outright harsh. Justified or not, this was my parting shot to make a point. I had been deeply hurt, feeling mistreated and dismissed by most of them. Having been declared as too old and irrelevant to be effective in ministry, I would take myself out of the picture permanently and hopefully inflict some well-deserved guilt in the process.

The notes written to my family were from a loving heart and mind, albeit, a very troubled and deeply confused soul that had lost his way. I sincerely believed they would soon be free of the nuisance I had been to them for so long. Nancy, my sweetheart for more than thirty years, had stayed by me through so many changes and hardships. She patiently waited for me to plod through one mid-life crisis after another. She was deserving of so much more. Though I had no idea the person it would be and how it would happen, I sincerely believed God would bring a man into her life, grounded and secure. He would provide a stable environment and sense of normalcy that had become almost non-existent living with me in Crazyville. I presumed to believe her new life would eventually erase any lingering memories of me and all would be made right in her future.

Even in my darkest moments, I was a hopeless romantic who dismissed the pain I was about to inflict on the very one who had loved me most and had devoted her life to me.

I had been convinced for years she simply tolerated me, though nothing could be further from the truth. Nancy had always loved me with an intense allegiance very few men have ever known in a wife and friend. Her love never wavered. If any man had ever been blessed with a true soul mate, I was that guy. How I could ever come to believe anything close to what I did early that morning in July, is simply a testimony to the power of the mind and the deceptive ability of the Prince of Darkness.

I convinced myself once the initial shock had passed, my kids would ultimately be relieved. They would be liberated from the burden of a father who had been a drag for so long, a lifeless weight to everyone who knew me. Everything, everyday, everywhere was misery. As much as I loved my children, I could no longer enjoy anything. In a room-full of laughter, I was the dark brooding chill. Always mourning something, I invariably discharged large portions of sarcasm from a heart alarmingly full of bitterness.

AND THAT WAS ON MY GOOD DAYS.

My daughter Lindsay would no longer worry about her Dad's emotional and mental condition. She would be free in her spirit to enjoy the love, comfort and protection her new husband Cory would provide as they moved on with their life together. My son Jason would learn a great lesson by the debacle of my life, to never be controlled by anyone but God Himself, or allow the joy of his life to be embezzled by those parading as trustworthy friends. Hopefully he would always remember the wolves in sheep's clothing his father had permitted to massacre his joy of life.

I prayed that morning, as I did constantly, Jason and Lindsay would learn from my mistakes. I pleaded with God to heal them of the wounds and distress, even though I knew they would find it hard to ever trust anyone again.

My fault. More guilt.

In those moments alone in my office, prior to driving away for the last time, I solemnly believed I was doing the right thing, cashing in my only option left. I completed my notes, leaving no hint of my destination. In actuality, there remained indecision about where my life's journey would come to its' premature ending. The locations had been narrowed down to Chicago, Minneapolis, Kansas City, or St. Louis, all of which were within a few hours drive from Cedar Falls. Just close enough that I could get there rather quickly and large enough that I would become very difficult, if not impossible, to find.

I left my cell phone on the office desk leaving no chance of being traced via GPS, then double checked my wallet confirming possession of a few hundred dollars cash, tucked away for weeks from a couple of funerals for which I had sung. How appropriate in my mind this was - money earned in performing at another's funeral would help to finance my demise.

No credit cards. No verifiable information given. Nothing traceable.

Certainly, tremendous caution must be employed. The last thing I needed was to be stopped for even the most routine traffic violation. As I turned onto the highway in front of the church, I made my choice.

MINNEAPOLIS. THE CLOSEST MAJOR CITY.

Only four hours away, I would be checked into my final resting place before anyone in Iowa even knew I was missing.

My first appointment of the day was scheduled for 10 am. I left the parking lot around 5 am. The math was in my favor. The streets were suitably free of traffic, as I made my way north through the cover of the early morning darkness. I was insanely paranoid of being detected, but there were no police in sight. Since the moment my morning alarm sounded, I had already consumed four Dramamine tablets. This was to combat the tenacious nausea I felt from the turmoil raging in my stomach. Additionally, the Dramamine would aid to numb any emotional or involuntary outburst of common sense that might deter me from following through with the task at hand.

I TURNED ON THE RADIO, THINKING ONLY OF THE NEXT STEPS.

There was no turning back now.

With every mile, it became easier. I lost track of time and even where I was. At some point, the sun had come up without me even being aware of it. Nearing the state line, I took a couple more Dramamine. I did not feel sleepy, just relaxed and undaunted. The dull whir of road noise beneath the Geo was almost itself like a tranquilizing sedative. At one point, I caught a glimpse of my own eyes in the rearview mirror. I quickly adjusted it so that would not happen again.

Without really remembering the miles behind me, I suddenly became aware of the southern suburbs of Minneapolis. The morning commute was still fairly heavy, especially compared to the local traffic encountered on the streets of Cedar Falls. I studied the unlimited array of signs, fuel stations, restaurants, hotels and shopping centers. Should I treat myself to breakfast? What part of town did I want to land in? Which hotel would accept cash without any form of identity verification? I must remain inconspicuous and undiscovered until they find my lifeless body. I remained fixated on the task. Choices I would make in the minutes ahead would be essential to my success. Every precaution had to be taken to insure that by the time anyone located me - it would be too late for rescue. Recovery of my vacated body would be the only option.

Spotting the first signs to the airport induced a stroke of genius. I would park the car deep within the recesses of the Minneapolis airport parking garages, hike to the baggage claim area, and catch a hotel shuttle to the inn of my choice. The odds were greatly stacked against anyone finding my diminutive white Geo in these mammoth parking buildings. Even if they did, there would be no trace of where I went from there.

PERFECT.

Selecting the most remote space available, I grabbed my bags and initiated a jittery walk to the terminal, following signage that seemed grimly appropriate to follow: THIS WAY TO TERMINAL.

I was consumed in the moment.

Arriving at baggage claim - there stood the bank of phones with direct connections to hotels around the Twin Cities. Which one to choose? This would be my final life choice so let's make it a good one. My selection was the Hampton Inn. I wanted to quietly pass from life in comfort, but accommodations had to remain within my limited cash budget. My intention was to pay for two nights in advance therefore insuring authorities would not find me in time for a rescue. There must remain nothing of life left to revive.

Now engaged in conversation with the Hampton Inn staff member, I became cognizant of the profusion of security cameras focused on the exact spot I was standing. My every move was now being chronicled in one of the most secure areas in all of Minneapolis.

Good Grief!

Assailed by convulsive paranoia, I hung up the phone, picked up my bags, and raced in the direction of my previously abandoned Geo, desperate to locate it quickly! The problem, I had made no mental record of its' location, never expecting to drive my little clown car again.

Overweight, out of shape and devoid of sufficient breath, sweating profusely and my heart racing for fear of detection, I finally found the Geo. I hopped in, pulling out of the space into which I had backed, snugly hidden between two very large pick-up trucks. Now shaken from my misstep, I looked to find my way out of the parking garage. Navigating through several floors, I managed to run over two different very substantial curbs, one nearly rendering the car immovable. Finally able to bounce the Geo free of the concrete island, my nerves were being lacerated by manic hysteria. Surely, airport security would notice this bizarre behavior of a sweat-drenched baby boomer erratically curb-surfing their building in a miniature car!

Good Grief!

In retrospect, this scene has actually become quite comical. I can just imagine the angels assigned to watch over me at this point saying, *"Of all the people in all the world, why did we have to be assigned to a nut-case driving a Geo? Who drives a Geo?"*

With only minimal damage and still undiscovered, I emerged into the bright sunlight, paid my minimum nine-dollar fee for a mere thirty minutes in long term parking and made my way back onto the expressway. Once again safely immersed in the flow of traffic, I motored north for a while, not looking to the left or the right but focused straight ahead, taking long and very deliberate deep breaths.

I WAS SAFELY ON TRACK, YET AGAIN.

Soon on the Northwest side of Minneapolis, just off the freeway, my goal was in sight. The Hampton Inn. Finally. I wondered if this could be the same hotel I had momentarily connected with at the airport? Pulling into a parking space, I sat quietly in the car for a moment. Closing my eyes, I absorbed the silence. There seemed to be nothing creating hesitation. No voices of any kind swirled in my head. No sense of guilt, anxiety or fear. Just silence. I could almost hear the blood rippling through the veins in my neck.

Walking into the lobby of the hotel, I was again aware of nettlesome security cameras. I did my best to get through this undertaking without appearing anxious. Everything must remain blandly ordinary. I have no memory of the desk clerk's face, making a concentrated effort to avoid eye contact. The question of the moment was how could I possibly check in by paying cash and without giving credit card information? Any traceable transaction was an option.

My registered name for the day was Doug Edwards, requesting a room for two nights and placing three one hundred bills on the counter. She asked for a credit card to cover incidental charges. My reply, *"I do not own one"*. My cover story was being in town scouting a place to live for permanent relocation to the Twin Cities area. The clerk graciously put the hotel as my home address.

ANOTHER CRISIS AVOIDED.

To my delight, the room was on the very end of the second floor, adjacent to the stairwell. Entering what I thought would be my final temporary residence I immediately thought how much Nancy would love this room. Warm decor, a sparkling clean bathroom and a cozy, comfortable queen size bed with big fluffy pillows. It was then I felt brutally alone. Tears welled up in my eyes. For more than thirty years, she had always been with me. We had shared every part of life together. Even on rare occasions when I had to travel without her, I called Nancy along every step of the way, to hear her voice and to let her know all was well.

NOT THIS TIME.

I took out the various photos of Nancy and the kids, notes, my Bible, and the two bottles of Ambien, carefully placing them on the table next to the bed. Attempting to think thru all the ways I could possibly fail at this attempt or be discovered too soon, my computer suddenly became a glaring issue. It could somehow be a tool in finding me, especially if I happened to go online once the Ambien kicked in. There are files full of cases where people have done innumerable crazy things they are entirely unaware of, after consuming Ambien.

Loading up the Mac, I jumped back in the Geo and drove about ten minutes away. Pulling

into an office park, I located a large dumpster in the back of the complex. It was quiet with very little traffic, I imagine due to the holiday week. Taking the computer from its' protective bag, I got outside and began the process of beating my MacBook Pro into splinters. Once again I got teary-eyed and very emotional. This was the beginning of the end. My Mac had been somewhat of a close friend. I was the only staff member at the church not using a PC, so in a characteristic way of thinking, I was destroying a symbol of my non-conformity. My iTUNES library, representing so much of what I had loved about life, was being systematically exterminated.

The Disney logo on the protective cover, a reminder of creative inspiration, innocence, career dreams and childlike joy, would now be destroyed as well. The massive digital photo album containing documentation of my career, ministry and most of all, the people who had been hurt because of my misjudgment and failure, were systematically disconnected from me. The suicide had begun. I tossed the fragmented remains of my Mac into the dumpster, soon to be buried in some landfill.

I knew I was next.

Now it was time for the last meal, certainly a cheeseburger was in order. Climbing back into the Geo, I decided to park some distance from the hotel, this way, should the car be spotted, it would not immediately disclose my location. Driving thru a newly opened dining and entertainment district, the local multiplex cinema advertised the new PIRATES OF THE CARIBBEAN movie, set to open on three screens at midnight that very evening. The presence of the Disney logo prominent in every direction opened the floodgate of memories with Nancy and the kids. For a moment, acute hesitancy surged thru me triggering a torrent of tears. The reality of never seeing my precious kids again or hanging with them at Disney, which had been our long family tradition, nearly revoked my self-execution.

After a few minutes, I dried my eyes and reengaged my focused resolve.

Somehow, I sincerely believed their life without me would prove to be far more beneficial. I carried on, selecting a restaurant very similar to Applebees. I don't remember the name of the place, but as always, it reminded of the Cafe. The plan was to enjoy the meal and then throwback a couple of very strong alcoholic beverages, knowing from my study this would significantly increase the potency of the drug overdose yet to come. Having never consumed alcohol, I knew it would have even a greater effect in my case. Sitting at the bar, I placed my order for a cheeseburger and fries, sipping on a Coke while watching ESPN on multiple flat-screen televisions. I made the impulsive decision to dispense with the alcohol consumption, assured the Ambien would be more than adequate to render me lifeless. Asking the attending server to change my order for take-out, I headed back to the hotel.

I left her a twenty-dollar tip.

Back outside, the afternoon temperature was wickedly hot, so rather than walking back, I decided parking the Geo at the hotel would not be that much of a problem. Let's face it - even if the decision would be made to search for me in Minneapolis, it would take days to find me. With no air conditioning in the car, I was soon soaking wet from my drive back to the Hampton Inn. I parked behind the building and took the back steps up to the room, avoiding any further encounters at the front desk.

Since my childhood, cheeseburgers had been my favorite food. I spread out my final meal on the queen-sized bed and pulled up a chair. A movie about United Flight 93, one of the planes involved in the attack on September 11, was on television. Watching the recounting of the events transpiring on that day, it reminded me of being in bed at home recovering from major surgery when the actual attacks had occurred. Nancy and I had watched together from our home in Louisiana as she was attending to my post-surgical recovery. She had faithfully and lovingly prepared meals just the way I liked them, watched over the proper schedule for my medications, and remained a close constant comfort thru the entire process.

As I watched the movie, I thought how she would never have to fret over me again.

Finishing the meal, I opened the first bottle of Ambien, a count of one hundred, and by the handfuls, washed them down, along with several more Dramamine, Lunesta, Phenegren and Zoloft. It was my hope the meal, along with the anti-nausea meds, would prevent it all from coming back up, thus thwarting my suicide attempt.

On that Thursday summer afternoon in July, while family and friends tearfully interceded on my behalf for a miracle, I flopped onto the bed, mindlessly staring at the television.

The last thing I remember was watching United Flight 93 fly into the ground.

CHAPTER 2

Waking up Dead

ALL BECAUSE OF JESUS I'M ALIVE

For the first few seconds, I had absolutely no idea as to who or where I was. My initial memory is of sitting on the floor, leaning against the wall and without any movement of my head, looking forward to see a blurry CNN logo on the television. Apparently, I had engaged in a bit of channel surfing amid those dark forgotten hours, consistent with my stellar reputation as a remote control wizard.

Sitting listless and staring at the side of the bed, I remember thinking: *"How am I still alive?"*

With a certainty gained from my exhaustive research of suicide, there was no question my kidneys and liver had suffered fatal damage and my heart was now destined to fail. Lifting my unsteady head and glancing back toward the television, I vaguely recall seeing the words Saturday morning. There is no way I should still be breathing.

IMPOSSIBLE.

In this pivotal moment, I did not choose to the right thing. There was no thanking God for survival. No repentance or remorse for the pain I was putting my family through at that very minute back in Iowa.

Instead, my singular thought was, *"I have to finish this".*

The memory of this resembles some sort of milky slow-motion hallucination that plays in my head when I close my eyes. Still sitting on the floor, I began to pick up Ambien spilled from the other bottle and scattered on the floor next to me - swallowing them one by one. Unquestionably, five or six more of the high-powered sedatives disappeared down the throat. After that - I remember little else and remain oblivious as to the time or duration of events. I only knew from the television it was Saturday.

In Cedar Falls, friends and family had been at our home around the clock since late morning Thursday, hoping and praying for a phone call from me, attempting to comfort Nancy and Lindsay. Multiple cell phones had been in constant use notifying everyone they could think of as to the situation. Across the country, friends and family were on the look out, attempting to determine where I might have journeyed. Several thought Disney World could be my destination. In East Tennessee, helicopters were employed to search for the white Geo. State and national parks were alerted as well as local authorities along the Cedar River and the nearby lakes in Black Hawk County. They looked at all my favorite places.

Even so, not a crumb of a clue existed as to where I might be. My bid to leave a very cold trail had met with great success. Remember, I left my cell phone in the church office and had mercilessly pulverized my computer. Friends in law enforcement, including the FBI, had been doing everything possible to unearth even a meager hint as to where I might be.

I COULD BE ANYWHERE, WITH NO VIABLE REASON FOR ANYONE TO LOOK FOR ME IN MINNEAPOLIS.

As the sun rose on Saturday morning, Nancy's hopes began to slowly wilt away. She continued to pray the angels were watching over me, yet reality was beginning to set in that I had succeeded in ending my life. Critical to that conclusion, this marked the first time in more than thirty years of marriage we had gone this long without contact. No phone call to let her know I was safe, or, when I would be home.

As the Clergy arrived on the scene, they began conversation with Nancy about the looming memorial service she faced once my body was finally located. Who would she want them to involve and how should they proceed in preparation? Keep in mind, since the discovery of my disappearance on Thursday, absolutely no prayer had yet been offered in person by the Senior Pastor with my wife, family and friends. This fact did not go unnoticed by the multitude gathered at our home.

Phones were ringing constantly with well - wishes, offerings of prayer, and volunteers for the search. Not really being up to answering all the questions from the well meaning and curious, friends had been answering her phone.

10:30 a.m. exactly as Nancy's phone rang and this time, for some reason, she answered it.

Her vanished delinquent husband was finally calling home. She screamed my name resulting in a mad scramble for three-dozen phones to pass the word I was alive and talking to Nancy! The sleep deprived and mournful group of friends who had been on the verge of accepting the worst-case scenario as imminent, were suddenly hysterical with newfound hope.

As the jubilation of this news overtook our home, poured into the front yard and neighborhood, then spread quickly across the county and country by phone, texts and emails, the immediate reaction of the Clergy became somewhat of a stunning development.

In the midst of this euphoric celebration, the senior pastor was overheard by several on the scene to be snarling in angry tones: "That little s---, he's alive". With great disgust and a flurry of enraged door slamming, the now unhinged ministerial delegation loaded into their vehicle, and scampered frantically back to the church boardroom to reexamine their existing plan of action, calling an emergency meeting of the Elders.

THE NEWS OF MY SURVIVAL HAD NOW THROWN A SIZEABLE WRENCH AT THE MONKEY.

Meanwhile, in the instant I uttered Minneapolis, multiple friends were calling to notify Metro law enforcement. Within minutes of the call, Nancy and Lindsay, along with several of our best friends were en route for a very long four hours north. What would they find? What would be my condition? At the moment, the best news was at very least I was alive and on my way to the hospital to be cared for.

Jason was in route from Orlando to Cedar Rapids, which included a scheduled stop in Minneapolis. The airline was notified of the situation and Delta representatives met him as he exited the plane upon arrival in the Twin Cities. He would be picked up at baggage claim by a couple of our friends who were making the trip in support of my rescue.

OUR FAMILY WOULD SOON BE REUNITED.

The only cognizant memory of the call home was hearing Nancy say my name. No awareness remains of dialing the hotel phone or the forty-five minutes of mumbling obscure conversation I had with her and Lindsay as they attempted to determine my exact location.

Beyond that, only snapshots of time and fragments of memory remain of Saturday morning:

- The police arriving at the door of my hotel room and the sight of the badges of two officers thru the *"peep hole"*. I have no grasp of faces, conversations or sequence of events.

- The sound of sirens and the sensation of being constrained within the back of a moving ambulance. I do remember looking down the length of my body and seeing something like a bag into which I had been secured.

- Looking into a very large white cup of vividly black liquid and someone yelling at me: "You have to drink it all, do not stop until the entire contents are gone."

'Turns out, that was the charcoal treatment applied in the emergency room. TO THIS DAY, NOTHING ELSE HAS SURFACED IN MY MEMORY OF THE MAJORITY OF THAT SATURDAY MORNING AND EARLY AFTERNOON.

Sometime mid-afternoon, I opened my eyes to see my son Jason standing at the foot of the hospital bed, along with friends from Cedar Falls, Dave Grimm and Jerry Swangel. I was now the latest admission to North Memorial Hospitals' population of attempted suicides, waiting to be seen by the resident psychiatrist. In a semi-private room, the guy next to me had attempted to suffocate himself with a plastic bag. Between us hung a plastic privacy curtain and the perpetual presence of a rather intimidating nurse, never more than arms length away.

Then Jason delivered those insightful opening words addressing his charcoal-faced father; *"Dad, what the hell were you thinking?"* A scholarly enlightened question followed by a lingering affectionate embrace. We have since shared laughter over that reunion quite often.

The expectation of the medical team was that an aggregation of physical complications was unavoidable, given the extreme lethal nature of the attempt I had made on my own life. I consumed almost ten times more Ambien than what is considered lethal, in addition to a potent cocktail of other meds. Emergency room personnel would later tell me they had never seen such a virulent attempt at suicide fail.

IN THEIR PROFESSIONAL OPINION, THE ONLY EXPLANATION FOR MY SURVIVAL WAS A BONA-FIDE MIRACLE OF DIVINE INTERVENTION.

I should have been found dead by the housekeeping crew, lying on the floor of the Hampton Inn, just as I had planned. However, I was not yet in any mood for celebration, brutally miserable and breathlessly anxious about what would happen now. I could not yet appreciate the supernatural intervention on my behalf.

Just after four p.m. Saturday afternoon, Nancy walked into the room, followed by Lindsay and our good friends, Dalen and Cathy. Though an enormous comfort to see them, I was more consumed by how I had once again failed them. It was impossible to look into their eyes without a deep sense of guilt. No one has ever known a sweeter, more faithful, loving and loyal wife than I have, and yet I had just put her through hours of harrowing terror and heartache.

True to form, the first thing she did was lavish me with hugs and kisses. The truth of the matter, she literally laid on top of me in the bed. No anger. Not a hint of *"how could you?"* Just pure love and sweet relief I was alive. Soon after, she proceeded to clean the residual charcoal from my face with a warm washcloth. Nothing ever felt more comforting than when Nancy had taken care of me in times of need. This was no exception. However, with a potent array of wires and tubes attached to my body, surrounded by a room full of family and friends all intently staring at me in some sort of stunned, not knowing what to say look in their eyes - I could hardly breathe.

IF I HAD EVER WANTED TO BE THE CENTER OF ATTENTION, THIS SCENARIO WOULD NOT HAVE BEEN WHAT I HAD IN MIND.

There was a sense of relief and fear at the same time. I was alive and awake, but what would life be like from here? Would my wife and kids ever trust me again? Even worse, would they resent or hate me for the pain I had put them through? I hate to admit it, but the preoccupation with self continued even in those moments of being reunited with those most precious and significant people on earth to me.

Physically, blistering headaches persisted, along with a tenacious sense of abject misery. Bloated, weak and exhausted - yet unable to sleep. God knows I had just gone through a fairly strong season of sleep over the last couple of days. Being incredibly overweight and out of shape intensified the discomfort. There would be no relaxation on a hospital bed that felt as if I was lying on a car hood with a cheap sheet stretched over it and a football for a pillow.

I remained in a cloudy funk that Saturday evening, yet was more than aware of the constant surveillance by the nurses, most of whom seemed to resent having to work over the weekend. That was gratifying, especially when they had to follow me into the bathroom. I was utterly tormented by the predicament and guilt ridden, insofar as I was the stooge who had put us all in this very bizarre and distressing moment.

Welcome to Eddie's Twilight Zone.

There were tender moments when Lindsay would hold my hand. Without a word, we would look at each other, both of us wishing we were in another time and place in our lives together. She was broken-hearted to see me like this, and I felt like the worst father who had ever lived. It was easy to see the arduous emotions running deep in Jason, trying to somehow make sense of what his Dad had done. They deserved far better than this. How could a man blessed with this kind of family and friends be so emphatically unzipped? Self-reprehension was pegging the meter as I had now successfully entangled myself in a web from which there appeared to be no escape.

IN MY MIND, I HAD NOW BECOME THE *"IN LIVING-COLOR POSTER CHILD"* FOR THE WACKY RELIGIOUS DYSFUNCTIONAL SERVANT OF GOD WHO HAD PREACHED ONE THING AND LIVED ANOTHER.

The thought kept running through my mind, if God was truly merciful - my heart, kidneys and liver would fail in the night and by sunrise Sunday morning, there would finally be freedom from the albatross I had become to everyone who remotely knew me. I closed my eyes and began to trace the paths I had taken to arrive at this ghastly place in time. I kept hoping this was some kind of junked-up dream brought on by the overdose, but the infernal nightmare was all too real. I grappled with embarrassment and guilt, overwrought with emotion and thoroughly numb. The weight of my situation pressed hard against my chest and head, as I endlessly rehearsed the details of my self-inflicted misery. Shallow breathing accompanied my anxious need to escape.

I FELT HORRIBLE AND LOOKED WORSE.

Watching my family and friends rotate thru the room in various small visitation groups, I quietly wondered how any of them could ever trust me again. What was going on in their heads as they sat there gazing at me? Extended durations of excruciating silence ensued due to the fact no one had a clue what to say. Taking your best shot at suicide has a way of sucking all the air right out of room. We were all wrestling with the awkwardness of the moment as best we could, while I remained frustrated at the lingering effects of the charcoal treatment, giving the appearance I was in recovery from addiction to Oreo cookies.

The rule for psych patients like myself was for all visitors to leave by ten p.m. That was not a bad thing for Nancy and the kids given the string of sleepless nights they had endured. About the time for them to leave for the hotel, I seemed to be more fully awake and present. With just the four of us now remaining, we indulged in prolonged embraces and loving kisses, as my wearied soul mate and our kids said a thankful goodnight and headed for the elevators. My prayers were for a safe, deep and restful sleep for each of them.

Meanwhile, my world of confinement spun up into full nocturnal torment, mumbling to myself and spitting up charcoal. My entire back wrenched into spasms generated by the devastating combination of anxious foreboding and the torturous mattress of Hades!

If that wasn't bad enough, the resentment of the night shift kicked into high gear. I overheard why everyone seemed to be in such a *"pleasant"* mood. A shortage of nurses resulting from labor disputes with hospital management, led to the need for people to work extra shifts against their will. We are talking threats of major walkouts and an environment of hostility directed toward everything related to the Metro health care system.

We had one thing in common, none of us wanted to be there.

Try having a needle in your arm attended to by a disgruntled nurse who had planned to be at the casino all weekend, now stuck baby-sitting a guy who tried to kill himself. I knew from the moment she walked into the room just after eleven o'clock, this was destined to be a night to remember. Let's put it this way, this particular staff of nurses scored very low on the compassion portion of their final exam. This seemed to be the longest single night of my life.

IT WAS PURE TORMENT. I wish I could tell you I devoted the night to prayer and Bible study, but that is far from what transpired. The realities of the mess I had created viciously haunted me. My only avenue of escape was the television, but any hope of pre-occupying my mind with I Love Lucy and Mayberry, seemed unconditionally futile.

Well into the night and in a sort of an *"Oh, by the way"* kind of vibe, the most recent attending nurse looked up from her studious attention to a crossword puzzle and gleefully broke the news: *"Since you were admitted to the hospital on Saturday afternoon, the mandatory suicide watch will actually begin on Monday morning. Darlin', you might as well relax, you're gonna be here for a while."*

This meant an unavoidable extended stay in Pleasantville until at least Wednesday afternoon.

In addition, Monday afternoon would bring the joy of being relocated to the second floor, a multiple-bed dormitory unit where family or visitors of any kind were not permitted. I would be required to attend group discussions involving other patients having attempted suicide. This was the initial stage of therapy required by the state.

It seemed the sun would never rise on Sunday.

The morning shift finally clocked in and the cyclical monitoring of my vital signs resumed with a new set of faces. Numb and weary from my night in sleepless purgatory, I scarcely remember anything of Sunday morning, inclusive of Nancy and the kids arriving back on the floor. Nothing stands out in my memory until about 3pm in the afternoon. Even though being examined by the medical doctor on multiple occasions since my arrival, we were still anxiously awaiting the initial visit of the attending psychiatrist.

I was very uneasy about this particular meeting, given it would be pivotal in determining my fate for the near future. The idea of being left behind in the psych unit for an untold number of days riddled me with anxiety. Friends and family would take their turns wandering down to the cafeteria for a snack and a break from the airless, over-crowded room. Everyone was in limbo, prayerfully wandering what the prognosis would be. The best news so far was my incredibly stable vital signs, a rather compelling surprise by everyone's estimation.

Nancy tells me that in early afternoon, the hospital staff relocated me to another room. I have no memory of that whatsoever. However, soon after the resettlement I do recall for the first time a bathroom visitation, during which I observed my face in the mirror. Looking into my own eyes again was painfully sobering and disconcerting. No question, I still hated myself. For years, I had despised the sight of my own reflection or photos including me. Now, here was a withered grotesque image staring back at me in the mirror, the face of a cadaverous-white, bloated loser with charcoal-covered teeth and sporting a frazzled six-day old beard. One might conclude I was anything but kissable.

AT THAT MOMENT, I QUIETLY DECIDED – STAY AWAY FROM THE MIRROR.

The room was now sleepy and quiet. No chatter. Jason and Lindsay had gone outside for a while to grab a little sunshine and fresh air. And where was that abominable doctor? Come on, who can be so busy that he can't at least stop by for an initial conversation! I had now been there for two days.

At this point, here is a note of interest for your consideration.

After nearly thirty hours of hospitalization, I had yet to hear from any of my fellow staff members at the mother church, either directly or indirectly. The Clergy were conspicuously missing. No offers of prayer or support. No signs of *"we got your back"* or *"we're here for you brother"*. Unbeknownst to me, church board meetings with the elders were continuing back in Cedar Falls as leadership agonized with the formidable question, *"What do we do about the "old poot" now that he survived?"* After all, they had been counting on a funeral to substantially reduce the average age of their staff roster.

Dalen came back into the room, giggling. Apparently, nothing had happened in particular to cause her laughter, Dalen just giggles and laughs a lot. That had long been one of the blessings of her friendship with Nancy. *"The girls"* were always a source of joy for Nancy, carrying her away on mini-vacations from the heaviness of my personal atmosphere. *"The girls"* were never very hard to find, given the raucous laughter filling the air of every room in which they landed.

As my ceaseless scanning of televised options kept me suitably preoccupied, the overseer nurse remained sitting quietly by the right side of my bed reading her magazine, primed to subdue her patient should I abruptly unravel into an unholy mess. The anticipated seventy-two hour mandatory watch was yet to go into effect, and yet the surveillance had remained unyielding since my admittance. My curiosity was at a premium as to what the subsequent mandatory watch would be like by comparison.

Nancy was sitting on the bed beside me, while Dalen sat at the foot of the bed, her hand placed on my left ankle and quietly praying for me.

THE SCENE WAS NOW POISED FOR SOMETHING AMAZING.

The sound of a familiar voice instantly directed everyone's attention to the television. TBN was broadcasting a sermon from the Potter's House Church in Dallas, Texas. The speaker was the fiery and powerful T.D. JAKES.

The instant I hit the channel, Bishop Jakes spoke these words: **"The spirit of suicide is on you and if God Himself had not come to your aid, you would be dead right now!"**

Everyone participated in the collective yet silently stunned, "Whoa!" Even the guardian nurse put down her magazine, turned her chair toward the television and began to give full attention to what else this prophet might have to say to us.

This instantly seemed to be far beyond a mere coincidence.

It was as though a direct feed had been established for T.D. Jakes to speak precisely to me, insisting God was ready and willing to free me from depression and suicide.

As Bishop Jakes spoke, it was as though God attached a very large hose to the top of my head and proceeded to flush anything from my life standing in contradiction to my healing and restoration. I wept uncontrollably from the deepest recesses of my soul, barely able to breathe. The security nurse was now reading the 23th Psalm from the Gideon bible she had retrieved from the nightstand, all while dispensing Kleenex around the room. Dalen tightened her grip on my ankle as she intensified the prayers for my healing.

Nancy lovingly wiped the tears from my face. I did not know until later, she would take those tears and anoint my forehead with them, passionately praying for God be set me free. The inhabitants of the room seemed to be linked together by one common denominator: We were all encountering the indisputable presence of God.

I WAS BEING AWAKENED FROM THE INSIDE OUT BY THE POWER OF THE HOLY SPIRIT.

I did not want to cry like this! If the psychiatrist chose this juncture to at long last walk into the room, he would assign me to the psych ward for months. Trying to get it together and reel in the emotions, Nancy held on to me, encouraging me to let it go. This was no time to hold back! I was finally being set free and introduced to an entirely new dimension of living. It would be early Monday morning before any of us would come to realize the full extent of what transpired over that hour.

As in the night before, Nancy and the kids were required to leave the room by the ten o'clock hour, but this time under very different circumstances and a great sense of relief. About eleven p.m. I actually began to relax, turned off the television and located Christian radio on my pillow speaker. The bed now felt to be much softer and surprisingly comfortable. The frenzied mania and consternation of hours before had subsided, replaced by a serene gratitude. Closing my still moist eyes, I sensed the Presence and love of God on me like a warm blanket. It was as if the Lord Himself was singing me to sleep. I dozed off with the song, **"I Am A Friend of God"** ringing in my ears and saturating my soul.

"The Lord your God is with you, the Mighty Warrior who saves. He will take great delight in you; in His love He will no longer rebuke you, but will rejoice over you with singing."
ZEPHANIAH 3:17

Early the next morning, I was awakened by one of the nurses of the new weekday shift, taking my vitals and reviewing my chart. She encouraged me to relax and snooze as she carried out her tasks quietly and respectfully. After a few minutes, she asked what sort of work I was engaged in, to which I responded with a single word…musician.

Her reply was absurdly comical.

My laughter interrupted the hushed tranquility of the early morning hour.

She declared that my vitals, heart monitoring, and the various results now available from the battery of tests over the weekend, upon her initial review, would comfortably lead her to believe I was a well-conditioned athlete.

I laughed more in the moments that followed than I had in months. She could be assured the only *"athletic activity"* in which I had participated was the possible erratic swinging of a golf club a few times over the past three years and I was anything but well conditioned.

"Just look at me! Do I look like an athlete?"

Our collective laughter now drew a couple of additional nurses into the room, curious to discover what was so funny. We talked a bit more, after which they moved on down the hallway, giggling as they went. I really did not think much about it until later, but during the moments of that new day, I had been genuinely laughing, out loud, for the first time in a very long time.

I was wide-awake and renewed by a flawless night of tranquil uninterrupted sleep - now feeling motivated to get cleaned up. Monday morning saw the welcomed arrival of the A-team nursing staff. They were remarkably more friendly and joyful than was the weekend crew of the past 48 hours. Then again, little did they know, I too was now more friendly and joyful than I had been in months.

The nurses graciously allowed me privacy to bathe and shave. After a full hour of thorough scrubbing, shampooing, shaving, teeth brushing and hair styling, I stood for an extended period of time before the mirror peering into my own eyes. Without exaggeration, there appeared a striking difference from the last time I went through this exercise.

I felt uncommonly alive.

Everything around me was inordinately vivid and vitally real. The softness and warmth of my terry cloth bathrobe was like some wondrous new discovery. The textures and colors of the USA TODAY delivered to my room were extraordinarily fascinating. I reclined in one of the chairs with my flip-flopped feet propped up on the bed, rubbing the pages of the newspaper between my fingers as if stumbling across the concept of paper for the very first time.

When breakfast arrived, I was mesmerized by the aroma and taste of this remarkable array of toast, jellies and fruit. There was no recollection of food ever tasting like this, as I savored each bite and morsel. The orange juice was heavenly and I remember being captivated by the texture of the pulp it contained.

I found myself listening to and taking in the sounds emanating from the hallway with great interest, suddenly aware everything had changed. I was awake and alive, present in the moment, peaceful and amicable.

Several different nurses came by to check in on me, take vitals, etc. - all of who remarked in some way of their surprise to see a person like me taking up space on the psych floor. There was no sense I belonged in the ward and maybe I had just ended up there because of a lack of rooms elsewhere in the hospital over the busy weekend.

Nope – as they read my chart and heard my story, some actually became teary eyed and sincerely thankful I had even survived. By all practical medical analysis, I shouldn't have. Through the morning, I am fully convinced every nurse on duty in the psych ward, came by to witness my transformation for themselves. By their account, I was the headline news of the day among the staff.

About 10:30 a.m. Nancy and the kids arrived. To say they were stunned at first sight of me would be the most extravagant understatement imaginable. Somewhere far beyond joyful, these three sets of dumbfounded eyes gawked intently at the incomprehensible miracle, that was their father and husband, sitting before them. The medical doctor arrived shortly thereafter, announcing the tests results had returned and every single facet of my body was functioning to perfection. She saw no further reason for concern in regards to any physical danger I might be facing.

Just after noon, the long anticipated visit with the psychiatrist finally ensued. He interviewed me for about thirty minutes, after which he stated his belief the psych ward was not the best healing environment for me. Then he posed the question, "What would you like to do, what do you feel is best for you to move on from this event?"

I desperately wanted to go home. The very idea of being locked in a dorm room with multiple psych patients sent a paralyzing chill through my entire body. I poured my heart out to him. With my promise to seek out professional counseling upon returning to Iowa, by his signature he waved the mandatory watch and released me to the protective custody of Nancy and my kids. By 10pm, we were huddled together at home, collectively rejoicing and humbly grateful for the miraculous intervention of God in our lives.

One final point here: the board of elders and pastoral leadership made the decision that afternoon, determining I would not be allowed to return to the church in any role or function. My employment had been terminated, effective immediately. The church would provide six months of severance and that would be the extent of any further involvement by them in my life. They notified Nancy of their decision via a brief and emphatically stern phone call from Pastor Hipster.

It would be several months later before she would share with me the details of that phone call.

THE VIEW FROM HERE

Nancy

I wanted to write this because I have been asked MANY, MANY, times how in the world did I not get mad and hate Eddie. My answer is ... *"Because."*

It was not an unusual Thursday morn. Four o'clock AM, I heard Eddie getting ready to go to the office at the church. He loved going in early because he could get more accomplished before the office opened. It always worried me when he would get up and go in that early because he was taking Ambien to sleep, which wasn't really working that well and getting up that early and driving could be dangerous. I always hated that drug. It seemed to do more harm to him and his *"mood".*

I saw him open the bedroom door, looked at me for a few seconds and shut the door. He couldn't tell I was looking back at him. As he left, I just rolled over and went back to sleep - nothing unusual.

We have had the blessing of working together most of our married years and he has always called me a lot during a day if we were not physically together, to usually say he loved me. As the morning time went on, I noticed he hadn't called me, which was odd. I knew he was having a meeting at 10:30 so I proceeded about my morning - THEN, the person he was to meet with called me, saying Eddie was not at the office. He was never late to any meetings, so I told her I would try to reach him. I got his voice mail, the first of the hundreds of times for the next few hours *(to this day I cannot bear to hear his voice on a voicemail, I have to hang up).*

Then about an hour later, Rick, one of the staff members, called me. He said he was coming to pick me up and had some news regarding Eddie. Even now writing this, I feel that panic-sinking feeling. I immediately called my best girlfriends: Dalen, Cathy *(and Lorna - she was on a cruise but she found a way to contact me and her and Kevin were THERE with us as soon as they arrived back to Waterloo).* Dalen and Cathy came immediately & joined me at the church office. The church staff had looked at the video of the office from that morning and it showed Eddie coming in 4:15 AM. Leaving the office at 5 AM with a couple of his shoulder/ duffle bags. They unlocked his office.

As I walked in, we found notes addressed to me, the kids, and various church staff, and we found his phone. I just plopped down into his chair. HE LEFT HIS PHONE. I knew life was going to change for me radically! Cathy called her son and he got in touch with Lindsay at work. They immediately came to join me. Lindsay and I hugged and she cried –hysterically. I knew, once again, I had to be strong, as times before, to show her and Jason that we believed in a BIG God and He will never leave or forsake us! Only God can help a person to be strong in such a tragedy.

> *He Himself has said, "I will not in any way fail you or leave you without support. I will not in any degree leave you helpless nor forsake nor let you down."*
> HEBREWS 13:5

The office began to fill with people as word was getting out that Eddie left notes saying he was going to help me have the life I deserved by taking his own life. That he was a burden and a failure and he was sorry. He was going where no one could find him, so it would be easier on Jason and Lindsay and myself. The notes to the staff were unpleasant because of some staff meetings he had had earlier that week, dismissing him from the *"platform"* - too old at 50!

The next 3 days ahead of me was to be hell on earth!

The staff and Elders gathered, which I thought was in support, but actually became a meeting of how to deal with this embarrassment. During these hours, friends from across the country were sharing information hoping to put together some idea of where Eddie might be. This is when the church learned that Eddie had disappeared before while we were living in Louisiana, but he was back by 10:30 that night, being so sorry for the pain, but he came back home. I was so hurt that this news came out because we had worked through this time so diligently. We never told anyone outside of our Louisiana friends who stood by us through this event. (*Thanks to the friends in Bossier City that stood with me*).

I knew Eddie was getting MORE dark, MORE self-hatred. He never, ever took that out on the kids or me, but the deep hole he was spiraling down was so painful to watch. I loved him dearly and nothing I could do or tried to do helped the matter. So we carried on the best we could every day and I would try to shelter others from seeing this side of him, his dark mood, withdrawal, disgust of himself and no interest in life. Exhausting task.

I didn't want anyone to see just how DARK it had gotten, even though friends realized Eddie had changed, they couldn't put their finger on what was really going on. I had no idea what he was planning, his thoughts of suicide or that he could ever hurt us that deep. I knew how he hated himself but we always knew how much he loved US. The only time he seemed alive was when he would minister from the *"platform"*. I knew very little about the meetings of the staff in Iowa *"taking him OFF the PLATFORM"*.

THIS WAS HUGE. This is what *"snapped the twig"*, so to speak.

I held onto the hope that like last time, he would be home by 10:30 that night. We all stayed at the office until 11PM. Not a call from him to my phone, neither to the kids. Reality hit me. Dalen, David, Cathy, Cathy's son, and Lindsay NEVER LEFT MY SIDE. They slept on my couches. They couldn't have been comfortable. They welcomed the people in and out of my home at all hours of the day and night.

I would continuously go to our bathroom and look in the mirror and cry and pray, BEG God *"TO PLEASE KEEP HIM SAFE. IF THE WORST HAS HAPPENED TO PLEASE SPARE HIS SOUL* because Heaven is the ultimate JOY that he deserved. No one loved to use his talents to tell others about God's mercy, grace and love like Eddie Anders. He loves you, God!" *I buried my face in my hands, crying loudly to God*

Dalen kept speaking the scripture with boldness, Ps 37:23 "The steps of a good man are ordered" - *"he's gonna be fine"* - that was a powerful encouragement, my only hope.

I will always be forever grateful for Dalen, David, Cathy, Cory, Lindsay, for never leaving my side. One of them would go home for no more than an hour at a time, which seemed like an eternity, but they gave up their whole lives for these days with me, God used them to save me. Then others stepped closer in as well. Cork and Becky were angels to us. Janice Ephriam made sure we had food for about 6 months, definitely an angel. I have to mention Connie Erpelding, she loves to write and would email me just about everyday during those six months with some hilarious stories in her life and beyond. She always made me laugh! Angel.

Laughter IS the best medicine.

In the meantime, Jason was contacted immediately. He lived in Florida and worked at Disney World, Eddie's favorite place on earth. So Jason stayed there until further notice, keeping a watch out for him to show up. I know that was so hard on him not to be with Lindsay and me. People in Tennessee were flying helicopters over the area, hoping he might be sitting at the door of *(formally)* Eddie's Heart and Soul Café, because we were still mourning what we considered *"the death of our baby"*. Our closest, dear friends in Louisiana, Cheryl and Randy Henson, Debbie and Pat Worley, Scott Kelly, Julia and Randy Walker were on watch just in case he showed up at their doorstep. I was so thankful for them!

Hundreds of phone calls came in, my friends and I had our phones lined up on my kitchen counter, answering the hard questions to say *"no news yet"*, family members staying in constant touch!! My sister, Judy and her husband, John, were packing to make a drive to Iowa to be with Lindsay and me. I didn't actually answer the phone many times, but I did when Pastor Polston and Ruth Ann called. His voice would always stir the Holy Spirit and bring comfort like no other, and it certainly did at that moment. Their prayer was powerful. Roger Breland called. My heart literally felt like it wrapped around that phone when I heard his voice. I will always be grateful for those two phone calls, a huge part of carrying me thru the battle.

That Thursday night felt as if it was a million hours long. I did not sleep a wink! Praying and crying, my heart pounding, eyes are swollen shut, my head hurting and my heart broken. I go downstairs that Friday morn, once again, Dalen reminds me: *"A good man's steps are ordered - he's gonna be fine"*, as Dalen,

Cathy and Lindsay and I would hold each other up, literally, crying out to God. It's all we had to hang onto, not with smiles, but with PLEADING to God His own Promise!

"The words and promises of the Lord are pure words, like silver refined in an earthen furnace, purified seven times over."
PSALM 12:6

The girls loved on Lindsay and me. They were our angels protecting us in our home.

Friday was worse than Thursday. No word. No sight. I was becoming weaker with all the crying and lack of sleep. Not knowing. Not hearing a word from Eddie - after thirty years of constant contact during each day, always working together wherever we landed, it was starting to feel hopeless.

Friday night was torture.

No sleep, praying and crying. Holding onto Lindsay, wishing Jason was there. Appreciating all the phone calls and all the visits. Most were genuine, some were curious. People didn't know what to say, wasn't like he was dying of cancer or tragic car wreck - it was that HE WAS MISSING and expecting the worst, but their presence and my girlfriends being protective hostesses, allowed me to breathe the next breath and make many more trips up to my bathroom mirror, crying and pleading to God. I do say, I always felt HIM holding me up.

Saturday morn. I am so weak physically. I require eight hours of sleep. I have not slept a wink since Wednesday night. Now facing people, still wanting to protect the person of Eddie Anders, extremely talented, loved God and had a tortured soul. No one has ever loved to minister with his many talents like Eddie Anders.

But, the depression - while being a Minister, he had a dark secret. He had helped and touched so many lives thru his teaching of God's Word and thru his music about Jesus, God, our Father. I was wanting to blame others and explain why he had the right to be at this dark place - and didn't want anyone to feel betrayed by his current actions, because *"he is a good man and His steps are ordered"* and hoped they all could forgive him.

When I get stressed, I just want to wipe and clean the counter tops. I'm strange like that.

So I was at the kitchen counter. I was doing this a lot, especially Sat morning. The pastor of the church was there to talk to me about accepting the worst. He wanted me to start planning a memorial service. I named a few like Pastor Polston and Roger Breland to lead the service. Oh my goodness, I couldn't think beyond that. My brain was scattered and fried and was not prepared to accept what could be the worst of news.

As he left, I began to wipe down the countertops, lined up with all the phones. It was 10:30 AM. My phone rang. It was the oddest long distance number I had seen. It rang almost at the time for voice mail to kick in. I picked it up and said, "Hello???" A few seconds of silence. Then I heard a voice speak in a very weak tone: "Nancy, I am sorry."

The voice was ALMOST unrecognizable – I answered: "EDDIE?????"

The room that had been buzzing with chatter came to a complete silence. I said "are you alive?" "Where are you?" The room ROARED with "PRAISE GOD!" "THANK YOU JESUS"! I had to step out on to our deck to hear: *"Eddie, where are you? Please tell me, where are you?"*

He refused to tell me for the longest time in that conversation because he was afraid the police would take him away. I would say, *"No, please tell me!!"* He finally told me.

Immediately, I told David Grimm and our *"policeman"* friend, Lionel, the hotel where he was in Minneapolis. David and Lionel jumped into a car that split second and started their drive to Minneapolis, handling the details to get an ambulance to him. I kept saying, "We are coming to get you. I need you. I need to smell you." *(Side note: Looking for clues in his closet, I would bury my face in his clothing, crying and smelling the scent of his cologne that we all loved.)* I need you with me - the kids need you. I kept him on the phone. It was obvious he wasn't as happy as I was that he was alive.

The miracle here was, he never knows my telephone number. I am on his speed dial and I had that phone he left behind. He called me from a hotel phone. He didn't remember even dialing the number. An angel of God dialed that phone and my angel literally made me answer that strange number showing up on the caller ID. This is the beginning of the MIRACLES of God laid out before us. I called it God's yellow brick road!

I kept him on the phone until an ambulance driver and policeman arrived at the door, there to get him to a hospital. He was not happy about that, but I promised they would not lock him up in the police station. Lindsay and I packed a few clothes. My brain was shutting down, but the girls and God's angels kept me going. Cory drove Lindsay, Cathy, Dalen and me on the longest four-hour trip EVER, even though it was record-breaking speed.

In the meantime, Cork and Becky were flying Jason to Waterloo. I was so grateful to them for that gift. On our panicked drive north to Minnesota, we realized Jason had a scheduled layover in Minneapolis!!! We reached him by phone just as he was walking onto the plane in Minneapolis. Cathy was able to contact the right person with the Airline to let him get off the plane. *THIS WAS A MIRACLE AND AN ACT OF GOD*. It is a nearly an impossible task to pull off a *"spur of the moment"* change with a major airline. God bless Cathy!

Following that gut-wrenching mission, Jason waited for David and Lionel to pick him up at baggage claim of the Minneapolis airport. God's perfect timing - oh my goodness!!!! Amazing! Jason, David and Lionel arrived at the hospital ahead of us. What an encounter Jason had with Eddie in his room. His Dad had no idea he was going to be walking in his door.

We finally arrived, in record time, but it felt like an eternity. The doctor walked us to his room, filling me in on the various tests they had performed. She prepared me to expect the worst with the overdose of drugs he had taken, sure to affect his kidneys, heart, lungs, etc. Lindsay and I, along with the girls, turned the corner into his room. He looked at me and I immediately crawled from the foot of his bed and laid on top of him with my face pressed to his and feeling his tears, him feeling mine and I kept say, "Thank you Jesus". He kept saying,

"I'm sorry, I couldn't even kill myself." I kept on saying, *"Thank you Jesus"*, you are "gonna be fine."

OUR NEW JOURNEY BEGAN.

I could NOT be mad at him nor hate him. He was a MIRACLE of God pulled out of the depths of Satan's lies. First of all, I love him unconditionally and I saw God do the miracle of my lifetime. I had to honor God.

I knew the good man God made Eddie to be, and now He was going to have 100% chance to do the great work in his life. God restored me totally from the pain immediately as He allowed me to crawl up on Eddie in that hospital bed. Little did I know the extent of the true miracle before our very eyes, as God would begin Eddie's complete healing the next evening.

A beautiful story of reality!

After some long hours of waiting in the hospital room and the next miracle of his quick release, I cannot tell you how glorious the ride home was on Monday evening, with Lindsay and Jason. They witnessed the healing. They saw the transformation before their eyes. We were a *"family of one"* whom God once again bound together thru this tragic event and are witnesses to a glorious miracle. I was to honor my God and tell of His miracle, loving Eddie with all my heart and soul, unconditionally. It was as natural as breathing, even though hard to explain. I'm thankful God breathed that into me. I never doubted for a minute nor hated Eddie for a second. No resentment, no distrust, no doubt. It was a crazy roller coaster ride, but I never had hate in my heart. It was about him and the journey of restoration for us together. Most of all, it was about Gods' healing grace.

The six months to follow were times of deep renewal, a new life in Christ - redeemed. Dalen and David, Cathy, Lorna and Kevin, Cork and Becky, surrounded Eddie, Lindsay and me like soldiers of Jesus. We saw God move *"road blocks"* Satan threw at us that made it seem impossible to get our back on our feet. We were given six months by the Staff of the church to heal, but officially informed we would have to start a new life *"somewhere else"*.

"Do not earnestly remember the former things, neither consider the things of old. Behold, I am doing a new thing; now it springs forth; do you not know and perceive and know it, and will you not give heed to it? I will even make a way in the wilderness and rivers in the desert."
ISAIAH 43:18-19

Those six months, not knowing our future, was the richest spiritual growth in our lives. We had been digging in God's Word like no other time, receiving preaching from God's men on tape, on television and in various reading materials. Being very selective and studious, the basic things we already knew became brand new and more tangible than ever before. 'Saw it all with different eyes now, being bathed in joy and freedom, rescued out of a desperate situation and totally dependent on God and His Word for survival. I watched Eddie transform before me and I hung on to God and Eddie's coattails very tight, the best of times. The miracles Lindsay, Jason, Eddie and I and the small core group saw, were as huge as the highest mountain and as deep as any ocean.

"The steps of a good man were ordered." He was gonna' be fine!

We lost some *"friends"* because of the suicide attempt. Some were very verbal, some just disappeared never attempting to reach out nor responded when Eddie would reach out to them. They vanished out of our lives. That was painful. We just had to let them go.

Attempted suicide, especially ten years ago, was the worst of sins in the eyes of most people. Our pastor told us it would have been better if Eddie had died than having to deal with him living. I have a feeling others felt that way as well. But God gave me the ability to feel that: *"It doesn't matter."* We just need to concentrate on healing, growing and spreading the word about God's mighty miracle!

"I shall not die but live and shall declare the works and recount the illustrious acts of the Lord."
PSALM 118:17

In these last ten years, the list has become longer and longer of ministers and others following thru and dying of suicide. Why was Eddie spared, I don't know, but I thank God daily for the miracle. I just want people to hear this great story of our lives so it might be a source of help. In the opportunities presented to Eddie to share, there has been a great impact. I pray the pages you read in this book will be words of life should you be hearing the lies of Satan and secretly planning your suicide. Your family is NOT better off without you and even though the darkness you are enveloped in hurts everyone, you are not a burden. They love you and need you. I began to realize loved ones rarely help anyone escape from depression and suicide by their actions or words. Neither tender love nor tough love - will ever change their mind.

Only God can.

"I waited patiently and expectantly for the Lord; and He inclined to me and heard my cry. He drew me up out of a horrible pit, out of the miry clay and set my feet upon a rock, steadying my steps and establishing my goings. And He has put a new song in my mouth, a song of praise to our God. Many shall see and fear and put their trust in confident reliance in the Lord."
PSALM 40:1-3

Nancy Anders
MAY 2016

A DAUGHTER'S POINT OF VIEW

Lindsay

Growing up, my dad has always been my hero. He is the king. He's strong, can do nothing wrong, and always knows best! In my heart resides a flash-view of me standing on his feet as we dance together, looking up at him, thinking he's perfect and how can anything go wrong.

When I was in 8th grade - thirteen years old - reality hit hard. After being in the trenches with my parents, building a dream literally out of dirt *(the cafe)*, everything came crashing down. The moment I saw the cracks in our triple glass office door, left there by the phone my dad had thrown across the room, I knew we were near the end of the dream. Worry set in, not about everything going away, but the pain my mom and dad were going through. That moment was a turning point in my life. I almost lost my dad physically on three different occasions. The stress from the Café wars hospitalized him soon after the move to Louisiana, which I thought was the scariest moment.

I was wrong.

I was in high school, doing my high school thing, knowing my dad was becoming more and more stressed and depressed, taking medication to calm his mind and hearing about the conversations that were being held between members of the church staff. Trying my best to not be angry at what was taking place at the church, my way of dealing with the stress was to ignore it and think everything will just be fine.

Then all of a sudden one afternoon, my mother calmly tells me: *"We don't know where dad is. We can't get ahold of him."* A cloud of confusion and panic rolled in. I will never forget locking myself in my room calling his cell phone over and over, begging God to protect him and bring him home. I was just so confused. My perfect dad is in pain and I just wanted to hug him. Meanwhile the pastor of our church was in my living room and it took everything in me not to scream and kick him out. My lion inside me wanted to pull the pain out of my father and disperse it on anyone who hurt him, to everyone who had pushed him to this point.

Suddenly my phone rang. It was dad! I can't even explain the feeling of joy. He told me he had driven to Texas and planned to end everything, but seeing a road sign saying he was entering a town named Lindsay, Texas woke him up like a bucket of cold water to the face. He turned around and a few hours later - walked in our front door.

I knew at this point, God is real!

We all talked about it and he promised me he would never do it again. I took that promise to heart because I knew he loved me, yet I also knew there was so much pain, hurt, disappointment, feelings of failure, embarrassment and confusion going on inside him, more than I could comprehend in my little teenage brain. The church didn't make any of those feelings easier. The one person in your life you would think might provide guidance and support, the pastor of our church at the time did none of that. He, along with others, only made it worse. They grew cold and more judgmental. No place of healing for my dads' soul, so once again, it would be time to move on. We had a new exciting adventure ahead. We were moving to Iowa for a fresh new start for all of us, leaving the pain behind and hitting the restart button.

My dad came alive again, thriving in a vibrant church with a younger pastor who seemed to understand life. This was a new heavenly environment where the whole family could heal and be surrounded by old friends, so much joy and love surrounding us all.

After some time had passed, I once again began to have a deep-gut feeling of *"uh-oh."* I started hearing negative things on how the pastor was running things, his views and reactions to people, including my father. I saw the stress and disappointment building in my dad. Just like old times. The familiar coldness resumed once again from the pastor, staff, and even just random people. My dad repeating: *"I'm just not good enough",* all the things I'd heard before. Warning signs. Once again, I just dealt with the situation by ignoring it, thinking, *"I'm *sure this is just a rough patch. I know he will be fine, and he promised me he would never try and hurt himself again."*

IT'S ALL-GOOD!

It was a normal day in my life, but for some reason, I just didn't feel very well and made the decision to stay home from work. It was still early and my husband at the time called me. He asked, *"Are you home? I'm coming back really quick."* 'Didn't think anything of it. He walked in, somewhat in a panic, sat me down and said as gracefully as he could: *"Your dad left a note and we don't know where he is."* I instantly stood up and starting saying no - no - no - no that's impossible! He promised me! Pure panic. We drove straight over to the church to see my mom. I was in pure disbelief. I thought this was it for sure. He was serious.

The next three days were a blur. We couldn't have survived without our family and friends. We all camped out in the living room together, sometimes falling asleep all holding hands. I sat on the front step throughout the day for three days straight, just waiting for him to drive up again. Praying again. God you did it once, do it again.

The morning of day three, I remember waking up, looking at my mom and realized she was staring at me with the look of, Honey it's over. He's gone. 'Still just didn't believe it. I went to take a shower- standing there just thinking - now what?

All of a sudden, the door flew open and all I heard was he's on the phone.

I ran out on the deck where mom was on the phone and fell straight to my knees when I found out it was true. HE'S ALIVE! I was in shock. I got on the phone with him as my mom called the ambulance to go help him. He just kept saying, *"I'm sorry"* and I kept saying. *"I love you!"* The whole gang jumped into two cars and drove as fast as we could to Minneapolis. Running into the hospital room, I will never forget the first words out of my brothers' mouth: *"Dad, what the h--- were you thinking?"* It is exactly what we all wanted to say.

I have so much unconditional love for him.

Holding on to my Dad I whispered to him: "You are one of the most important pieces to our family puzzle. We can't do life without you! "

That first day in the hospital began the healing for each of us, but most importantly his! The question always being asked: *"Aren't you so mad at him?"* I heard it from everyone, asking my mother and also directed at my brother and me.

Our answers we always the same in our own words: "Absolutely not. I don't blame him!"

Watching just a glimpse of all I thought was going on, and so much I didn't know, how could I blame him? He's such a hard worker, sensitive, people-pleasing warrior. He's never had a moment to heal from past pains before new ones happened. How could anyone be ok after watching a dream crumble right in front of him, never feeling like he could ever be good enough? No one ever gave him the space to own and live out his greatness.

He has always been ahead of his time and there was no one who could keep up. I've always seen his greatness. So I couldn't blame him. I've seen the glory and the struggle. I just wanted my dad home and have the space to heal. To this day, I still see him as my hero as I stand on his feet, dancing, looking up saying I love you and feeling he can do nothing wrong.

It's been amazing to watch my dad heal and grow, as well as see my mother in an even brighter light. To witness the strength and grace she had through it all, bringing to life the meaning of true love and marriage, never giving up on each other and loving one another through everything.

Dad's life experiences have taught me to let go, not to harbor feelings toward others or carry emotional wounds and burdens.

That will literally kill you.

Our success has been found in our failures. We can do whatever we dream, and if we don't make everyone happy along the way, it's ok.

Let it go.

Let it be.

Lindsay Victoria
MAY 2016

CHAPTER 3

"Learning to Perform... Religiously"

LIVING LIFE TO PLEASE THE PIOUS AND OTHER SEMI-SACRED ADVENTURES

HERE'S THE TRUTH, PLAIN AND SIMPLE; **"I took my own life – and God gave it back to me."**

The attending physician in the Minneapolis emergency room addressed what he had seen in my case: *"In my thirty-five years at this hospital, I have never seen that lethal of an attempt at suicide fail. You do understand, Divine Providence in the one and only reason you are even alive. Do you get it? You are a miracle!"*

He spoke with such surprising and passionate conviction - I dared not doubt his word. Tom had, without question, seen more than his fair share of everything imaginable operating within the ER of a major inner-city hospital over more than three decades. And yet, with the Lord and my wife as witnesses, this crusty old Emergency Room veteran embraced me in a sustained bear hug, and with tears streaming down his face, begged me to do whatever it took to never repeat such an attempt against myself.

"Never forget, you are evidently very special to God. So never, ever, even think of f---ing doing this again!"

Yep…that is exactly the way his closing admonition was pronounced.

THEN – ONCE MORE, THE HUGGING CONTINUED.

I imagine all of us who have made a suicide attempt, or even contemplated such action, have what we think to be justifiable reasons. Hopelessness and despair are more commonplace than people are willing to admit. We have learned to perform for one another, falsely projecting an image of wellbeing and spiritual health, but for so many it is only that, a perceived image. The plaguing question, *"What will people think?"* drove me to mask the self-doubt, fear and worthlessness by manufacturing a shrewd veneer I hoped would keep my instability undiscovered. The goal in life was to appear normal, whatever that is.

The reason no one recognized I was in abysmal trouble and desperately needed help, I had become a professional Christian. I had achieved *"black belt"* in performing within the parameters of what was expected, both professionally and socially, acting out the part of a strong confident leader who demanded excellence from himself and everyone in his charge.

My vision and unforgiving persistence to broaden the small thinking and radically narrow view of what genuine Christianity should look and sound like, was born within the deepest regions of ultra-conservative fundamentalism. Being raised within the fortresses of granite affectionately known as *"Old-Time Religion"*, one quickly discovers the ruthlessness directed toward anyone who might choose to actually think independently.

Should you conclude to walk a divergent path, you are hastily branded a theological scoundrel and social outcast.

IF YOUR HAIR'S TOO LONG...THERE'S SIN IN YOUR HEART

I will always remember this pivotal point in my life, an incident serving as the genesis and significant determinant of my future approach to ministry.

A perfectly sunny fall day, we were gathered for our regular Sunday afternoon youth group meeting. This weekly function was always held just prior to the Sunday evening service and was identified as the Training Union hour. To this day, I remain ignorant as to the origin of that particular event title, one I believe most contemporary congregations have abandoned, both in name and function. In essence, "Training Union" was the evening version of Sunday school.

Numbering a dozen or so, we huddled on the steps just in front of the main entrance to the sanctuary excited a new face was among our ranks. A schoolmate, by the name of Mike, had accepted our invitation earlier in the week to be a part of our group.

Not yet a convert to the faith and wholly unaware of any of the church guidelines established for proper attire and grooming, Mike arrived dressed in his normal gear, blue-jeans, a plaid long-sleeve shirt, and Converse canvas sneakers. Living just down the street, he had made his way to the church via his bike. Without question, he was one of the *"coolest"* guys at school, with his relatively long hair and scruffy sideburns, a maniacal working knowledge of the current rock music scene, and a starting line-up position on the high school basketball team. The girls all loved him and the guys wanted to be him.

As the sun began to set behind the expansive hillside just to the west of the church, a gentle breeze sent the autumn leaves swirling around our feet. The fire of a nearby farmer clearing his garden filled the air with smoke and the aroma of smoldering corn stalks and husks. It felt like football season was supposed to feel.

Enjoying the moment, we all loved the fact Mike seemed stoked about being with us at church. It wasn't often new people showed up to join in our group, especially someone like him. Due to this occasion being savored by all involved, our sense of time was lost. We had inadvertently blown-off the formal start of the youth meeting. This was feverishly brought to our immediate attention by the pastor's wife, who without warning appeared in our midst, forcibly communicating her crazed displeasure at our tardiness and glaring lack of respect for those in authority.

It was then she noticed Mike.

You have to get this picture in your mind. Mike's appearance was radically different from those of us who had been properly indoctrinated as to church etiquette and dress code. The girls were modestly dressed in skirts of appropriate length and the stereotypical blouses, sweaters, etc. which adhered to the codes as established in the student handbooks of Bob Jones University, the school for which we were all being prepped to attend.

The guys were decked out in our standard issue polyester pants, dress shoes or at very least - penny loafers. Our various pastel dress shirts were freshly cleaned, pressed and firmly tucked in. Ties were not required, but were encouraged and worn by some, as were sport coats and blazers. Hair was basically G.I. regulation cut. Anything exceeding said length was to imply a propensity toward subversive allegiance to the anti-Christ.

Standing next to Mike, our youth group looked like Mormons at Woodstock.

The pastors' wife targeted him like a deer in the crosshairs of a bow-gun. What happened next would impact my life forever, and most assuredly his. She informed Mike in no uncertain terms as to her displeasure with his appearance.

"Young man", she said, *"this is the house of God and your dress is not acceptable. I'm afraid until you cut your hair and change those despicable clothes for something proper you are not welcome here. That is just the way it is. We expect our teens to look respectable, not like the world".*

We were all stunned, especially Mike. No one in the group dared to say a word, knowing a sure heavy-handed reprimand would be in store for anyone who came to his defense. He simply glanced around the circle of friends and quietly said, *"Sorry guys"*.

That was it. He grabbed his bike and took off down the hill for home. To my knowledge, he never went back to church again, at least not that one. 'Can't say that I blame him. That moment changed my world forever, cultivating the seeds in my heart and mind that would ultimately lead to my commission as an ambassador of change in the church.

THE ATMOSPHERE OF RELIGION I GREW UP IN, WAS TENSE AND TEDIOUS.

There was continually a sense of someone looking over your shoulder, investigating your loyalties to the kingdom, a devotion measured mostly in terms of your appearance, vocabulary and piety. In addition to the litany of the scheduled youth functions, I also attended the adult choir rehearsals with my father, singing with them on a regular basis. It appeared as though I was something of a mascot for them. It was during this time I was first introduced to the idea of me being labeled as *"cute"*. I loathed being described as cute.

I made a public profession of faith at the age of six and was baptized by immersion soon thereafter. An undefeated champion of the *"sword drills"* in Vacation Bible School, I was enlisted at the age of ten to be a member of the adult visitation / evangelism teams, due to my working knowledge of scripture. These teams would visit the homes of people who had recently attended our church for the first time, and would determine thru survey-type questions the level of faith held by the various family members. Most often, regardless of their responses to the questions, we would share the plan of salvation and challenge the families to declare their trust and belief in the Lordship of Jesus Christ.

The lion's share of these encounters would find me sharing my faith and a rapid-fire barrage of scripture verses. Over a period of about two years, I was privileged to lead several adults, as well as some of their children, to relationship with the Lord Jesus Christ. *The absolute truth of the matter,* I have always secretly hoped those conversions were genuine, as opposed to peoples' simple fascination with my *"preacher-boy"* presentation as a child. Again, the favorite adjective used by most adults to describe my life at this juncture was predominantly the word *"cute"*. I was becoming known as the cute little preacher-boy.

Let me be quick to say, I appreciate the *"fundamental"* Bible teaching I received in my childhood and adolescence. The basics of life and faith were woven into my DNA and I continue to draw from the benefits of that life experience each and every day. I learned respect for authority and a strong work ethic, all of which are necessary and have served me well in my lifetime. I did my best to pass along the very same fundamentals to my children.

Because of the focused application of the Bible into my life as a child, without question, I was saved from a multitude of bad choices and the resulting consequences, rather than having to be saved out of them. For all of this, I am deeply grateful to God and to those who invested into my life as a child. There are many wonderful and Godly people, walking a fully devoted life of faith that taught me valuable lessons and helped establish an infrastructure upon which I could build my life.

However, along with all the good also came the bad, a truckload of extra baggage, which proved to be very bewildering over time. Joyless, driven and cold personalities turned up the heat on the legalistic approach to Christianity as I grew older in the church, resulting in more and more of my friends bailing on the idea of devotion to Christ. To all my peers, this heavy-handed approach to faith sucked any and all vitality out of life. There was no appeal to be derived from the long litany of lifeless regulation and fuddy-duddy rules of the church, especially in the minds and changing bodies of young Turks wanting to experiment with the shiny new inventions of an evolving pop and hippie culture. In the meantime, I developed into the poster child of compliance of our religious sub-culture, replete with vast amounts of knowledge and information about God, well-armed arguments and apologetics in defense of the Gospel message, yet wildly missing a genuine intimate relationship with the God of the Bible.

THIS WAS THE RELIGION OF MY CHILDHOOD.

Religion resembles a flu shot. They administer just enough of the virus to make you immune to the real thing. It is having a form of Godliness that denies the transforming power. As a result, I struggled to maintain footing spiritually. Everything felt forced and contrived, rather than being an outward expression of the indwelling presence of God.

It was, as a friend of mine put it, **"Just enough of God to make you miserable and not enough to set you free."**

I grew up reading and studying about the joy of the Lord being our strength, yet literally never saw the reality of that joy being fleshed out. It was a culture of accusation, condemnation and suspicion. I believe this pernicious and destructive environment was a direct result of so many people leading a double life. The Gospel of Grace and the love of God seemed far removed from the military-like and legalistic approach applied to daily living. The reaction of our Pastors' wife to Mike, best exemplifies this contradiction. His jeans and hair were far more of an issue than was the condition of his soul and relationship to God. It really became hard to listen to lessons from her concerning the love of God after that encounter.

I was taught by example from most everyone around me that what happened in church on Sunday had very little to do with everyday life on Monday. It still seems to me a contradiction of major proportion for a person claiming faith in Christ, to also be known as an active card-carrying member of the Klan. And yet, that sort of duplicity was rampantly normal in the *"hood"* where I was raised.

My father sang in a southern gospel quartet in those days. He was what is referred to as a *'week-end warrior'*. Each member of the group held normal day jobs, and yet they would rehearse in the evenings and perform on the weekends at various churches, revivals and *"singings"* in the region. We would travel in multiple cars to venues up to three and four hours away. Many times they would share the stage with some of the biggest names in the industry.

I grew up around the Happy Goodman Family, The Blue Ridge Quartet, The Oak Ridge Boys, The Statesmen and my father's favorite, The Blackwood Brothers. My fathers' goal for me was to one day play the piano and sing for one of these groups. He always longed to sing professionally, and in many ways I believe he eventually lived out his dream vicariously through me. Growing older and regularly hovering in backstage areas of these gospel events, I was rudely awakened time and again to the realities of life. While some of these icons of the southern gospel culture no doubt had a genuine and devoted walk with God, the scene I witnessed first-hand was deeply confusing as I was trying to get my spiritual legs under me.

Many of the Gospel songsters developed legendary status for their sexual exploits, open use of drugs, free flowing hard liquor, pot smoking and use of language embarrassing to even the grittiest of sailors. The hardest part for me to get my head around, was seeing the same cast of characters who had just worked thousands of loyal southern gospel enthusiasts into a frenzied jubilee of revival and shouts of glory, now diving into a lifestyle having absolutely no resemblance to anything they had just testified to or sang about on stage.

It was distressingly baffling to me. Disillusionment took root as I witnessed the hideous inconsistency of what was trumpeted from a stage versus what was actually being lived by those who were well-paid purveyors of the *"truth."* My personal on-going discovery of deceit in the world of faith, ultimately led to deeply rooted cynicism. I had just seen more than my share of too much, and it eventually began to wear me down emotionally and spiritually, more than I even realized.

From that cynical viewpoint I continually wrestled with the question, what tangible difference has this gospel charade made in the life of anyone I know? Growing up in the Carolinas, our home was an airless vacuum of expression, passion or emotion. While never being the victim of physical or sexual abuse, family communication was close to non-existent and routinely limited to instructions - clean your room, do your homework, mow the yard, say your prayers, etc.

It was all efficiently driven by indoctrination and discipline. I'm not sure if our family life was a reflection of our church life, or vice-versa. It was a sterile and colorless existence, where duty was the only tie that bound us together. And the sad part, our family seemed to be the norm and not the exception. I never recall hearing the words *"I love you"* coming from the lips of my mother or father at any point in my childhood.

I know they loved me, and they provided for me in every way, and I'm sure they most likely did say it from time to time, but with God as my witness, I do not remember it if they did. At the very least, any tangible expression of affection was far from regular practice. The first time I ever actually recall hearing those words from my father was long after Nancy and I were married.

Even following my suicide attempt, not a single phone call originated from my father to check on me, nor did conversation of any kind transpire between us. The effort to take my own life was apparently not deemed worthy of his interest. Whether that sort of dismissal on his part was willful or simply a part of some habitual oversight, a lifetime of his disinterest helped to create my paralyzing lust for approval.

Many say this personality trait - the less than demonstrative show of affection, was true to form for most adults of that particular generation, which makes this even more disheartening. Accepting this as normal thinking endorses the idea that environment and circumstance trump the power and love of God. You are forever relegated to being a victim of generational baggage, family heritage and cultural parameters that have no escape route whatsoever, or so it seems.

I'm glad to say I have personally learned from experience - God's Name and power are higher than any cultural conformity, abuse, abandonment, bloodline or generational curse ever contrived by the enemy of our souls. You very well may have been a victim of some kind at some point in your life, but there is freedom to be found from your past.

REV. COSBY ANDERS

MY UNKNOWN FAMILY AND THE ANGRY FUNDAMENTALIST

I had hardly known my paternal grandfather when he passed of a heart attack at age fifty-eight. I only remember being at his house twice, and vaguely recall him visiting our home once, arriving late in the evening and departing very early the next morning. We did, however, make it to hear him preach several times over the years. There is absolutely no recollection of any conversation I ever had with him on any topic. I do remember on one of the visits to his home, he presented me with a Remington single-shot rifle purchased with his allowance money as a child. I treasured that gun for years as my only real connection to him, until some thug from Mayflower stole it during one of our moves across country in the nineties.

There was some sort of deeply murky estrangement in the relationships within my fathers' side of the family. I know nothing of what created this distance and conspicuous tension, all of which remained firmly entrenched until the day of my father's passing. Without hesitation I tell you, I would not know my Aunt Betty or Uncle Paul if they walked up to me eye to eye on the street and said hello. I own no single or collective photos of any one of them, nor have I ever seen a photo of them in the home of my mother and father during my entire lifetime.

Cosby Anders was an impassioned fundamentalist circuit preacher in the mountains of Virginia and North Carolina. I remember his sermons vividly, not so much the substance of the messages, but the style and flair in which he delivered them.

The jacket came off, the tie got loosened, the sleeves were rolled up, and for the next hour, it became open season on everyone and everything. Honestly, he was a little scary to me and most likely, frightening to everyone in attendance at the small frame church houses in which I heard him speak. My remembrance of him on the platform was not unlike most other preachers and evangelists who dominated the landscape of my childhood, thundering against anything remotely associated with sin. Always loud and audacious, you never had a problem staying awake or paying attention during his sermons. It was something like being at a track meet featuring cross-eyed javelin throwers, you kept your focus on him at all times because you never knew what was coming your way.

There were times at the close of his message, during the prayerful invitation for people to come forward in response to his sermon, if no one moved out into the aisles to come to the altar, Grandfather Cosby would himself leave the platform and make his way to a select person in the congregation. With his arm draped around the shoulder of the *"sinner in question,"* he would emphatically implore them to come to the altar with him to make amends with God.

TALK ABOUT THE POLAR OPPOSITE OF THE SEEKER-FRIENDLY MOVEMENT!

I was at the hospital the night he died. I remember the intercom blaring code-blue on several occasions thru the evening as we sat in the ICU waiting area. Due to a snowstorm over the next several days, I was left at home with my other grandparents, not permitted to attend the funeral. In the weeks following however, I recall the heated battle between my father and other assorted unknown relatives at the auction of my Grandfather's meager estate, all of which seemed very little to be combative over. This intense altercation obviously had much more to do with the long-held dissent among them, than with the scant accumulation of knick-knacks and trivial possessions of a mountain preacher being auctioned in the front yard of his home.

It would be years later I would find out, quite by accident, that my sin-chasing, pulpit-pounding, fundamentalist circuit preaching grandfather had in real life been a full-blown closet-alcoholic and drug addict for years. Not only that, he had been known to frequently distribute prescription meds to a few select congregants throughout several counties, for a small profit of course.

The revelation of this activity was capped off by the additional new knowledge he had been quite the womanizer, discovered to be having an affair in his later years of life and ministry. Though moderately stunned, it really didn't come as an epic jolt. After all, this fit the discrepant persona perfectly. The otherworld behavior I had witnessed behind the religious props and facades of distant pretenders suddenly came home to my doorstep. My grandfathers' condemnation and accusation aimed at so many through limitless sermons over his life span, was blown to dust in the actuality of his own life, seemingly void of a genuine devotion to the faith he declared as vital. Maybe this incongruity had something to do with the salient detachment between our family life and his.

We all make mistakes and poor life choices. We are all sinners in need of grace. God knows I stand number one in the line marked **"Acquire Grace Here"**. This is why Jesus had to die, to make provision for our personal redemption and to save us from ourselves. However, due to this new discovery of moral and spiritual failure within the family tree, the playing field of my life shifted substantially. I had come to the realization, not only was the contradiction of faith versus action a learned behavior in my life, it was firmly entrenched in my very DNA.

The arrogant hypocrisy I had grown to despise was in my very own bloodline.

Was my faith real or was it as fraudulent as so many others, including my own grandfather? Was I walking a life of integrity, or just fooling myself and everyone else? Without really being aware of it, I set out to prove my authenticity and to win the approval of others, for in their affirmation and acceptance, I would find peace in knowing I was one of the good guys. I wanted desperately to prove to everyone, including God and myself, I was the real deal, and that in my case the proverbial nut had indeed fallen a very far distance from the family tree.

Ironically, that very ambition would prove to be at the root of my personal destruction.

I continued to be copiously devoted to God, but plagued with a self-imposed goal of personal perfection, one that would never be satisfied, no matter the accomplishments. Due to my unfettered appetite for approval, the slightest hint of criticism would paralyze me emotionally. While the depression developing in my life was eventually to be diagnosed as event-triggered and not bipolar in nature, major adrenal fatigue was one of the issues brought on by constantly pegging the extremes of my emotional meter. Riding the high-flying melancholy roller coaster would eventually take a very large toll.

Once the enemy of your soul discovers your vulnerability, he will lay siege to that area of weakness and exploit every opportunity to destroy you from within. I unwittingly set myself in agreement with his destructive plan by developing a constant confession of defeat, failure and frustration over my life, rather than verbalizing the Word of God. While continuing to proclaim and teach countless others of the overcoming power of the Gospel, I routinely declared myself immune from the benefits of the same. Supernatural intervention would eventually be required to deliver me from a ferocious inability to ever love myself.

Only then could I ever believe His Love was unconditional.

CHAPTER 4

LET IT BE

DISCOVERING GOD IN THE MOST UNUSUAL WAYS

SUMMER WITH CHICAGO

In the summer of 1971, I was privileged to attend the Cannon School of Music at Appalachian State University in Boone, North Carolina. I had unlocked a healthy measure of purpose and identity as first chair French horn player in our high school concert orchestra program, being selected to the North Carolina All State Band for two consecutive years, as well as being named Directors' Assistant.

My objective in attending Cannon would be the disciplined rehearsal and focused study of French horn and classical music. My band directors and guidance counselors were encouraging me, knowing this track could provide very productive opportunities for my college education, should I vigorously pursue the development of my talent.

The hallways of my dorm that summer overflowed with a wildly assorted mix of music. It was in this setting the music of the CHICAGO TRANSIT AUTHORITY wholly captured my attention. Recently inducted into the Rock and Roll Hall of Fame, they would come to be known simply as, **CHICAGO,** the rock band with horns. I had heard their music on the radio, but really had not paid much attention in my headphones.

Invited to a spontaneous afternoon gathering of fellow music students in a large rehearsal hall, we charted out the chords for a few of the tunes from **CHICAGOS'** first album, a double disc set. We would spend hours together in the days to come, learning songs such as *Beginnings*, *I'm A Man*, and *Does Anybody Really Know What Time It Is*.

And - I LOVED IT!

Here's a novel aspect of this: years of piano lessons, singing hymns and Gospel songs in church since the age of six, a fascination with my new Fender guitar and the music of the Beatles, and now a season devoted to the study of classical music and the French Horn, all led to a rehearsal hall at ASU where I found myself playing bass guitar for the first time in an impromptu jazz/rock band experiment. I had no idea, in that moment, how significant the bass was to become in my future music career.

That summer was remarkable.

I loved playing French horn and performing weekly concerts as part of a seventy-piece symphony orchestra would quickly prove to become habit-forming! The pure joy of bringing to life works such as Tchaikovsky's 1812 OVERTURE, Shostakovich's FIFTH SYMPHONY, Dvorak's SYMPHONY #9, and Handel's WATER MUSIC, is far beyond my ability to translate into words.

Successfully navigating through this music was a sizable challenge - especially being thrust into the midst of much more seasoned and accomplished players. And yet, with each rehearsal my confidence grew exponentially. Surrounded with highly skilled musicians certainly did help to *"raise the level of my game"*. Adding to the profusion of adrenaline, a highlight of our outdoor concert performance of the 1812 OVERTURE was the firing of actual cannons on cue from their positions on surrounding rooftops. These heart-pounding moments would go a very long way in reinforcing my enthusiasm for flamboyant production and the use of special effects in my future career. Performing in an ensemble of this magnitude and experiencing the power of the music we were creating was unimaginable, igniting an unquenchable desire to spend my life creating music.

FEBRUARY 1972

Midway through my sophomore year in high school, my family moved to York, South Carolina, a cozy little town just across Lake Wylie from Charlotte, North Carolina. I had been concerned my fertile musical environment had vanished into thin air with the closing of the moving van doors. Fortunately, that would not be the case.

Quite to the contrary, I believe it was totally a *"God thing"*. The band program at York High School was one of national prominence and my focus on a career in music only sharpened. Our band director, John Bostic, took a vitally different approach than I had grown accustomed to. Where the North Carolina program was more a bit more laid back and refined, Bostic expected a gritty and tenacious level of discipline that at times was merciless and severe, to put it mildly.

Hours of rehearsal became a predominant aspect of daily life, practicing until the instrument becomes an extension of your nature and the music an expression of your soul. There were sessions of rehearsal when it would be necessary to wipe the blood of my shredded fingers from the strings of my acoustic bass. He taught us to never settle, for with great preparation will come great opportunity. That mantra has proven to be impeccably true yet today.

I will always be grateful to John Bostic for helping to instill within me this level of discipline and focus. On more than one occasion, I have thanked him personally for the impact he made on my life. His influence and guidance engrafted a relentless commitment to excellence that has remained a strategic part of my life.

SEPTEMBER 1972

The Jesus Movement and the song - Let It Be - come together to create a defining moment.

As a teenager, there was never a time I walked away from faith. My youthful rebellion would be relatively subtle in nature. Though my relationship with God would go through dormancy at times, it was never lifeless.

THAT, HOWEVER, WAS ABOUT TO CHANGE.

The fall of 1972 brought with it marked anticipation for what was to be my junior year in high school, reconnecting with friends who had all gone our separate ways over the summer. A couple of those friends, George and Danny, attended a major youth event in Dallas, Texas known as Explo'72, sponsored by Campus Crusade for Christ. Among others, featured speakers included Billy Graham and Bill Bright, with music presented by a group known as Andrae Crouch and the Disciples.

The significance of this festival brought the Jesus Movement to the forefront of the youth counter-culture. Multitudes of hippies and flower power advocates were turning to Christ.

What began in Southern California with leaders such as Chuck Smith at Calvary Chapel was now spreading like a raging brushfire across America.

My friends spoke of their spiritual encounter in Texas with breathless exhilaration. In addition to their stories of personal renewal, they returned home in possession of cassette tape recordings of the music and messages delivered during their three days in Dallas, wanting to share with me all they had heard and experienced.

Intrigued by their newly found enthusiasm, I listened intently for days, also utilizing my recently acquired GOOD NEWS FOR MODERN MAN Bible in further studious consideration of those cassette messages. As you might imagine, my origin being the King James Version only crowd, to even own a copy of this paraphrased version of the Bible was in itself, blatantly aggressive heresy. To this day, one of my childhood peers swears this is where I strayed from *authentic faith*.

The subject matter of Explo'72 was all extremely familiar and in no way a theological departure from what I had learned in my youth. What did seem distinctive however, was the extraordinary joy and vibrancy radiating from everyone who spoke or sang. This alone served to capture my undivided attention and fascination. For two solid weeks, I studied those tapes tirelessly, engaging in daily conversation with my friends over the fact each of us were being awakened to a new awareness of God.

One particular morning, due to repair work being done on my car, mother drove my sister and me to school. Along the way, the Beatles song, **"LET IT BE"**, came on the radio. With mom and Linda up front, I was sitting in the back seat alone, eyes closed and listening intently. In fact, for three minutes and ten seconds the rest of the world temporarily disappeared from my conscience awareness. As the song concluded, a distinct sense of revelation swept thru me, as if some lingering heavy fog had suddenly lifted, unearthing a first glimpse of brilliant colors soon to supplant my heretofore, monotone existence.

What I came to realize - God *"spoke to me"* through this song.

I have always described this as my "burning bush moment", something similar to Moses hearing the Voice of God originating from a tree ablaze on a desert mountainside. Only for me, it was God utilizing the car stereo to say: *"Be still, pay attention and listen. I've got some important things to tell you"*.

And listen I did. With my entire heart and soul.

While risking accusation of being exceedingly melodramatic, this was the sort of WOW moment that dares you to find a way to sufficiently describe. Using the lyrics and melody of a familiar song I loved, God reached into the commonplace and unlocked my soul. A fuzzy black and white existence was being upgraded to full-on Hi DEF color.

An uncommon and soothing peace settled over me.

You know, that *'clean sheets on the bed'* feeling.

That sense of freshness in the air after a storm has finally passed through.

LET IT BE.

To all my questions, there will be an Answer.

In the darkest night of my soul, there will be a Light.

When I am still and choose to listen, my Father's voice will lead me.

He will speak the words of wisdom I can follow.

Even though many factions of people around me are divided by prejudice, bigotry and convoluted theology, there remains the hope they can see the Truth.

LET IT BE became my new Amen.

Whatever God has spoken in His Word - LET IT BE!

Whatever God wants to happen in my life - LET IT BE!

Arriving at school, I was thoroughly distracted by this brush with Divine epiphany. The first two classes of the day were a vapor, lost in some sort of esoteric daydream. An otherwise routine morning commute to school had become a transformative catalyst in my life. Amid the human chaos that is a high school corridor during class change, I knelt in front of my locker to exchange books. While there, I uttered a brief and simple prayer of thanksgiving to the Lord for reaching out to me. I had been on a quest to discover the reality of God for as long as I could remember. Yet here, in this most unlikely of places, I was fully aware He was listening.

This impromptu conversation with Yahweh was nothing akin to the normal drill, routinely composed of me clamoring before Him for an answer to some brewing dilemma. This was radically off script. God reached into the unremarkable normalcy of an ordinary day to engage in dialogue with me.

Nothing at all routinely religious in nature took place.

Kneeling in the dusty bedlam of a thousand shuffling feet, for an instant this commonplace corridor of York High School became an altar of praise and gratitude, completely unnoticed by all those who passed by.

How cool was this – lost in a fuzzy blur of religious activity and roleplaying for most of my childhood and adolescence, now God had used a couple of my shaggy-haired cohorts and of al things, a Beatles song being played on the radio, to get my attention.

MASTIN ROSE
THE OTHER SIDE OF "LET IT BE".

He was my maternal grandfather, Mastin Rose. In his younger days he had been employed by the railroad, as well as serving among the ranks of fellow coalminers. He had been an alcohol driven, tobacco-chewing brawler, farming eighty-eight acres on the hillsides of Virginia's New River Valley with two plow-horses and rugged blistered hands. He was small in stature but a giant in terms of his *"street sense"*.

PawPaw, as I called him, raised primarily tobacco, strawberries and corn, in addition to overseeing a small dairy operation of a few hand-milked cattle and a very productive hen house. The farmhouse was, as you might imagine, outfitted with linoleum floors, wood stoves, a tin roof, feather beds and handmade quilts.

If ever a man was born again, it was Mastin Rose. I did not personally know the untransformed, roughhouse version, but rather was raised by a post-conversion, loving grandfather who spent hours in conversation with me about how God had reshaped everything about who he was.

PawPaw was as real and genuine as anyone I have ever known, and I knew him well. Through about my sixth grade year, we were together constantly and I loved him dearly. He literally raised me. My parents and grandmother all held full-time jobs, whereas my grandfathers' work schedule allowed him to invest his life into mine. Wherever he went and whatever he did, I went with him.

Fishing, hunting, hiking, building model cars or working the garden together, I was always learning from him. He was in no way abusive or heavy-handed, and yet never withheld discipline when needed. Even his Grandfatherly correction seemed to come from some offbeat place. He never once hit me, but his most subtle rebuke carried an immeasurable amount of influence with me. I knew I could trust him and without question, I respected and treasured him.

Among the most cherished memories of my childhood, are the countless hours spent talking deep into the night, sitting under the stars in his squeaky old rocking chairs. Painted hunter green, one of them had a slight nick in the left-side rocker arm, creating a little bump as you rocked back and forth.

He thoroughly loved bluegrass music, which at the time just nearly made me sick to my stomach. I hated it. Long before my musical tastes had broadened to be far more inclusive, I marveled at his knowledge and enthusiasm for these fiddle songs of Scottish and Irish origin being created in the hills of Appalachia. And this was the real stuff, raw hard-core mountain music, where even Bill Monroe himself seemed slick and commercial. As we took turns in the car listening to radio stations featuring our chosen styles of music, he would educate me as to why certain tunes were his favorite, singing along while tapping out the rhythms on his steering wheel.

It was awful, but I played along and enjoyed his enthusiasm.

I loved him and he made me laugh.

On the opposite end of the spectrum, Pawpaw set me up in his basement with a makeshift drum-kit comprised of a real snare drum he had purchased for me, surrounded by various sizes of heavy cardboard boxes and shiny lard cans to finish out the kit. (*A note to all my percussionist friends, large old lard cans make killer floor toms.*)

With a mono phonograph close beside me, I would thrash away for hours to the Beatles, the Monkees, and Paul Revere and the Raiders, with PawPaw as my audience.

It was awful, but he played along and enjoyed my enthusiasm..................

He loved me and I made him laugh.

I will never forget the sight of him sitting on a stool, tapping his foot to my lard can rhythm, all the while dipping snuff or hand-rolling cigarettes with his own tobacco. He was funny and playful in many of the things he taught me about life.

Many were the times we assembled model planes, cars and ships together, an activity always revealing my proclivity to rush the process. My exuberant and fidgety plan was to layout all the pieces on the picnic table, quickly glue them together, paint it right then and put the decals in place - all in one sitting.

Patience was never my strong suit.

Still isn't.

As a master gardener, he diligently attempted to teach me how to grow vegetables. After sowing seeds in the soil together, within two or three days I would begin digging around the planting rows to see if anything was happening, hoping to witness immediate results. The same was true on our mountain hikes up to his favorite fishing lake. I preferred the rapid-fire gratification of catching little Blue Gill and Sunfish at the rate of about forty an hour. This was my idea of a worthwhile and productive outing. However, Pawpaw wanted to teach his grandson the fine art of landing the big prize, requiring a more hushed and agonizingly patient approach. This version of fishing seemed supremely tedious until I discovered for myself the rush of reeling in a fighting, six-pound mountain bass.

In every instance, I remember his instruction:.........

"For this to turn out right - you gotta glue the first pieces together and then let 'em dry. Don't mess with it. Just let it be for a few hours before ya move to the next step."

"Bait up the hook and toss it out there to just the right spot, then just let it be still. Let the fish come to you. If you get a nibble and jerk the line too quick, he'll be gone. Wait for the float to completely disappear under water before you try to set the hook. Just let it alone."

"When you get the seeds in the ground, you got to let 'em be. You can't be digging 'em up all the time to see if something's sprouting. You'll kill it all. Let it be."

How many times in life I wish I had remembered the words of my PawPaw to just Let It Be.

For all my impatience with people, projects, and relationships - for all the frustration I ever had with myself - for all the times I felt the need to fix everything for everybody so they might approve of me - how I wish I would have remembered his words, which coincidently happened to be the very words of John Lennon and Paul McCartney.

LET IT BE.

CHAPTER 5

ON THE ROAD

IT WAS THE BEST OF TIMES - IT WAS THE WORST
OF TIMES

I love to travel. When seeing a plane overhead, my initial thought is almost always; *"I wish I could be on that flight going anywhere"*.

Tour buses along the highway always capture my attention and the familiar aroma of diesel fuel exhaust quickens my step. I never seem to weary of airports, hotels, sound checks or a constant change of scenery. Some of the most incredible adventures of my life have been performing alongside legendary musicians in many of the most magnificent concert venues and recording studios in the world.

Those experiences have also been wildly eclectic, sharing the stage and/or studio with a list of artists including Michael W. Smith, Bill & Tamara Champlin, Emmylou Harris, Dr. John, Mylon LeFevre and Broken Heart, Dolly Parton, Al Dimeola, Dann Huff, Phil Keaggy, Percy Sledge, Whiteheart, Steven Curtis Chapman, Sam Bush, The Gaither Vocal Band, Amy Grant, Tom Hemby, Danny Seraphine of CHICAGO, The Speer Family, George Marinelli, Kerry Livgren of KANSAS, Lenny LeBlanc, 4HIM, James Burton and a myriad of others.

Normally, the broad majority of professional musicians devote themselves to a certain genre such as Jazz, Southern Gospel, Bluegrass or rock and roll. I have been fortunate enough to cross most all those boundaries and savor the creative flavor of just about every sort of musical dish found at the table. As a result, I have never been a purist concerning certain styles of music, only the substance and quality.

Often times, a week of normalcy has included multiple studio sessions, creating radio jingles or album tracks for a pallet of wildly diverse clients, then turning my attention to the concert stage with someone like Steve Lukather of Toto on Friday night, performing with the cast of Country Tonite Theatre on Saturday evening, and completing the week by leading praise and worship on Sunday morning.

I love the musical mélange that has defined the greater part of my career.

WHAT A BLESSING TO SPEND LIFE DOING THE THING YOU LOVE.

Countless people opened the doors for those opportunities, not the least of which is my longtime friend and mentor, Dr. Roger Breland. From the first moment I saw them take the stage, my dream/goal was to be a member of his award winning group, TRUTH. For more than thirty years, a great many of us converged on Mobile, Alabama from across America to take our place on the Truth bus. The sun never sets on our alumni, with more than five hundred singers and musicians sharing the TRUTH heritage scattered across the globe, including Steve Green, Dann Huff, Dick & Mel Tunney, Russ Lee, Andy Chrisman, Mark Harris, Kirk Sullivan, Marty Magahee, Kim Noblitt, Natalie Grant, Jody McBrayer, and Gordon Twist. We now share the joy of being collectively inducted into the Gospel Music Hall of Fame as former members of TRUTH.

It would happen after several years of prayerful persistence that Roger would graciously invite me into the fold. My dream not only became reality, I would be the only member in the full thirty-year run of Truth to play bass guitar, sing on the front line as a principal vocalist, and then eventually, take over as keyboard player. One more year in the group and I might have made the horn section. In an effort to broaden the sound of the band, we added Dick Tunney to cover the basic piano sounds, while I would deliver the *"colorings"* of keyboard-generated string parts, organ and clavinet. Also continuing to contribute as percussionist and vocalist, I surrounded myself on stage with a world of synthesizers and percussion instruments.

Three hundred or more concerts a year traveling with twenty other people wedged inside the confines of a forty-foot bus and a single equipment truck, sometimes performing up to five times a day. That astonishing fact was accomplished by way of our concert dates at various theme parks, multiple church services on just about each Sunday of the year, daytime school assembly programs, television broadcasts and much more.

I have told *"Mr. B"* countless times thru the years how, with great regularity, I utilize wisdom and insight gleaned from him personally and my time within the Truth organization. Additionally, that single bit of personal history and experience chronicled on my resume has opened multiple avenues of opportunity throughout my career, including my professional affiliation with Gaither Music and continuing later with Gary McSpadden.

Our record producer, Bob MacKenzie, was also longtime producer for Gaither recordings and their live concerts. After working with Bob in the studio on several Truth recordings, including our first Christmas album and the only Direct-to-Disc recording in the history of Christian music entitled *"DEPARTURE"*, the invitation was extended shortly after those sessions for to become a member of Gaither's touring band and session musician at Gaither Recording Studios, all based just northeast of Indianapolis in the quaint little town of Alexandria, Indiana.

Dr. Breland currently heads the music department at the University of Mobile, where he continues to mold and fashion the careers of thousands of young people from around the world entering music and creative arts ministry. I am sincerely grateful for his guidance and more predominantly, his friendship over all these many years.

As I ventured through my darkest of days, he was one of the first to reach out to Nancy and me, which really came as no surprise.

The education gained through this sort of exposure has been priceless. Learning to adapt to varying audiences and their unique local cultures, as well as observing the wide ranges of response, worship styles, and methodology one encounters on the road, has enriched my life and greatly enhanced my discernment. What an amazing thing to meet and work with a lifetime of astonishing people and artists from around the world. The joy of cherished friendships and memories of our creative interaction along the way is a priceless treasure.

Then comes the yen to the yang where the romance and adventure of the last four decades, gradually becomes tainted to a great degree by life's ugly realities. Paraphrasing the Apostle Paul's account of his experiences, I have been stunned, shunned, shocked, wounded, surprised, tormented and in many ways, corrupted by some of the things I have encountered on the road and learned from life behind the curtain.

IDEALISM & CHASING DREAMS

Once upon a time, I was a boisterous advocate for Contemporary Christian Music and its validation in the church, playing a very small part of the pioneering force helping to bring the art form to life in the seventies. The enthusiasm generated by the Jesus Movement, opened the church to a new sound of worship and strategic tools designed to creatively communicate the message of the Gospel to the youth culture. However, there was a storm brewing on the horizon. I vividly recall extended, heated arguments with an infinite array of red-faced clergy getting up in my grill with a vengeance over their passionate belief contemporary music had no place in the church. Those of us who brought this new music into the sanctuary were ceremoniously defined as evil and malicious in our intent. I knew better, yet people do have a way of judging your heart and motive if they do not embrace your style and customs.

HUMANS SEEM TERRIFIED BY THINGS THEY DO NOT UNDERSTAND.

I will always remember being met at the door of a church in southern Georgia as we stepped off the bus, guitars and amplifiers in hand. The pastor, adorned in yards of thick beige polyester, greeted us by firing an immediate warning shot across the bow. We would be more than welcome to sing and testify in 'his' church with one non-negotiable caveat; He would first escort us to the nearest barbershop for a vast reduction of the unsanctified mess that was our hair. Then and only then would we be allowed to load in, set-up our sound equipment and present our concert.

WE TOOK THE NIGHT OFF.

Drums were evil, guitars were loud and those who played them were deemed offensive. The anticipated volume of our band, the clothes we wore and our outlandish *"hippie"* hairstyles, dominated these confrontational dustups with our critics on a regular basis.

During those days when my hair was much longer and the glasses I wore were of the wire-rimmed variety, a combative church elder ranted: "You remind me of that nut-job, John Lennon." He had no earthly idea of the compliment just extended in my direction. My response to his intended insult was a gleefully simple, *"Thank you!"*

Please remember this crucial fact: It is not as though we were setting up gear in protestant sanctuaries to throw down on Jumping Jack Flash and Helter Skelter. Our nightly set list included songs such as The Church Triumphant, Because He Lives and Majesty, with scripture verses and testimonies woven among the music. A formal invitation for concert goers to publically acknowledge Jesus as Lord and Savior was almost always a part of our presentations, resulting in thousands of people a year coming forward to make that proclamation. And yet, to witness the reaction of many of our critics, you would have thought we were something akin to LED ZEPPLIN arriving to incite hedonistic chaos.

On one particular Truth tour, we dealt with the ongoing complaints about the volume of our band by adding a very large *'dummy fader'* to the house sound console, labeling it with bold red letters - *"Master Volume"*. As the predictable attacks on our sound engineer would once again ensue, Mark humbly complied with their demand, turning down the *"Master Volume"*. This acquiescence was invariably met with great exuberance. In the estimation of the church representative, the volume was now far more tolerable and reasonable, thanks to his bold intervention on behalf of the congregants in attendance.

He would receive the congratulatory *"pats on the back"* from his peers and/or subordinates, even though nothing had really changed in the slightest, given the *"Master Volume"* fader was attached to <u>absolutely nothing</u>. It was pure psychology and misdirection. Astonishingly, the ploy worked 100% of the time on that entire tour. Administering doses of our placebo volume control calmed the anxiety of many a hyperventilating deacon across America and beyond.

Another interesting fact discovered by our sound engineer on that particular tour, in several venues our decibel meter readings proved scientifically conclusive, the volume of our band, at full throttle, registered beneath the volume level generated by the house pipe organ during congregational singing and offertory within the same worship service.

WE JUST LOOKED MUCH LOUDER.

For all our success in ministry and music, some people refused to be anything other than violently exasperated by our mere presence in their sanctuary, especially when we were scheduled as part of a regular weekly church service. Before we counted off song one, sulking deacons and vexed church-members were already scheduling meetings to insure Truth, and groups similar to us, would never darken the door of their church again.

In light of this consistent reaction, my personal struggle for acceptance and approval continued to escalate through the years of establishing credibility for this new form of ministry.

CORPORATE CHRISTIANITY

As the untapped potential for generating cash flow in Christian music and ministry became realized, everything began to rapidly change. The pioneers of contemporary music and ministry launched out of the Jesus Movement, never envisioned that what began as a move of the Holy Spirit on the beaches of Southern California and in the hearts of generals such as Pastor Chuck Smith, Bill Bright and Billy Graham, would someday morph into the current soulless corporate version.

Ministry through the tool of contemporary music gradually became a profit-driven business rather than a prophet-led endeavor to fulfill our Great Commission.

There was a day people actually prayed and sought the instruction of God concerning the direction of their ministry, which happened to incorporate the use of music. More than anything, we believed music was a tool of communication to share the gospel. People would often listen to music and engage with an artist long before they might *"tolerate"* someone preaching at them. The movement was initially driven by a passion to creatively share the message, yet the "suits" slowly began to discern the potential of a massive income stream.

In the earliest days of my tenure with Truth, our record label executives relentlessly pushed Roger Breland to change the sound of the group. In meeting after meeting, they articulated the need to make us more *"radio friendly"*, developing an updated trendy pop sound. This would be the only way we could go to the next level. The problem quickly became, we no longer sounded like Truth. They longed to move us from the church to the concert hall. It became far more about sounding like the Bee Gees and how the group looked in jeans than it was about the anointing of God.

Christian music was becoming a commercial product and little else. It was a big deal that we now had our own section at Tower Records. In time, Christian music also proved to be somewhat of an entry-level artist development scenario for many artists, who would eventually "cross-over" into a more mainstream secular career.

The majority of what happens in Christian music is derived from secular corporate examples of successful entrepreneurs and their business models. You can place your bets in Vegas on this one: Mark what is *"hot"* today in the secular music arena, then watch to see that influence rise to prominence in the Christian market about two to three years from now. That has long been the trend.

U2 became all the rage a few years back and is one prime example of my claim. Though they have been successful from their outset in the eighties, they did, in fact, become the biggest band on the planet during the nineties and into the twenty-first century. Their concert tours sold out the world's largest venues within minutes of tickets going on sale. What resulted in CCM about three years after U2's career and industry peak was male-dominated, guitar-driven worship music, absent keyboards, horns, etc. Everything being produced in the Christian marketplace, sounded like U2 and much of it still does.

THIS MODEL BECAME THE NEW TRADITION, RUT AND BIAS

The adaptation of this sound has been the blueprint for the modern *"worship"* movement. If you intended to be on the radio, lead worship in contemporary church settings, or be remotely relevant in music ministry, this has been the model most recently perpetuated by the marketing gurus and trendsetters.

At the outset, we hoped the Traditionalists would surrender their jacked-up bias against our music. We simply wanted our own music style we could enthusiastically embrace. The *Traditionalists* were locked into a form of worship completely out of step with contemporary culture and irrelevant to the non-religious world. We wanted to add to the tools in the box.

Sadly, our accidental success was in creating yet another subculture and new tradition that is just as biased and narrow in it's thinking as the old one ever was. It's the same old drivel tossed into a new box: **"If it doesn't look and sound like what we accept as genuine, then it has no place within the parameters of our worship experience"**.

In others words, more self-serving religious foolishness that has nothing to do with honoring or worshipping God. It is all about promoting our own agenda and personal preferences.

THE MORE THINGS CHANGE, THE MORE THEY REMAIN THE SAME.

We are just better at it now.

Here's the burning question: has the resulting commercial success of the Christian Music industry impacted our culture with the Gospel? Again, let's be honest. The answer is a resounding no! Quite to the contrary, the world culture is in fact, impacting Christianity, especially in the West. The focus slowly shifted from effectively sharing our faith thru the vehicle of music, to one of radio and chart success, major label deals and the ultimate prize, crossing over into the secular market.

WE WANTED TO BE IMPORTANT AND ACKNOWLEDGED AS LEGITIMATE. *We lost focus of our true mission.* **We became professional Christians.**

Everything around me reinforced the performance mindset on a daily basis. It was all about perception and image. In Christianville, we have taught one another to become comfortable with each other's veneer, all the while ignoring what lurks and simmers just below the surface, even in ourselves. We jockey for position, justify our actions, juggle lifestyles and close ranks to protect one another's investments in the industry.

This all went into developing who and what I eventually became. I will never blame anyone but myself for the steps I took and the paths I chose. Yet it is absolutely no wonder people are confused and hurt. Friends of mine who have been worship leaders for many years, in order to be relevant and acceptable as their churches adapted the new model, either had to learn to lead the congregation with a guitar slung over their shoulder and doing their best version of Bono, or they were relegated to some behind the scenes grunt job. Even worse, many have been dismissed all together, though their gifting and passion for leading in worship is as strong as ever.

AFTER 35 YEARS IN MINISTRY – THAT CAN BE DEPRESSING TO ANYONE.

This was precisely the basis of my ouster as worship leader in Iowa.

CAN WE JUST GET REAL FOR A MINUTE?

Since childhood, to my own detriment, I have been behind the scenes in the church, on the road, and in concert halls and studios. I have sat with friends at church camp coming off of bad LSD trips and been on gospel tour buses overridden with the smell of pot. My very own Fundamentalist, fire-breathing preacher of a grandfather, died as an angry alcoholic and living in an affair. I was in closed-door planning meetings with Jim Bakker and some of his PTL Singers about producing a new recording for them only weeks before everything imploded. Everyone knew more than anyone wanted to say. The fact is, everyone was afraid to say anything to anyone about anybody. No one wanted to be the guy with the pin in his hand when the balloon finally disintegrated. The PTL gig was a sweet ride no one wanted to surrender. The corporate gurus at PTL, some of them my friends, were drunk on their own power and known to be volatile and irrational people. Operating within the context of absolute power and virtually no oversight, provided the gatekeepers unfettered freedom to play things loose for a very long time. The misuse of that power finally proved fatal to the ministry and the joyride was permanently cancelled.

In another time and place I witnessed a group of renown and prominent southern gospel singers raising enormous sums of money in support of a campaign called, *'BIBLES FOR RUSSIA'*. This was at least a twenty-minute presentation in their *"show"*, urging those in attendance to donate to this worthy outreach, a vital part of their mission work abroad. The campaign proved to be a great success, resulting in a few cases of bibles making their way behind what was then, *"The Iron Curtain"*. In reality, the majority of the money raised in the campaign went to finance the group members' new cars, make payments on the condo at the beach, restock liquor cabinets and entertain the countless groupies hovering nearby in church parking lots. Sadly for the party planners, that particular cash cow rapidly dried up once President Reagan convinced Mikhail Gorbachev to tear down the wall.

In fact, I was told personally by the owner and manager of this musical Animal House, there was a ledger kept in their booking office listing all the various areas the group would never be able to return for concerts, due to the numerous blatant sexual exploits one of their vocalists had engaged in within those communities.

LIGHTS, CAMERA, ACTION

During the frequent trips we were making into Christian television and various high profile ministries, we were introduced to the legally binding non-disclosure agreement, and Lord knows I've signed my share of them. You were bound by the agreement to never discuss with anyone the things you witnessed or learned about while *"behind the curtain."* Everyone had to simply ignore all the obvious questionable practices if you wanted to maintain your place at the trough.

More recently, as a member of a worship team, I was backstage at a Crusade of one of the world's most famous Christian television personalities to participate in a called meeting with said personality. In that impromptu gathering of the band and singers, he told us we must learn to separate who we might see him to be in his private life versus who he was in his office and anointing on the platform. There was the man and then there was the *'man of God'*, and the two do not necessarily have to reconcile. We were strongly charged to understand this distinction in order to see beyond what might be construed as contradictions in what he taught versus what he lived.

HMMM, 'SOUNDED LIKE MY OLD SOUTHERN GOSPEL BUDDIES TO ME.

Though referred to in different terms within various cultures, the driving force behind much of what goes on in Christianville is most often about notoriety, money and fame. Whether it is Southern Baptist or Charismatic, Conservative or Liberal, Fundamentalist or Universalist, hip or cheesy, ministry has become a very lucrative business. There are those few personalities in Christian television and radio broadcasting, as well as on the road, known by everyone on the inside to be complete frauds. The amazing thing, they are brilliantly productive at raising millions in donations for all the various ministries, especially television. As a result, everyone chooses to play ignorant to the obvious, or even worse, they simply look the other way. Herein lies the reason why the general public can never get near some of their spiritual heroes. The standard response given is *'the man of God'* must be secluded from the people in order to maintain his anointing and focus to mission.

The truth is, they are afraid to expose who they really are.

While some might challenge its theological implications, Gloria Gaither regularly offered this prayer in our concerts: *"Lord, may I never lose hold on eternity…and not even know it."* I understand the content of her supplication now better than ever. Success and popularity can and do pollute spiritual discernment just as powerfully as an obsession for approval. Be it a massive ego and a depressed soul, they share in a common attribute, that being a self-centered focus. Our culture is obsessed with achievement and doing whatever it takes to realize prominence.

The slow drift from a life of personal devotion and passion for ministry to one dominated by demographic studies, marketing strategies, trend assessments, career management, image construction and product placement is subtle and dangerous. It happens to many people without them even realizing it. Power does corrupt and absolute power does in fact, corrupt absolutely.

Being surrounded by a lifetime of contradiction can be depressing.

IT CAN TAKE ANOTHER LIFETIME JUST TO WORK THROUGH IT.

Instead of focusing on the voice of our Shepherd, it is easy to be overwhelmed by the cacophony of big deal industry executives and image-makers who want to manage your career. Hell tormented my mind for years, manipulating me into constantly second-guessing myself and doubting the call and anointing of God upon my life, all because some wise guy with a corner office, a hot car and his own private parking place, felt the overwhelming need to voice his indisputable opinion about my calling, talent, and future.

During a time when I was faithfully rehearsing and working hard, prayerfully determined to skillfully extract the gift God had placed inside me and be ready when the opportunity came to share my faith thru music, one of the Captains of the industry sat me down in his office and pronounced over me: **"If you ever have to use your voice to make a living, you will eventually starve to death"**. I knew then and know now that really was not true. However, his voice and those words played over and over in my head for years and the enemy of my soul used it to nearly permanently derail me. One thing for sure, I was never gonna' just *"Get Over It"*.

God knows, I have been guilty of prolonged sessions of self-pity, some of them justified and many others the result of my own vivid imagination. The truth is, on spiritual battlegrounds, Satan's thugs will attempt to find the weaknesses in your defenses and exploit them. For me, and others like me, striving to perform at a level that wins the approval of your peers, especially in something as subjective as music and the arts, can make you incredibly vulnerable to your critics.

Self-pity was only the springboard for me. I hate many of the things I've seen and experienced. What I grew to hate more, is what I allowed myself to become as a result. My sin and failure – and the basis of my eventual self-destructive actions, was the misery I created in my own soul from working so hard to win the approval of people while equating their approval with pleasing God.

PLEASING PEOPLE IS A HORRIBLE ADDICTION.

I've never been drunk from alcohol a day in my life. In fact, I have yet to taste my first beer. I have no idea what smoking a cigarette feels like, let alone a joint. I have remained steadfastly loyal and faithful to Nancy. I love my children, giving up the life of full-time road gigs to make sure I was not an absentee father. My goal has always been to serve and perform in each assignment with excellence and integrity.

And yet, I became my own worst enemy. I allowed life to become all about me. Cynicism ruled my head and my heart, causing the joy of the Lord to become of no effect in me. Therein was the tragedy.

I hated religious phonies - and yet I was becoming one.

The industry makes it about the image – God looks on the heart and the intent.

We worry about who gets the credit – then when it fails, we look to fix the blame. That is pride and legalism in operation at it's very best.

I proclaimed the peace of God to others and yet found it to be absent my own life.

I claimed Grace was a gift of God and yet worked endlessly to prove my worth to God.

SATAN'S BEST WEAPON IS CONDEMNATION.

Bill and Gloria Gaither gathered the band and singers into their living room informing us that following the European leg of the current tour, they would be taking an indefinite period of time away from a full-time concert schedule in order to stay close to home in support of their three children, all of whom were now cruising through their teenage years.

Who could blame them for such a crucial decision? It was both understandable and commendable of Bill and Gloria, for which I bestow sincere kudos for actually living what they preach. Conversely, this disclosure stunned me to the core, instantly crushing my best-laid plans for the near future. I had it in my head to ride the Gaither bus for a very long time to come. The Gaithers were enjoying their greatest commercial success to date, demonstrated each evening with sellout crowds in every major venue we played, and we played them all. Our musical guests on different segments of the tour schedule included Don Francisco, Carman, Amy Grant, and Sandi Patti.

My band-mates, Dann Huff, Billy Smiley and Mark Gershmehl had all been writing new songs with the idea of forming a music group modeled after TOTO, a rock band out of Los Angeles composed of top tier studio session musicians. Dann, who was already a monster guitarist, studied the technique of TOTO legend, Steve Lukather, tirelessly. It was rare to see him without headphones on and/or a guitar in his hands rehearsing.

Once they had a few songs ready to record, Dann's brother, David, and I would join them in the Gaither Studio beginning about 11pm and work through the night. With free reign of the studio at that hour there were no distractions, given no one else in Indiana seemed keen to the idea of spending the night in the studio. Most often, we would lock ourselves away in the hours just prior to an extended road trip, work until call time for departure, then pile on the bus and sleep our way to the next concert stop.

With Dann on guitar, Smiley on guitar and vocals, Mark at the keys and vocals, David Huff on drums and me on bass guitar, we began the process of developing the sound of what was to become known as WHITEHEART. In time, Steve Green would become the lead singer for the first album release. Steve and I had been in Truth together and now were rejoined with Gaither, where he served as one of the background vocalists for the Trio, an original member of the Gaither Vocal Band, and the primary sub for Gary McSpadden. Steve's wife, Mary Jean, and Nancy would pack *"food suitcases"* for our road trips and would make dinner in the dressing rooms for us.

THE GAITHER VOCAL BAND

I was there, backstage following sound check one afternoon, as The Gaither Vocal Band was born, really quite by accident. Bill was sitting at a piano and began to play and sing an old Southern Gospel song, YOUR FIRST DAY IN HEAVEN, made popular by such groups as the Imperials. I remember Gary and Billy Smiley being there, along with Lee Young, our bass singer. In each concert, Bill would always reminisce about listening to quartet music as a kid in Indiana while doing chores on the farm, sometimes late into the evening.

We were just messing around as we all began to sing along with Bill. It was then, a very definitive bright light, obvious to everyone, began to emanate from Gaither's eyes. He immediately fell in love with the idea of putting the song into the concert that evening.

During this time, The Gaither Trio, composed of Bill, Gloria and Gary McSpadden, had become much more contemporary, at least for them, in their musical approach to the Trio recordings and in concert. This was especially true when you consider their touring ensemble was made up of musicians who loved rock and roll, and were corporately about to launch a trend setting contemporary Christian band. Concert reviews in several prominent newspapers and industry magazines were very complimentary of the fresh arrangements of the standard

Gaither catalogue being presented by our band. There were, of course, those who hated change.

To Bill's credit, I think he knew in his heart, dropping a wild-fire southern Gospel quartet favorite into the set list would be a enormous crowd-pleaser, as well as serving to appease some of the critics who believed the Gaithers' sound was moving too far away from their core audience and fan base. His intuition proved to be spot on as the impromptu quartet made up of Bill, Gary, Steve Green and Lee Young, were cheered into three encores of the song by the ravenous crowd, hungry for more. Gaither knew he had struck gold, a vein so rich he continues to mine the assets more than thirty years later.

THE GAITHER VOCAL BAND WAS BORN & BILL FINALLY HAD HIS QUARTET.

The new discovery and unhinged enthusiasm for the Vocal Band did not change the course of action for the immediate future however. Once Bill and Gloria had delivered their living room communiqué, everyone promptly began the process of relocation, with Nashville being the apparent destination of choice.

Gaither management assumed most all the team would pursue session work and songwriting, relocating the band only four hours away in Music City. The relative handful of Gaither concert dates over the next two or three years could still involve the same personnel on stage, the bus would simply pick up most of the band and singers in Nashville. This appeared to be the win-win solution for everyone involved.

While the Nashville option was radically more glamorous, my true passion had always been the ministry aspect more than the music itself. I believe music is a tool and my calling is to communicate the Gospel, utilizing it as a vehicle to accomplish that end. In addition, Nancy and I knew the idea of me being on the road and her having babies at home, was just not for us. We have many friends who have pursued that lifestyle, yet we loved each other's company far too much to consider that to be a viable option. I made a promise to myself very early on, long before I had even met Nancy, I would never put my career as a musician ahead of my wife and children.

It was a pledge made before God.

One routine late night at a Denny's, a friend who is a household name in the Christian music industry said to me, tears streaming down his face, that his kids had grown up and he had missed it all. While he traveled the world, they had become adults and he didn't even know them. In that incredibly vulnerable moment, the realities of a career perpetually on the road seemed to be far too costly a price to pay. While I certainly imply no disrespect toward all the countless friends who have spent their lives fulfilling a career calling and trusting to God the challenges of absentee parenting, I knew it was not for me. *(Bear in mind, to this point in my career and since our wedding day, Nancy was always on the bus with me as we traveled with the various groups and concert ministries.)*

The idea of pursuing a career in Nashville was set aside and prayerful consideration began for what the next step would look like in my and Nancy's world. Leaving the road would prove to be difficult at times, especially given my love for a steady change of scenery and the concert stage. A much more monumental conflict would be realized as I carried my fondness for theatrical production into the church, an attribute soon to raise the ire of more than a few inhabitants of the pew, as well as the resident sentinels of ritual and tradition.

THE TRANSITION BEGINS

It was at this point, session bassist Gary Lunn was recruited by Dann to assume my role in the Gaither band. In the months to follow, the ensemble of my former band-mates would morph into WHITE HEART as planned, taking their place as some of the most influential songwriters, session musicians and recording artists in history. And yes, I second-guessed and kicked myself for a very long time for choosing to leave and go another way. I believe this moment was one of several significant openings where a spirit of self-loathing and regret took deep root in my soul. My double-mindedness expanded to an entirely new level and the groundwork was laid for the turbulence and inevitable war about to be launched in my head and heart.

AN IMPERIAL INVITATION

To only complicate my internal discomfort, I received one of those phone calls I had always hoped for. Having arrived on the scene of our new church assignment, Nancy and I were literally unpacking the first few boxes of our belongings when Armond Morales called.

Armond was the founding member and owner of what was then the premier Christian music group in the world, THE IMPERIALS. They were at the very peak of the industry in every category. Grammys and Dove Awards by the armfuls were being won by this group, composed of Jim Murray, Russ Taff, Dave Will and Armond, all being guided musically by the skillful artistry and production of Michael Omartian, himself a multiple Grammy winner as keyboard player for Steely Dan and record producer for artists such as Christopher Cross, Rod Stewart and Donna Summer. Paul Smith was just beginning his stint as vocalist in the group.

Armond's invitation, delivered via his silky smooth bass voice, was for me to come to Nashville to be a part of the Imperials band as bass player. In doing so, I would be reunited with my old band-mates, Tom Reeves and Dick Tunney, along with one of the principal session guitarists in Nashville, Tom Hemby. One of my long-term goals had been to eventually be on stage as a part of The Imperials. Now, here was the opportunity at my very fingertips, along with the dishes I had been unpacking while watching a blizzard through the living room window of our new apartment.

The first thought flooding my mind was pure elation. Of course I would do this! I would be a lunatic not to. Think of all the musicians on the planet they could have called, and I got the invite, without an audition no less! This had to be the will of God. Everyone would just have to understand and if they couldn't, then they could just get over it. This was my dream job, which would surely lead to more incredible opportunities. In Christian music, to be a part of the Gaither entourage, followed up with climbing on board the Imperials bus, would be a privilege only a handful of people would have ever known. There was an overwhelming sense of gratification, as everything I had dreamed of seemed to be materializing. I asked Armond for the opportunity to prayerfully consider his offer overnight, thanking him for the honor of his invitation. He graciously granted my request and said he would expect my answer the following morning. *Nancy basically began to rewrap the dishes and put them back in the boxes. She knew what this opportunity meant to me.*

Then suddenly, the sound of common sense was heard crashing into the room, resulting in the abrupt need for me to sit down. The pastor and his congregation, in a significant vote of trust and confidence, had paid to move us across country, setting us up in our home and making provision for our future there. I couldn't just flippantly say, *"sorry, my bad"*, then head off for the bright lights of Music City, especially after making the prayerful determination that God Himself had wanted me to take a course other than the music business. If He had wanted me traveling with the Imperials or even remain with the Gaithers, I would have felt the need to move to Nashville with everybody else.

MOST RELIGIOUS PEOPLE WOULD SAY GOD WAS TESTING ME....... ACTUALLY, THEY DID SAY THAT VERY THING.

However - could it be God providing a way of escape? Maybe this was His way of saying, *"You are under no obligation to do this."* Besides, I had felt prodded by family and friends about this church thing anyway. Maybe I wasn't really called into the local church ministry after all. It seemed far more natural to be hanging with the Imperials in Nashville, not to mention the southern climate being a much better fit for Nancy as well.

After an exhaustively sleepless night filled with prayer, pacing and heart-wrenching indigestion, I arrived at the very painful and final decision.

I turned down the offer from Armond Morales and the Imperials.

Without the slightest hint of exaggeration, you must know that particular decision was one of the toughest I would ever have to make. There was no euphoria or noble sensation of dying to self. I was heartsick and hyperventilating. I mumbled and muttered my way through prayers of frustration, simply asking God to cut me a little slack for doing the *"right"* thing.

I was completely distraught for weeks over the choice I had made.

Then - I felt guilty.

Out of sheer discipline and commitment, I turned my full attention to the new role into which I had now been cast. Besides, surely this vibrant church setting would prove to be much closer to the utopian environment I deeply longed for - relatively free from the contradictions that so often seemed to plague the various music and television ministries.

I HAVE NEVER BEEN MORE MISTAKEN.

CHAPTER 6

ORDAINED AGONY

LIVING WITH A STAFF INFECTION

12 MARCH 1980

T his is the date of my ordination. At the time, Nancy and I had been married nearly four years. There seemed no doubt in anyone's mind God's anointing was on my life to minister to people. It was a toss-up where my calling might eventually lead, but anyone paying attention at all, knew it had zero chance of being conventional or anywhere near normal.

A handful of people were unrelenting in their belief I should pastor a church, declaring I would never be satisfied until I did. By their definition, my music career and other creative approaches to ministry were more of a diversion from God's will than a fulfillment. One significant individual in my life made the bold prediction: *"God will take your children from you if you are not obedient to His call".*

How very comforting and profoundly motivational!

Being one susceptible to the strong and outspoken opinions of others, this sort of nonsense can prove to be excessively unnerving. The troublesome question always lingered as to whether I was ever in the right place doing the right thing. Critics taking cheap shots from the gallery only added to the nasty habit of second-guessing myself.

"Why are you here when you should be doing much bigger things with your life?"

"God has so much more for you than this."

"You should be in Nashville".

"Why would you ever leave a situation like that? Your calling is ministry not the music business. *"*

The people making those statements meant well, but the cumulative effect only aided in producing additional doubt in myself, and any ability I might possibly have, to ever *"get it right"*. It has been said opinions are like navels, everybody as one. At issue was the fact I was becoming more driven by those opinions than anything else.

In addition, there was always another menacing issue dangling nearby - my genetically challenged attention span. Years of concert touring only served to greatly intensify that problem. I became bored far too easily, especially with the sameness of every day. Routineness was not my friend and waking up daily in the identical environment was hardly exhilarating. I was accustomed to large thinking, big dreaming and at the very worst, marginal enthusiasm. Making the shift from that scenario to one of recruiting reluctant semi-religious people and attempting to train them to be at least moderately enthusiastic about volunteer church work, all proved to be, at times, achingly frustrating and brutally tiring.

The drone of small thinking and stagnant movement depleted life from me at a rapid pace.

Furthermore, I learned in short order how people of every stripe are deathly allergic to change. If they do not like a certain style of music or ministry, they declare it to be vain, vulgar and unacceptable to God, all the while doing their best to stir up opposition.

I was prematurely becoming tired and discouraged. Then – I felt guilty.

FROM SWEET COMFORT TO SOUR TORMENT

I never intended to create controversy or conflict, but somehow, I always seemed to find clever, inventive ways to keep it stirred up.

It had come to my attention just how effective Calvary Chapel had been in impacting the youth culture of Southern California. Literally thousands of hippies, yippies and young people were coming to faith in Christ, being baptized in the Pacific surf. By way of Explo'72 in Dallas and the Jesus Movement, I had searched out much of what was happening on the west coast. One of the many bands I grew to love, originating from that very movement, was the Sweet Comfort Band, their lead singer being Bryan Duncan.

As student pastor of a church located on the east coast, I was visited by the far-fetched idea of bringing SCB across country, engaging them to reach youth who would never be interested in anything remotely *"churchy"* or religious. Here was this amazing band rockin' with the best of them, while the lyrical content of their music addressed faith and belief in Christ. Having been so incredibly effective in the western Youth Revival, surely they could have the same impact in our community. Sweet Comfort was such a predominant force on the California music scene they had just opened for Journey in several cities on their West Coast Tour that particular year. MTV was about to be launched, bringing the medium of music to an even more influential role in youth culture.

THE TIME WAS RIGHT AND I WAS STOKED.

Taking it to staff meeting, I surprisingly received immediate approval from the Senior Pastor and fellow staff-members on the first ballot. I was authorized to proceed in *"selling the concert"* and familiarizing the locals with the band. This was a challenge, given the only Christian radio stations were stacked wall-to-wall, morning to evening, exclusively with southern gospel singing and preaching of the most conservative orientation. No place existed to present the music of The Sweet Comfort Band on radio. Nevertheless, I booked the local civic auditorium to assure a neutral "non-religious" setting and spent months laying the groundwork. We distributed albums, music cassettes, videos and posters of the band to various youth leaders within a ninety-mile radius, doing all we could to educate people about SCB and our vision to reach the youth of our region with the Gospel. You must take into account Evie, Sandi Patti and B.J Thomas, all were considered to be radical cutting-edge contemporary artists within most religious circles at the time.

Yes Virginia, you have guessed correctly. Trouble was brewing on the horizon.

During this same era, I had creatively unlocked endless ways to irritate the religiously comfortable, including the formation of a rock and roll band of our own for youth meetings. A member of this musical ensemble was the son of my then next-door neighbor. The family was not members of our congregation, nor had they even attended our church, but I got to know their son and simply grew to love him. He was an amazing piano player with a love for Christ, a beautiful smile and great attitude, so I invited him to join us.

THE PROBLEM FOR GOD'S PEOPLE, HE WAS AFRICAN AMERICAN.

To recruit a funky little black kid to play piano in a Southern Baptist, pasty white, "good ole boy" church - was like slapping a 12- foot gator in the face with a chicken.

In the hostile opinions of many of the *'saints'*, it was already dreadful enough to have Junior and his family just living in our neighborhood. For me to invite him to join our youth group, and then actually put him on the platform as a musician, was far beyond the pale of tolerance and acceptability. I had reached much too far to endorse him as a leader and role model for the other students. He was a black child, for heaven's sake!

There were many meetings - I was the subject matter.

To repeat, there were many meetings.

The night came for the concert and our band was set to open for Sweet Comfort! More than eleven hundred tickets had been sold, though about one third of those chose to actually not attend. We were rehearsed and ready with a kickin' thirty minute set, including some of our favorite tunes from Phil Keaggy and a little known band called Petra. We dared to include Paul McCartney's song, EBONY AND IVORY, which lyrically calls for racial harmony in the same way the black and white keys of a piano coexist and collectively function to produce melodies, rhythm and chords. Long before it was fashionable or quasi-acceptable, we used a secular song in a Christian event, made even more radical by the fact it was the music of a former Beatle. I was playing secular music at a Christian event with a black child in the band.

THERE WERE ABOUT TO BE MANY MORE MEETINGS.

Then came time for the Sweet Comfort Band to take the stage. The lights go down, the band walks out to a small and reluctantly polite smattering of applause from the crowd of just under a thousand people, and launched into a burning arrangement of the song *"Valerie"*.

It was awesome! The sound was huge, Bryan's vocals were amazing, Randy's guitar playing was clean and powerful, and the building shook with the energy coming from the stage. Sanctified rock and roll had come to town and I was ecstatic!

And, as evident by what happened next, it was just all too much for God's people. Led by my very own Pastor who was seated on the front row, two-thirds of those in attendance systematically stood up and walked out of the auditorium before the Sweet Comfort Band could even get through the opening song. Leaders from other churches instructed the youth in their charge to head for the vans and buses. This was entirely unacceptable!

The second song of the set was the title cut from the new, soon to be released album, *"Perfect Timing"*. If the opening tune was revving the engine, now the guys kicked it into overdrive. It was exhilarating and terrifying all at once. I would later discover the band had no idea of the mass exodus occurring on the other side of the lights.

By the time SCB had muscled their way through song two of a fifteen-song set, less than a hundred and fifty people were left scattered throughout the seats of the lower level of the venue, a room with a capacity of three thousand. I made my way to the balcony where I sat alone to survey the wreckage and contemplate impending confrontations. This was bad - very bad. I stared at the stage that now seemed a hundred miles away. The only thing I could envision was a Deacons meeting with an ireful Pastor, soon to be convened in my honor.

Here's a little extra-added spice; Nancy was confined to the hospital, having just given birth to our son Jason the day before. I went to the lobby and called her from a pay phone, lying to her that all was well. 'Just wanted her to know I was thinking about her and Jason. The truth is - I needed to hear her voice.

Months, even minutes earlier, a concert featuring the Sweet Comfort Band had seemed to be a magnificently visionary idea.

NOW ON SECOND THOUGHT, NOT SO MUCH

My young evangelistically enterprising veins had been coursing with life, unbridled enthusiasm and passion for our mission to reach the youth culture with the Gospel thru concerts with artists such as the Sweet Comfort Band. Now my demise and departure were all but imminent.

I took the SCB to Shoney's afterwards and we talked. I loved them - but hated myself.

Today, thirty-four years later, that exact same church utilizes a rock band, theatrical lighting, smoke machines, and HD video presentations in their contemporary worship service.

Quite frankly - they owe me an apology.

TORPEDOES AND TUGBOATS

DID I HAPPEN TO MENTION - PEOPLE DO NOT LIKE CHANGE?

One approach to implementing change within the church I like to refer to as *The Tugboat*. The movement is slow, pragmatic, and gentle. It is a long and steady process of guiding the ship safely out of dock and into the open waters of the vessel's mission. The Tugboats themselves, while crucial to the success of the transition, are diminutive almost to the point of being unnoticed. The launch is carried out in such a way, the passengers and crew on board are hardly aware of the transition into the deep.

Professional Clergy and their parishioners collectively prefer *The Tugboat* approach as opposed to the favorite alternative of my youth: *THE TORPEDO*. *The Torpedo* approach is simple, clean, and straight to the point. Identify the objectives, target the obstacles that prevent realizing said objectives, and systematically blow them out of the water. Then, proceed at full throttle to implement the mission objectives as efficiently and expeditiously as possible.

In other words, GET 'ER DONE. Let's do this thing!

What are we waiting for? Time is of the essence.

Be not afraid of innovation!

The price of progress is the pain of change!

This is why I terrified people over the years. I loved *The Torpedo* approach. A relative few appreciated my energy and creativity, while most, chose to watch the Eddie parade from a safe distance.

Please allow for my learned pontification at this point: *The Torpedo* is not a wise approach in the world of stoic tradition and theological paradigms. Most congregations have no real desire to see things change, improve or be remotely innovative. To the contrary, they simply want to hire non-visionary staffers willing to stir the stew of complacency and manage the weekly minutia without disrupting the congregants' comfort zones, religious habits and normal expectations.

Somehow though, I had gotten the misplaced idea that people attending church might actually enjoy encountering creative changes week to week in the environment, lighting, theme and/or style of music. I have always loved constant movement in staging and presentation to keep things fresh and interesting, implementing an eclectic blend of musical styles. Approaching this mission with boundless energy and enthusiasm, I believed the results would surely render the critics not only silent, but actually convert the original dissenting opinions into solid votes of confidence in my inspired leadership.

I COULD NOT HAVE BEEN MORE WRONG.

Their rejection only intensified my determination to reach that illusive goal of winning their approval. I was consumed by their dissatisfaction and lack of acceptance. And please understand this, they critiqued everything - the songs, the arrangements, the volume, the clothing, the hair, the lighting, the approach, the set-up of the platform, the use of the choir, the lack of a choir, the use of the organ, the unplugging of the organ - everything.

I was accused as being hyper sensitive and taking things way too personal, many saying I cared too much what people thought and needed to lower my expectations. I must cease from people pleasing and toughen up if my intention was to be a successful leader. Upon reviewing these accusations, I attempted to correct those conspicuous shortcomings by becoming more emphatic, less approachable and blindly confident. At that point, I was labeled insensitive, uncaring, defensive and self-centered by even the people considered to be my closest friends.

NO WIN.

No matter how I played it, I always fixated on the response of my peers at some level, the vulnerability most exploited by the enemy. To my discredit, overreaction was my normal go-to response. I would almost always fret over people having the wrong impression of me. I realized they may not like everything I did, but how could they ever think I was evil? Such harsh judgment paralyzed and consumed me internally.

Meanwhile, life on the road accommodates individuals suffering my inclinations with a very different and pleasant proposition; if people do not like you, for whatever reason, you'll be gone in the morning. The damage is short-lived and with every new venue there appears a fresh set of faces and the added benefit of getting another shot.

With the acceptance of a pastoral staff position in a local church, no such luxury availed itself. I was now firmly entrenched in relationship with a *"permanent audience"*, those who loved me were seated just down the pew from those who were my loud consistent critics. The pattern would soon be established for the foreseeable future of my professional life. Sixty percent of the people would love and support my work and vision for change. Twenty-five percent would tend to be reliably uncomfortable and less than enthusiastic with my leadership, but somehow be able to *"grin and bear it."*

THE REMAINING FIFTEEN PERCENT WOULD RISE IN ONE MIGHTY CHORUS TO PROCLAIM ME AS THE DEVIL HIMSELF.

In fairly short order, staff meetings became extended mental doodle sessions for me, daydreaming of far distant places I would much rather be.

Internally - my patience was frayed and a simmering resentment was always brewing just beneath the surface toward stubborn deacons, small-thinking leaders, beginner musicians and prima-donna choir members. Meanwhile, I watched from the gallery, as my former band-mates were becoming rock stars and world-class studio session players.

As you might imagine - those feelings are somewhat embarrassing to admit, yet they are nonetheless true.

Externally - I attempted to put on the face of joyful determination, putting forth the best resolution to carry out the work of the ministry with excellence and verifiable results. Some would judge me, even now, as pretentious or not being genuine, but I really never saw this behavior as fraudulent. I was simply performing as a Professional Christian.

I redefined success as meeting the expectations of others, no matter what I felt inside.

The church had succeeded in teaching me to perform, far more than had the concert stage. It appeared that honesty was synonymous with weakness, so you learned to perform as a way to cover your true feelings. Pretense seemed to be heralded as strength. Never let 'em see you sweat. Put your best foot forward. Square your shoulders and *"give the world a smile each day"*, to quote the Blackwood Quartet!

I was already in survival mode. In no way would I ever admit to anyone I had made a major mistake in my decision to turn down the Imperials. That would call into question my spiritual discernment and maturity, as well as the commitment I had made to Nancy and our yet to be born children. However, this was the infancy of a sinister and disturbing trend soon to be woven into my very DNA. No matter where I was, what I was doing or how successful it proved to be, I always seemed to gradually develop an insatiable appetite to be somewhere else.

I longed for something, or more likely someplace, that did not exist. The concert world was void of the spiritual emphasis and depth I longed for, while the church was suffocating me in her bourgeois and pious bickering, as well as the complete disregard of anything original and innovative. All of this was followed by the constant onslaught of guilt for feeling the way I did, none of which I ever talked about to anyone with any transparency whatsoever. The slow burn to self-destruction had been kindled, and there was to be plenty of fuel for the fire.

TORTURE IN TEXAS

Square Dancing, Designated Drivers & Other Goofy Adventures of The Misguided

It would necessitate volumes of written testimony to chronicle the details of my pastoral adventures through the years, so at this juncture we will embark on more of a high altitude flyover of the landscape, without descending into the weeds of detail. Enjoy just a few select snippets of my close encounters of a religious kind.

Let's begin with another side-note: With God as my witness, every single pastor I ever worked for would say in his own paraphrased version something to the effect: *"You only have to worry about pleasing one person, and that is me."*

For the record, let us clarify – That is what they said, this is what they meant: *"I'm wanting to try a whole bunch of radical new ideas and put you on the point. My goal is to change this church at its' very core. The music, worship and overall environment in the main services will be where we focus our efforts. If the plans succeed and everyone is happy with the changes, I'll thank you for making me look really great! If the people hate the changes and our new direction, then very simply, you will get the blame".*

GET IT? GOT IT? GOOD!

That statement of clarification is without the least bit of exaggeration. This represents the life I lived as an agent of change in the world of the contemporary church, no matter the name of the denomination or pastor on the sign out front.

PASTOR PERFECT - In a very intriguing exit interview at a prominent church in the West, with tears streaming down his face, Pastor Perfect acknowledged he had wrongly used me as a shield to protect himself as he moved the church toward a Willow Creek *"seeker-friendly"* model. The response to our efforts had been less than enthusiastic from the traditional, mission-oriented congregation, and vehemently opposed by many. Thru the two-year process, he had covertly laid any blame for the experiment in modernization at my feet, even though I was guilty of only one thing: *loyally implementing his specific instructions.*

As we hugged good-bye, he dolefully sought my forgiveness for the blatant abuse and thanked me for my faithful service and friendship, then, of course, Pastor Perfect had me sign a non-disclosure agreement prior to surrendering my final paycheck. To be clear, my employment was not terminated. I voluntarily resigned my position, accepting another music role in a far distant land. I could no longer function, due to the many issues hidden behind the curtain, of which only a few select people were even remotely aware. Once again, rather than poke the bear, I chose to quietly exit the cave before the lights of reality came on.

Months later, Pastor Perfect would resign after being discovered having an affair.

IN A FAST GROWING CHURCH - I served as Student Pastor and Assistant to the Music Director where the student population of our youth ministry flourished from a dozen kids to over three hundred in a matter of months. Concurrently, the inclusive church growth was exponential as well. Pastor Powerball hastily revamped his personal style to become a full-tilt, hyper-demanding, tirelessly driven rising star wannabe within the burgeoning contemporary church movement. He hired a slick nickel counter and gatekeeper from the town called Tulsa and we were up, up, and away! The mission was soon being accomplished in spades. Power replaced purity and many of the typical troubles ensued. 'Dude got a Mercedes and a gold chain necklace. 'Hung with all the television heavies. 'Demanded the best of everything. Got the best of everything. Became elusive and proud.

I knew Pastor Powerball had been having an affair for months.

Unknown to him, his seductive mistress, a member of the support staff at church, lived in an apartment located just across the parking lot from my mother and father's home. Ooopsie! Without question, many of his so-called *"field visits"* to parishioners, included regular and extended sessions of afternoon delight with his Honey Dew. Rather than being the whistle blower, I quietly moved on to accept a music position in a far and distant land. Though I kept my knowledge of his indiscretions perfectly undisclosed, he was furious at my departure. Months later, following my *"escape"* back to the Midwest - Pastor Powerball was forced to resign amid a deluge of allegations and revelations concerning his vile lifestyle. He did get to keep the car. *Woo-hoo!*

I HAD BEEN FORWARNED ABOUT TEXAS - A very close friend and former road-mate had served as Minister of Music for Pastor Hellion for more than three years. This was just long enough for my friend to acquire a perfectly formed bleeding ulcer. To quote his wife, "Working with this Pastor is like working for a demon from hell".

I WENT ANYWAY.

I flew to Texas to meet with Pastor Hellion, where he made a contrite confession of his prior ugly issues, assuring me a dynamic encounter with Jesus had shown him the error of his ways. For some regrettable reason, I accepted the invitation to join his staff.

To no one's surprise but mine, he continued his historic onslaught, living up to his reputation of being ruthlessly contentious with everyone, even those who fully complied with his notorious leadership. Deeply involved in Texas denominational politics, fights were always brewing on several fronts at state and national levels. He was enraged by something all the time and accusatory toward most everyone in life. No one could do anything right but him.

Brother Hellion was unashamedly verbally abusive toward his wife and family, even from the platform. More than once, I listened in stunned disbelief, as he openly reprimanded his teenage daughter from the pulpit, selectively using her youthful indiscretions as sermon illustrations of how not to live and choices not to make.

In a hotly contested staff meeting, Brother Hellion abruptly removed from church leadership one of our best volunteers in the music and arts ministry. I was furious! Once he discovered my friend had chosen to continue his employment at the local Budweiser plant following his conversion to faith in Christ, Brother Hellion demanded I remove him from any position of leadership until which time he resigned from the brewery.

I, of course, made the significant mistake of asking Brother Hellion if he would pass the same judgment on his daughter, who was employed as checkout clerk at a local grocery store, given the fact she marketed and sold the exact same Budweiser and countless other brands to the general public. Additionally, she personally rang-up copious amounts of whiskey, scotch, vodka and wine for massive numbers of patrons from our community, some of which were no doubt members of his own church!

Yet again, I had smacked the very large, proverbially angry bear right across the nose!

During an unplanned and extended period of silence in pastoral staff prayer time, Pastor Hellion suddenly jumped up, slamming his genuine leather throne into the solid walnut credenza, violently hurling his large print King James Bible across the room and bellowed, *"If no one on this stupid staff will pray with me, then I'll go find someone who will!"*

MEETING ADJOURNED.

Brother Hellion was proudly humble to send his luminous reports to the State Denominational Office of more than three hundred baptisms each year and yet, his greatest success went conspicuously unreported! He was most effective in creating substantial growth among the congregations of other local churches, as the constant flow of wounded and embarrassed members of our church family quietly escaped by way of the back door.

I voluntarily resigned after six months, accepting another music position in a far distant land.

The Music Pastor following my departure abandoned the ministry altogether after two years of service under Brother Hellion's acrimonious leadership. His tearful mother shared the details of his egression as we stood in front of our theatre in Pigeon Forge years later. We prayed together that day for his personal healing and restoration.

DESIGNATED DRIVER

On our journey to a three-day church leadership conference, I was appointed Designated Driver, given that Pastor Hipster and his new favorite Elder loved to throw back an abundance of distilled brew following a brutal day of spiritual seminars and lectures. *I was proud to serve*, though being sufficiently accosted for my less than mature decision of choosing not to participate in the brotherly consumption of said spirits.

As I commandeered the wheel of Pastor Hipsters' car, the atmosphere now reeking of alcoholic belching, the occasional passing of brisket-fed gas, and the pulsating sounds of AC/DC rocking us down the highway toward home, it was almost like being in high school again. The truth is - in my heart and head I felt guilty for always being the prude and Victorian throwback. I also realized something had significantly changed in my relationship with the pastoral staff that day. I was now once again on the outside looking in, due to my pronounced lack of hipness and non-participation in the fraternal alcoholic consumption.

SHEER AGONY – A Few Mere Glances @ More Amazing Misadventures

- I pleaded with Pastor Pontificator to please believe me and my professional sound engineer friends, the church was headed for an acoustical nightmare if we proceeded with the plans for our new worship center as submitted by the Design and Build firm he and the Building Committee had hired. *He ripped me a new one, telling me in no uncertain terms to never speak to him of it again.* Twelve years and three million dollars over budget later, the sound and acoustical problems persist. By the way, he retired and the new guy has inherited the mess.

- Pastoral Staff meetings were attended by the wife of Pastor Henpecked during my four years at this church, where she systematically and ruthlessly attacked various people within the congregation viewed by her as some sort of a threat, insinuating everything imaginable about their personal lives to build a case for removing them, first as leaders, then from church membership entirely. *Her success has rendered the reputation of that ministry greatly diminished and seemingly scarred beyond repair in the region where they are located.*

- **Never**...hang parachutes in the ceiling of the sanctuary, fill the platform with colorful banners and theatrical lighting, create music videos featuring the faces of the hundreds of children attending the wild and crazy Vacation Bible

School, nor give free rides each morning on tethered hot air balloons to kids as they arrive in the parking lots with carloads of friends they are bringing with them to church for the very first time. *Never ever even think about doing any of that, not if you want to keep your church gig. Just sayin'.*

TAKE NO THOUGHT – No More Thinking, No More Dreaming, Just Shut Up and Have A Good Time

A longtime friend once offered this perfectly well timed advice: *"Eddie, find a nice place where you would like to live. Move there. Then, for the love of God, do not have an idea for the next five years".*

While I may not have seen it all, my experiences have brought me to a place where I am certain of two things; nothing would ever shock me and absolutely anything is possible. Not only does the cynicism of the general public toward organized religion and the contemporary church not surprise me, it really is a wonder anyone would ever go near a church door again, except to exit the building.

Over time I have been tried and found guilty of living a life of escapism, running from place to place looking for an elusive spiritual nirvana that will at last heal my plagued hungry soul. Many say I could never be satisfied. *"Eddie has developed a lifelong pattern of a wanton unwillingness to deal with life among other human-beings."* This was the critical definition of my greatest perceived weakness given by a friend in the Midwest.

And yet – as you review the history contained within this text, the question must be asked: *DO YA' BLAME ME FOR WANTING TO ESCAPE?*

Granted, we are all imperfect and in desperate need of Grace.

Like the Apostle Paul I would say, no one more than me.

In the quiet darkness of many sleepless nights, I wrestled with the guilt of not sticking it out in many places I loved. I continued to allow silly people to steal my joy by way of their cheap shots, accusation and childish behavior. Sometimes, I would fire back with cheap shots, accusation and childish behavior.

THEN - I FELT GUILTY.

Years ago - I was already becoming incredibly weary and discouraged, showing early signs of serious depression. Hurt, cynical and frustrated for all I had experienced - yet I still believed it would be weak and needless to surrender to normal. I was wired to be radical and stubborn.

I've never been afraid of a challenge.

God places a visionary spirit inside of us for a reason.

On late afternoon bike rides with my kids in the Rockies or while wandering thru the Mall with Nancy, I continued to dream about and mentally rehearse untested ideas. Quietly and prayerfully I began to explore the possibilities of a radically alternate approach to ministry, simmering on the back burner of my *Heart & Soul* for a very long time. Maybe there was a decidedly better way to fulfill the calling on my life.

DREAMS WERE ABOUT TO BE REALIZED.

However, I would also soon discover that with new levels come new devils.

We were about to move from mere skirmishes to full-blown warfare.

Photo Section

SCROOGE - DENVER - 1991

PERFORMING @ THE RYMAN

ON STAGE WITH
Jason Anders

TRUTH

ON STAGE WITH ALBERT LEE

EDDIE ANDERS

ENTERTAINMENT

FRIDAY, JULY 10, 1998 ✦ THE MOUNTAIN PRESS

DIARY OF A DISCIPLE

AFTER PERFORMING AT A BILLY GRAHAM EVENT WITH MICHAEL W. SMITH

Voted Best Restaurant!

CHAPTER 7

EDDIE'S HEART & SOUL CAFÉ

A DREAM COME TRUE BECOMES A NIGHTMARE

IT HAD LONG BEEN A DREAM OF MINE...A family entertainment venue and restaurant borrowing from all the best elements of Hard Rock Cafe, Cracker Barrel, House of Blues, and the like, coupled with the visionary "seeker-friendly" aspect of churches such as Willow Creek in Chicago.

Traveling the country extensively through the years, I knew firsthand no one had even attempted a concept like this. Granted, there were small Coffee Houses or a few Christian bookstores sporting a petite coffee/dessert area where local groups or singers could present a Friday - Saturday night set of music, serving as a gathering place for high school or college kids to hang out.

However, no one was presenting the *"multi-million dollar"* version, competing on the level with Hard Rock Cafe and Planet Hollywood. My dream was of a truly unique place where people of all *"stripes"* and from various cultures, ages and demographics would come for the unsurpassed quality of food, service and entertainment. We would set our sights on being the best of the best, to win awards and acclaim for the food and the *"vibe"* of the environment we created, a world-class family entertainment venue and critically acclaimed restaurant.

I would never want to be known as exclusively a *"Christian place"*, or to win the support of the religious community due to a *"fish"* or a *"cross"* positioned within our logo, along with the various trivial accouterments people somehow think classifies a business as *"Christian"*. We fully intended the Cafe to be known as far more than just a Gospel music performance venue, even though Gospel music would always be included. I would perform music from the Beatles, James Taylor, Billy Joel, Chicago, Vince Gill, Nat King Cole, B.B. King and John Denver, and blend it with movies themes, television songs, bluegrass, gospel, instrumental, and an endless array of diverse styles.

To create such an environment, pleasing to Senior Adults as well as their grandkids, would prove an enormous undertaking, but I knew it could be done.

We envisioned the Cafe a giant, cozy living room, giving prominence to a massive stone fireplace on the west end of the dining area. Opposite the fireplace, the east end would feature a high-tech stage including a multi-screen video wall, a dramatic circular keyboard set-up and state of the art sound. Patrons would enjoy multi-level seating designed to enhance sightlines to the stage from any of the 250 seats. Our approach was never one of a conventional dinner theatre, yet a warm relaxed ambiance featuring live entertainment during lunch and dinner, again borrowing from House of Blues or Hard Rock Café, yet far more eclectic and diverse in our musical identity.

We were not interested in the nickel and dime remodeling of some worn-out leftover space in the basement of a church building or in creating a cut-rate imitation of Chuckie Cheese. Our goal was the development of a concept with the potential of capturing the attention of the service and entertainment industry. To compete at the highest level was imperative.

From the outset, words of instruction years earlier from my esteemed friend, Derric Johnson, proved vital to our success: *"What you do on stage earns you the right to be liked by the people, and if they like you, then they will listen to what you have to say"*.

This became bedrock principal and crucial to the core values of Cafe. The allurement to the public would be the quality of our performance and presentation at every level. The by-product of this success would be the realization of our primary objective, utilizing the Café as an apparatus to creatively share our faith.

Also paramount to our constitution was the idea life is not separated into the secular and the sacred. For me, a thread of the sacred is at the core of everything. God is Creator of all things. Humans simply manipulate His creation. Having personally been spiritually impacted thru the music of Paul McCartney and James Taylor at very determinative moments in my life, I knew if God could use *"secular"* music to reach into my soul, He could use the very same music in the lives of our guests in similar fashion.

Our presentation of faith would be creative, yet without apology or compromise.

NATURAL.

GENUINE.

Faith is meant to be fleshed-out organically, cultivated and shared with others in the routines of our daily lives. Most of humanity only knows of the one dimensional window-dressing brand of Sunday morning Christianity, relegated to a few devotional minutes in a sanctuary and having little hope of actually transforming a life.

To this point, I had spent most of my adult life operating as an agent of change within the church, attempting to move congregations to adopt new styles of ministry, expression of worship and creative outreach. Not only did they resist and oppose the idea of change, they most often reacted to my proposals with outrage and fury directed toward me personally. In time, I determined I must have been blessed with the spiritual gift of irritation, frightening normal occupants of classic Protestant pews to the point of hysteria.

The Café served as an alternative to this dilemma, a place the church could actually use as a strategic tool to share the Gospel, yet posing no threat to any religious tradition. The ultimate goal was to see EDDIE'S HEART & SOUL CAFE as a featured attraction of Downtown Disney in Orlando. To be located as a neighbor to Wolfgang Puck, the House of Blues, Gloria Estefan's, and Planet

Hollywood, and for EDDIE'S HEART & SOUL CAFE to become one of the *"must-see"* places on every Central Florida tourists' agenda would be a lofty, yet attainable goal.

It is indeed as Walt Disney said: "If you can dream it, you can do it".

A good friend always encouraged me with these words: "Everything you do needs to contain great value - always make it unforgettable."

As we walk through this part of the story, please keep this fact in mind: *I had never worked in a restaurant, let alone cook, serve in or come anywhere close to designing one.* Being a Chef was not a club in my bag. I had no real skills or knowledge about the *"back of the house"* operation in the food service industry. I did, however, know the things people loved and I certainly knew how to market, build relationships and perform on stage. Most important and strategic of all - I knew how to pray.

PLANNING, PROMOTING, PERFORMING & PRAYING
MY ROLE: ATTENDING TO THE FOUR P'S

I was not about to launch into a venture of this size on presumption and pretense, being fully mindful of the requirements to fund and construct the Cafe, even though I had no money of my own. Nancy and I were basically living from paycheck to paycheck. It would be a bona fide miracle of egregious proportion to sell investors and bankers on a new and untested restaurant concept, with the identity based around a guy who had never earned a paycheck working in a restaurant a day in his life, let alone having one named after him.

Granted, the same could be said for restaurants named for Michael Jordan, Jackie Gleason, Ronnie Milsap, Alabama, Alan Jackson, or Dolly Parton's Dixie Stampede. Even Planet Hollywood was initially built on the celebrity status of Arnold Schwarzenegger, Sylvester Stallone and Bruce Willis, not their years of experience in the food service industry.

However, allow me to posthaste acknowledge the obvious; my name was not one uttered by multiplied millions around the world. I did have a hit song on a couple of radio stations in Holland about this time, but that was a very long way from the mountains of East Tennessee and would prove to be a ridiculous commute for the small contingent of Dutch who loved me. I most likely would not be able to build the business on their enthusiasm for my music.

Another famous Walt Disney quote: "It's kinda' fun to do the impossible!"

In addition, most themed restaurants were developed by existing powerful food service corporations and *"pitched "* to marquee personalities. Should they decide to *"buy into the idea,"* the celebrity received a negotiated share in the profit for the rights to simply use their name. In my case, we were raising the money, designing the building, recruiting and hiring management, creating entertainment concepts, and personally engaging the attorneys in matters of the corporate legal structure and fiscal budgetary planning.

AND YET, SOMEHOW I NEVER SEEMED TO BECOME WEARY.

Against the projections of all the odds makers and skeptics, my vision slowly morphed into a structured architectural design on paper and eventually, model form. Through the entire laborious process, there remained an unquenchable determination to vigorously press on. I knew if we prepared properly and attended faithfully to the minutia of the task at hand, the opportunity to see our dream realized would soon present itself.

I had been to multiple locations of the Hard Rock Cafe and similarly themed restaurants all over the country on countless occasions, studying and researching for years their successes and failures, interviewing managers, chefs, partners and owners. I learned from corporate leaders deep inside the industry some of the specific issues, which closed the doors of many of those same themed eateries so quickly. Planet Hollywood had to shutter many locations, simply due to relying far too much on the *"star factor"* for their success, while failing to concentrate on the basics of food quality and service. Strong as the concept was, the novelty alone was not enough to sustain the business long-term, even among unbroken streams of tourists.

During a private meeting in New York City with the newly hired Executive Chef of Planet Hollywood, he explained in great detail the issues bringing the restaurant chain to an urgent need for the reshaping of their priorities and focus.

"When each of our locations go on a two or three hour wait every evening of every week of every year, after a while local management begins to think, 'so what if thirty percent of these people never come back, we're built on tourism, of which there seems to be an endless supply of enthusiastic movie fans who will visit PH at least once. Turning the tables was our number one priority, not the fully satisfied experience of our clientele. It was about milking this concept for all it was worth without any thought of developing loyal returning customers."

My friend had been recruited and hired to lead the rescue of Plant Hollywood. He revamped the menu, streamlined the operation, redesigned the management structure, and basically, for the first time in their existence, actually focused the training of the staff on food quality, attention to detail, upscale service, and building a loyal consumer base.

THE INFLUENCE OF CRACKER BARREL

There was also a great deal of insight I was blessed to receive from the awesome leadership team at Cracker Barrel. Their concept presents a store that also incorporates a restaurant, promoted as Cracker Barrel Country Store. In the nineties, up to sixty-five percent of their per-store profit came from merchandise sales. Guests would arrive, waiting for seating while browsing a store loaded with impulse purchase items designed specifically for their target demographic. This concept was not the result of some secondary happy accident but was a very strategic plan. Rocking chairs, a huge fireplace, biscuits, gravy, country ham, catfish and pancakes. Quality, family oriented, and with very reasonable prices. Genius!

When locating a store in Pigeon Forge, Cracker Barrel leadership considered it to be a very serious risk - this being the only time the company had opened off an interstate highway. This was a monumental decision for the corporate bean counters, one made with a great deal of reservation and caution.

The last I heard, the original store at the south end of the Parkway in Pigeon Forge, as well as their second location next door to our Café, have consistently led national sales since their opening. With each return to town, out of sheer curiosity, I still check the parking lots at those particular Cracker Barrels, always to find they are still rockin' it all these years later.

ON OUR WAY TO BEING ON OUR OWN AT LAST

Grateful as I was for the mentoring and valued insight these brilliant people graciously shared with me, I was steadfast to not merely construct some rehashed, tweaked image, of any of them. OUR DNA WAS DIFFERENT. The procedure of finding expression for that uniqueness in our building design, branding, product development and marketing, was tedious and expensive, yet vitally crucial.

The flagship Cafe had to prove strong enough to be replicated in other markets, not simply built around me, the personality of our family, or our personal strength of relationships in the local region. This would be the only way to achieve the national success we envisioned.

Day by day, all the various elements began to evolve and take shape. More and more people became enthusiastic about our vision. I presented the details of our plans to my friends at the PIGEON FORGE TOURISM DEPARTMENT. Without hesitation, they believed our concept and the family oriented culture of the Smoky Mountain region were made for each other. They in turn shared the high points of their plans, already well underway.

The city was developing a theatre district to be known as Music Road, not as expansive as Branson, and yet home to multiple high quality venues featuring marquee names. This district would certainly require stellar restaurants for Pigeon Forge to realistically become a bona fide competitor with Downtown Disney, Broadway at the Beach, Branson, Nashville, and other major tourist destinations.

THE TIMING WAS PERFECT!

No one believed for a moment our arrival was coincidental.

BACK TO THE FUTURE

SMOKY SHADOWS & THE GREAT AMERICAN OPRY

To properly familiarize you with the backstory leading to the creation of EDDIE'S HEART & SOUL CAFÉ, let us travel back through the mists of time for a few minutes.

IN THE SUMMER OF 1976, I was recruited by the Director of Campus Ministries at Carson Newman College, Jerry Brittingham, to be a cast member for the family variety show he was producing in Pigeon Forge. The school granted a full scholarship along with housing for my participation as a vocalist and keyboard player. The show was designed as a ministry outreach to the increasing number of people visiting the Smokies throughout the tourist season, which at the time, primarily consisted of Memorial Day weekend through Labor Day. Long before DOLLYWOOD, these were the days of GOLD RUSH JUNCTION and a relative handful of t-shirt shops, home grown motels and a couple of miniature golf courses.

Our approach was to creatively combine musical variety and theatre with the presentation by an artist, center stage, crafting clay sculptures of famous personalities while telling the stories of their lives, accomplishments and contributions to our culture. The popular icons featured throughout our season included Walt Disney, Theodore Roosevelt and Will Rogers. Each of us in the cast were students at Carson Newman, whose first role of the evening was serving dinner to those in attendance, prior to surprising our guests by taking the stage as the musicians and vocalists.

SINGING WAITERS & RESTAURANT RUNS

While not turning the world on its ear or securing any of us a place in someone's Hall of Fame, the show did prove to be a moderate success! That summer was also my introduction to the concept of *restaurant runs*; a high-energy, hit & run, two-minute presentation in multiple restaurants during the breakfast hour, a quick song and distribution of promotional brochures, along with discount coupons to our evening show. It proved to be a win-win-win for everyone involved. A fun surprise for the patrons, entertainment value added to the restaurant, and the shameless promotion of our show. I particularly loved the cavernous acoustics of the local Arbys at the time. Like singing in the shower, the room greatly improved our sound, not an easy task for vocalists at 8AM.

Our venue was the Smoky Shadows Conference Center - located at the south end of the Parkway in Pigeon Forge, last stop on the way to Gatlinburg. We entertained our guests with stories of character, courage and conviction - using secular music, the biographies of pop cultural personalities, and a few well-placed scripture verses and songs lyrically communicating our faith in Christ. In those days, no template yet existed for something of this nature. Throughout my career and life's work, I have been blessed to consistently be associated with innovators utilizing contemporary art forms as a viable tool of communicating the Gospel.

Little did I know an entrepreneurial seed was planted deep within my soul, one eventually maturing to full fruition twenty years later at the other end of the parkway in Pigeon Forge. Nancy and I would be married that September, making our home in Greenville, South Carolina for only a few short months. Then our life together on the road would begin.

RETURNING TO PIGEON FORGE & THE SMOKY MOUNTAINS

Having maintained close friendship since our days with the Gaithers, Gary McSpadden graciously extended the invitation in 1991 for me to become his music director, keyboard player and featured vocalist in the show he was introducing in Pigeon Forge, resulting in our relocation from the Rocky Mountains of Colorado to the Smoky Mountains of East Tennessee. This move was received as cheerful news by grandparents and family, since our new home would be just a few hours drive from everyone, as opposed to the formerly insane distance spanning two time zones.

We purchased a house and dug in deep, anticipating The Smokies would be home for a long time to come. Over the next two years, each member of our little family were all involved in THE GREAT AMERICAN OPRY, proving to be significant training ground for the journey ahead. Nancy was active in the operations of Gary's tour company, booking bus tour groups into our show and area hotels; Jason assisted in the lighting production, and Lindsay took her place on stage as our featured dancer. Gary McSpadden has remained one of the most respected names in Gospel music through the years and given his notoriety and influence, my role in his organization opened door after door in the community for me to become associated with local business leaders, politicians, real estate moguls, and other entertainers.

Our home theatre was a very boutique venue seating just over two hundred people, proving to be one of the most positive aspects of our presentations.

The intimate setting meant audience members were up close and personally interactive with the performers during each show. Being the consummate professional, Gary's stage presence and heartwarming style of hosting gave us a distinct advantage in winning over a crowd and obtaining a loyal following in the market.

At the time of our arrival on the scene, in addition to the amusement park DOLLYWOOD and their dinner theatre DIXIE STAMPEDE, which opened it's doors in 1988, there were only five other theatres in Sevier County, all very organic, home-grown and relatively small in scale:

- **SWEET FANNY ADAMS**
  A VERY EUROPEAN MONTY PYTHON KIND-OF VIBE LOCATED IN GATLINBURG.

- **THE SMOKY MOUNTAIN JUBILEE**
  THE ORIGINAL FAMILY VARIETY SHOW FEATURING COUNTRY MUSIC AND "HEE HAW" TYPE COMEDY.

- **MEMORIES THEATRE**
  HOME TO EDDIE MILES' TRIBUTE TO ELVIS - AS WELL AS OTHER LEGEND TRIBUTE ARTISTS.

- **BONNIE LOU & BUSTER**
  THE SHOW FOR BLUEGRASS AND TRADITIONAL "OLD-SCHOOL" COUNTRY MUSIC LOVERS, VERY POPULAR IN EAST TENNESSEE DUE IN LARGE PART TO THEIR LONG-STANDING ASSOCIATION WITH THE LEGENDARY PORTER WAGNER AND HIS SUCCESSFUL TELEVISION SHOW.

- **THE RAINBOW THEATRE**
  FEATURING ENTERTAINERS DICK DALE & AVA BARBER FROM THE LAWRENCE WELK SHOW

One additional show had long been a local favorite, featuring HEE-HAW host and comedian, ARCHIE CAMPBELL. He regularly performed as a solo act in a small Gatlinburg venue prior to moving to his own Pigeon Forge showroom, closing after his death in 1987. As a side note, several years later, one of the most popular shows in the region, THE COMEDY BARN, would be built on that very location.

All of these shows gained loyal followings over the years in a market not really known as an entertainment destination such as Branson. Outlet Malls were just beginning to soar, along with the go-cart tracks, leather stores, a multitude of miniature golf courses and small gift shops loaded with cheap t-shirts, Smoky Mountain souvenirs, postcards, and key-rings. The Smoky Mountain National Park continued as the main draw with the majority of the eight to nine million tourists a year being from surrounding states. Visitors were almost exclusively a *"drive-in"* demographic, with nearly two-thirds of the population of the United States living within a days' drive of the popular tourist destination.

Traffic had been a major headache in Sevier County for years. The billboard laden highways accessing the Smokies had never been adequate to handle the volume of vehicles, resulting in two-lane parking lots stretching for miles, especially in the summer and fall seasons. The mountains, Rod Runs, car shows, the University of Tennessee football games, and of course, DOLLYWOOD, all contributed to the millions of people making their way to this blue collar resort. The average stay was then and continues to be three days. The majority of motels were of the homegrown variety, the most exclusive and swank accommodations being found at the Holiday Inn in the center of town. Restaurants were of a similar kind with branding such as THE APPLE BARN, THE APPLETREE INN and THE GREEN VALLEY RESTAURANT. That was all about to change as commercial growth in Pigeon Forge began to accelerate rapidly.

SEVIER COUNTY BECOMES A YEAR-ROUND DESTINATION

Once again, I found myself to be an intrinsic component of innovation as THE GREAT AMERICAN OPRY dared to challenge the long-held traditions of the seasonal show calendar. In the Autumn of 1992, all of the shows, including DOLLYWOOD and their wildly successful offspring - DIXIE STAMPEDE, would close for the season by the end of October at the very latest, not to reopen again until Mid-April.

As we looked around, there appeared the hint of a golden opportunity on the immediate horizon. Streams of people continued to flow into The Smokies for weekend trips, enjoying shopping at the new Outlet Malls, Tennessee Volunteer football, the brilliant colors of Fall in the mountains, fishing, hunting, car shows and uncomplicated relaxation. More and more hotels and restaurants were being constructed, realizing significant success through the unofficially extended tourist season.

Maybe we were naïve and foolishly optimistic, but it seemed the obvious was being ignored.

Thousands of people were actively pursuing ways to be entertained at any given time, even during the *"off-season"*. We made the decision to keep the lights on and the OPRY open for business as the "only show in town", an overture people responded to with astounding joy. The tourists, as well as the locals, bought tickets as never before and we enjoyed our greatest success to date. Being the first to introduce a long-run Christmas show in Pigeon Forge facilitated our becoming an instant hit.

Our first NEW YEAR'S EVE IN THE SMOKIES resulted in three sold-out performances in one evening. A small upstart cast, housed in a tiny two hundred seat boutique theatre, shifted an entire paradigm for the Smoky Mountain region, resulting in an insurgency of commerce and economic growth unlike anytime in it's history. Within months, all the performance venues, shopping centers and hotels in the county were hard at work retooling to expand the tourist season far beyond the previous long-standing parameters.

Even if on a relatively small scale, our success had helped to awaken a sleepy giant.

Within two years, the newly formulated **"Winter Celebration"** had transformed Sevier County into a solid ten-month entertainment destination. The weather, normally mild through December, allowed the traffic count to maintain substantial growth, especially from points south such as Atlanta, Birmingham and the Carolinas.

Real estate values realized an exponential curve upward, creating many new local millionaires. Jed Clampett hit oil again, this time in the Smoky Mountains of East Tennessee. In 1976, according to a classified advertisement in my well-preserved copy of The Mountain Visitor newspaper, an acre of property on the Parkway in Pigeon Forge could be purchased for less than Five Thousand dollars.

That remarkable fact promptly became a mere faded memory.

By 1994, the aforementioned acre lot on the identical segment of highway frontage would easily yield in excess of one million dollars, creating happy, happy, happy times for the handful of families who had owned these Tennessee farmlands for generations. Just to reemphasize what was transpiring, one million dollars per acre on the Parkway.

Dollywood announced plans for a 2,500-seat theatre called Music Mansion, initiating the launch of Music Road. Country music artists T.G Sheppard, Louise Mandrell and Lee Greenwood were all soon to follow with their own theatres. Gaylord, the Herschend Family Entertainment Corporation, and other monolithic companies began to view the area with renewed interest and speculation. As the big money began to roll in and competition swiftly escalated to capture the richest pieces of this newly discovered pie, Gary McSpadden's enthusiasm began to wane. It is one thing to operate a quaint theatre in a sleepy little town where entertainment options are minimal. It is an entirely different proposition when the neighborhood becomes home to multi-million dollar productions housed in state of the art theatres, featuring marquee names and a multitude of talent from across America. With the area poised to make a run at becoming another Branson, Gary concluded competing against corporations with extremely deep pockets was not something in which he wished to engage. Soon he would close the show and make his way back to Nashville.

I knew in my heart this was the perfect opportunity to go after my dream.

EDDIE'S HEART & SOUL CAFÉ 1994 - 2000

A couple of the most loyal fans of our show were landowners on the Parkway, three acres of which they had proposed to roll into in a partnership deal with Gary for the construction of a new home for the Great American Opry.

He graciously - yet immediately - turned down their offer.

Several months after Gary's dismissal of the theatre offer and following a rather extended season of personal prayer imploring God for specific guidance, I requested a meeting with those same landowners for the purpose of presenting my sketches of EDDIE'S HEART & SOUL CAFÉ.

My prayers were answered, they agreed to a meeting.

Over breakfast, my simple rough draft, hand-drawn on a few pieces of college ruled notebook paper, was met with substantial enthusiasm and the creative wheels immediately began to spin. There was every appearance of this being the proverbial "match made in Heaven", with every resource needed represented at the table.

Forward movement was without delay and aggressive.

We formed a Limited Liability Corporation - the partnership comprised of Nancy and me, the landowners, my father-in-law, Leonard and his brother Jerry. Three equal shareholders of thirty-three percent (33%) each, with one percent assigned to EDDIE'S HEART & SOUL CAFÉ, as the general partner and operating entity.

Jerry and Leonard invested three hundred and fifty thousand dollars up front, providing capital for the architect, surveys, attorney fees and various startup costs. The landowners agreed to pledge the real estate to the bank as collateral to secure the construction loan, while my and Nancy's contribution would be pure sweat equity. And, sweat we did.

Months of planning meetings with our partners, architects, bankers, loan officers, local county and city government officials, attorneys, insurance agents, restaurant suppliers, promotion companies, and Pigeon Forge Tourism, culminated in the eventual approval of our construction loans with the bank, along with the business plan and architectural design of our proposed project being approved by the city of Pigeon Forge and Sevier County.

Following the ceremonial groundbreaking with the Mayor and Tourism officials, construction began on the Café in the fall of 1994. We experienced our share of challenges stemming from any undertaking of this magnitude, yet when the day arrived for the ribbon cutting ceremony, we had succeeded in opening the building at five thousand dollars under budget, a good day for a project with construction costs just north of 1.5 million dollars.

My greatest personal challenge during this time, was the ongoing demand of performing in daily shows while supervising the construction of the Café and laying the groundwork for the opening on the horizon. That being said, I excavated endless energy and enthusiasm seeing my dream rise from the ground. There were no misgivings about this being a Divine appointment. Everyone connected to us knew there was something special in the air.

EDDIE'S HEART & SOUL CAFE was destined to become an extraordinary place.

Our hilltop location overlooked the Parkway. Cracker Barrel, Country Tonite Theatre, Ruby Tuesday and Alan Jackson's Country Restaurant were our immediate neighbors. For months I had walked through the dense brush and thorny ground of our site, praying for God's favor and anointing. To fill an entire other book describing the miraculous provision along the way would be relatively simple. As grading was completed and the foundation was beginning to be poured, there was not yet paved access to our location. The town council and planning department approved the construction of a new, city street - allowing me the distinct privilege of selecting the name.

SHOWPLACE BOULEVARD.

The fanfare and joy were not without my fair share of punches to the gut, some of which could have put anyone in need of oxygen. One example for your consideration: the cost of installing city water and sewer lines to our new building; $48,950.00.

Yep! The price we paid for less than two hundred yards of pipe buried in dirt. And yet, those sorts of moments went a very long way in helping me to trust in the provision of God more than ever. Without fail, He always came thru to meet the needs. There was a day my leadership team realized additional equipment was needed in our kitchen to improve our service, news delivered with a price tag of almost seventy thousand dollars. I had no idea how to finance this purchase, given the fact we were already maxed-out in every line of credit. Updates to our menu that would significantly add to our sales potential, were the driving force behind acquisition of the additional equipment. I knew it was my task to find a way.

I TOOK DECISIVE ACTION. I decided to go play basketball with my daughter.

Lindsay was on the basketball team at school and wanted help from *"Diddy"* with her practice routine. It seemed exactly the right thing to do. I didn't head out the door to our driveway with some dismissive or presumptive attitude, just a simple confidence God had started this and He will most certainly finish it.

Enjoy the moment with my baby girl, He'll show me what to do.

As we played and laughed together on that sunny and cool fall afternoon, a neighbor was walking by and stopped to say hello. After a bit of small talk, my friend said he and his wife had been watching our progress from a distance and respected the approach we were taking in our business. He had been praying about exploring any options there might be of investing in our Cafe and wanted to know if this was an opportune time to get involved, to which I proclaimed "most certainly". Basketball in hand, I described the need for additional equipment and what the cost would be.

With that, he simply took out his wallet and wrote a check for eighty thousand dollars ($80,000.00).

GOD DOES NOT RESPOND TO NEED – HE RESPONDS TO FAITH.

Allow me to clarify: I quickly acknowledge there is a fine line between presumption and faith. However, even with my long heritage and upbringing in the church, no one had really shown me what it looked like to genuinely live by faith. In our circles, faith was something dealing mainly with the eternal post-death future of a person and seldom seemed to have much bearing on the present cares of this life. I was learning first hand how God responds to faith. Even more, there is absolutely no room here to boast about my level of faith, for even faith itself is actually a gift of God.

He truly is the source of everything we need, including faith to operate in the place and on the level to which He calls us. What a joy to be surrounded by the love and Presence of God in the commonplace minutiae of ordinary life. I had always said I wanted to be a part of something so overwhelmingly impossible - I couldn't take credit for it even if I wanted to.

Here was exactly what I had wanted in full and living color!

We opened the Café on DECEMBER 18, 1995, three months later than our actual projection. Somehow, delays always seem to be part of the mix in building projects. The enthusiasm for the completion of **Eddie's Heart & Soul Café** would be confirmed by hundreds of people accepting the invitation to attend our Grand Opening. The joy of the evening was short-lived, however, as I contemplated the inevitability of the calendar. The brutal reality of what little time remained until the *"off-season"* would arrive, challenged my enthusiasm, knowing vacant hotel rooms and deserted cabins were only mere days away.

January and February were the weakest months for any and all business in the Smokies. Our first winter in the Cafe was slowed even more due to banner snowfall, draining financial reserves after two weeks of steady frozen precipitation and repetitive road closures. Any business owner in the Smoky Mountain region will tell you, just the mention of snow in the mountains on The Weather Channel resulted in inescapable cancellations from our patrons to the South. Residents of Georgia, Alabama and the Carolinas were wickedly quick to envision the worst-case scenario. They unconditionally wanted no part of being stranded in a winter storm on backcountry mountain roads, especially following the major snowstorm in 1993 that stranded thousands of people for days.

Due to our extreme late opening, the Cafe had missed the financial provision of the fall season. As the parade of new-year snowstorms extended closure for eleven days straight, I was faced with an eighteen thousand dollar mortgage payment and payroll of nearly twelve thousand dollars. On this particular Monday morning in question, the balance of our primary business account was just over sixteen thousand dollars. The loan payment and payroll were due on Wednesday. It was still snowing and our doors remained closed, leaving us without means to generate the needed income from sales of any description.

I decided to go hang out with God, getting as deep into the mountains as I could and pray until I got some semblance of an answer.

As I approached the entrance to the National Park in my Geo Metro, the gates were closed, as the snow had now become enough of an issue for the state to postpone any plowing of the roads until after the storm was over. I found a way to maneuver around the gates, one of the rare benefits of owning such a tiny automobile. We had bought the Geo in Colorado and I was always amazed at how well it performed in the snow.

Three to four inches of snow covered the road, increasing as I drove higher in elevation. After a slow but steady motoring through the icy white confetti, I decided to pull into the parking lot of a popular road-side picnic shelter, grabbed my Bible and commenced the impromptu uphill hike to a yet to be determined destination, high above the tourist site. Walking along an ice filled stream cascading down the mountainside, I prayed out loud, knowing no other human beings were anywhere to be found within at least a two mile radius of my location. The bears were snoozing and the squirrels had taken cover from the storm. The freshly fallen blanket of snow had silenced most everything but the sound of my foot divots and minimally labored breathing.

I vacillated between prayers of faith and impassioned pleas of "what do I do now?"

Walking, praying, breathing, listening - further up the mountain I moved with my eyes focused only on the ground directly in front of my feet. It was then I came upon some very large rock formations, glancing from the ground for the first time during my upward trek to determine what was ahead in the distance and the path I should take. As I raised my head, directly in front of me was a boulder of somewhat imposing proportion, stopping me in my tracks. What actually brought me to a complete standstill however, was not the craggy stone obstruction, but rather the unexpected appearance of a small object resting on the pinnacle of this epic, snow-covered boulder.

Perfectly positioned at the precise center top of this stone at eye level, was a baseball cap. In the center of that cap, located where a team logo would most normally be positioned, was a patch embroidered with three very familiar and yet incredibly auspicious words:

NEVER GIVE UP!
Seriously? How much more patently cliché could it possibly get?

I stood motionless. It seemed all breathing was momentarily suspended.

How could someone pull off this gag? Even I had no clue where I was going when I left the Cafe an hour before. GPS was not yet a part of our lives.

Without moving my head - I slowly looked to the left.

Then, even more slowly to the right, and then refocusing on the cap.

Really? Seriously? Never...Give...Up.

Miles from anyone, trudging through a substantial snowstorm and mumbling prayers to God for some sort of Divine instruction, far beyond the padlocked gates of a 524,000 acre National Park and at least a quarter of a mile into the woods and halfway up the mountainside - a baseball cap magically appears on top of a colossal rock directly in the path of an unplanned hiking excursion, telling me to not give up.

Just then, a slight giggle bubbled to the surface. This was ridiculously amazing!

My arrested stance in the accumulating snow remained unchanged for several moments as tears welled up in my eyes. I can still taste, touch, smell and hear that moment, with my gaze frozen on the cap, not from the cold but held in the grip of being stunned and relieved all at once. Looking around me to be sure mine were the only footprints in the snow - I simply uttered the words, "Thank You".

The tears I shed were gentle and my faint yet audible giggling was now combined with a slight shaking of my head from side to side, startled by the reality of a caring and involved Heavenly Father Who had creatively intervened in my prayerful sojourn to send a decidedly personal message. Though His instruction lacked any specificity as to how to deal with the impending financial challenge or what His implied provision might look like, I knew I had heard from Jehovah.

For the moment - that would be more than enough.

After a minute more of marinating in what felt to be the very Presence of God, I gently pivoted in the snow and began my descent to the Geo, repeating the words *'thank you'* every few yards, at one point breaking into shouts of gratitude that ricocheted through the woods, abruptly shattering the wintery silence. It seemed as if all creation joined in my celebration, as though everything around me was aware of what had just occurred in my life. Like the *"one that got away"*, no one would ever believe what had just occurred.

Once back to the car, navigation through the additional couple inches of newly fallen snow was effortless. The Geo seemed to be floating on a cushion of air across the abandoned road. The existing tracks left by my recent inbound trip had all but disappeared in the fresh snowfall.

Arriving at the Cafe, I was prompt to call Nancy, describing in unimpaired detail my mountainside experience. We were in agreement this was a well-timed postcard from Heaven meant to strengthen our faith and resolve. Then our conversation was interrupted by the intercom, announcing a long distance call for me on line two. Saying a quick goodbye to Nancy and picking up the other call, I was stunned to hear the voice of my dear friend Malcolm from Colorado. It had been years since our last conversation.

After a normal exchange of the usual obligatory greetings and chat up, he revealed the precise motivation for his call. Earlier in the morning and two time zones away, having his coffee and morning devotional in the kitchen of his home overlooking the front range of the Rockies, Malcolm was troubled deep within his spirit that I was struggling in some way and began to pray for me over the next couple of hours. Once he had arrived at his office and attended to the first appointments of the day, he placed a call to directory assistance for the number of the Cafe.

In response to his caring inquiry as to my well being, I chose to not elaborate, speaking only in somewhat vague generalities. Anyone who knows me at all would tell you I have never been one to shy away from being transparent, most often, well beyond the fault line. In this conversation, however, I did not share the details of my prevailing financial dilemma or the events of my morning.

THE PARAPHRASE VERSION OF MY DESCRIPTION TO MALCOLM WENT SOMETHING LIKE THIS;:

"It's the usual challenges of opening a new business and dealing with the seasonal impact of the area in which we're located. Snow has really slowed things down and I'm currently having my share of those pressures, but overall we're doing well. I simply have to get through the next couple of months and then I believe things are gonna fly."

I continued on for a bit about the success of our Grand Opening weeks before.

Malcolm was ardent in his encouragement and assured me of his ongoing intercession for Nancy and me. Our conversation concluded, free of any specifics regarding the financial chasm before me. My eventful day came to a close with no solid answers from God or definitive action on my part. I simply continued to be captivated by the postcard from Heaven received on the mountainside earlier in the day, assuring me everything was firmly under God's jurisdiction. I needed only to press on in courage.

THE CHECK'S IN THE MAIL

Tuesday began early as usual, now only twenty-four hours before the looming financial deadline. Back into the Geo, I chose the drive to one of my favorite areas a little closer home - there to again petition the Lord in prayer and meditate upon the biblical wisdom needed to deal with the issues at hand. The snowstorms of recent days had now passed, leaving the sky icy blue and the cold air easy to breathe. Arriving at the Cafe about ten o'clock, preparations for lunchtime were well underway. My inbox was fairly normal in its' volume of contents, with one exception; there was a FedEx envelope propped against my office door.

It was from Colorado.

Tearing off the top of the package revealed a very simple regular sized business envelope inside, which I quickly dismantled. The contents: a single check in the sum of twenty-five thousand dollars ($25,000.00). No note of any kind was included. The signature was the only way of knowing it was from my friend Malcolm. After another brief session of stunned silence and wonder, I made the predictable and self-explanatory call.

My first words: *"Maybe a small bit of clarification might in order, given the contents of the package I have just received from you."*

In his gentle manner he said, *"It's just something God instructed me to do. I hope it helps. It is no way a loan and there are no strings attached. I simply love you and Nancy and I believe in what you are doing".*

THE MIRACULOUS PROVISION CONTINUED - NEVER GIVE UP!...................... The battles were soon to intensify.

The payments now made and moving toward spring with renewed confidence, the atmosphere in and around the Cafe became notably more energized. Now well underway, we implemented the decision to extract Nancy's family from the Partnership, transferring their stock ownership to a new partner with years of experience and ownership in the food service industry. This was imperative for several reasons, not the least of which was to limit the Hall's financial exposure in our infant endeavor. Their initial investment would remain in place, yet this action would relieve me from the intense pressure that came from having my in-laws as personal guarantors to the bank and our other creditors. This was the intent from the beginning, for them to aid in the startup then be replaced by someone new.

It is significantly easier to actually show potential investors the physical reality of your visionary plans rather than soliciting their help with only a bag-full of blue-sky propositions in hand.

Thanks to Leonard and Jerry's investment - that option was realized.

Even the closest of friends, knowing of the Cafe from a distance, could not grasp the significance of what was happening on the hill in Pigeon Forge until they actually drove into the parking lot and walked through our doors. Word spread quickly we were in the game to win on the big stage and the Cafe far surpassed any preconceived expectations.

We were blessed with major endorsements from every quarter: Leaders in ministry, the music industry, college and professional sports, and politics. The very idea *Peyton Manning, Dolly Parton, Jerry Falwell, Charlie Daniels, Third*

Day, George Beverly Shea, CHICAGO, and *Paul Harvey* - the young, aged and in between - old school and contemporary - Gospel and rock & roll - could all become exuberant about the same place was pretty cool.

The years of life on the road and the flexibility acquired by that experience, was proving daily to be critically fundamental in my role at the Cafe.

Being able to adjust stylistically to an audience while not compromising personal values to do so, has served me well over time. That very characteristic has sent observers scratching their heads in bewilderment at how I could transition musically from *"On The Road Again"* to Mozart to *"Staying Alive"* to *" I Bowed On My Knees And Cried Holy",* all in a single performance set. 'Seems perfectly normal to me, but not so much to others. I am a fanatical purist about quality, but not about style. For me the more diverse the music styles, the better.

Forget thinking outside the box – there are no boxes. **No one ever promised this would be easy, but when everything was working as designed, it was most certainly worth all the effort.**

Into our second year arrived national recognition and awards for our food and concept. The Cafe was voted the Best Restaurant of the Year in Pigeon Forge three years in a row. Glowing reviews appeared in major publications and newspapers across the country. Throughout much of the year, one hour wait times for seating became customary. Most significantly, my hope of attracting the attention of Disney began to gain traction.

Without a hint of hesitancy, I have always been persistent in recognizing our success was in no way due to my prowess, wisdom or energy. Our progress was undeniably a reflection of the unmerited favor and blessing of God.

MY GREATEST TASK WAS TO MAINTAIN THAT AS MY FOCUS.

The bankers were in our court, as were the food vendors, the media, the city, county and state government officials, and most strategically - the Tourism department. We invested back into the community through channels such as The Friends of The Smokies, The Boys & Girls Club, The Red Cross, The Save The Eagle Foundation and others. We certainly had our moments of organized chaos, especially with personnel and managerial adjustments, yet brand development and public relations within the Smokies marketplace was on target.

In our fourth year, plans for replicating ourselves in other markets began to take shape. Deposits were made on various buildings and/or acreage in two other states. Our greatest cheerleader and authentic friend in this project from the very beginning was Evelyn Ogle. She and her business associate, whom we shall refer to as *"Mr. Hardy"* going forward, were one-third of our corporate partnership. She was a mover and shaker real estate guru in East Tennessee who knew everybody and whom everyone seemed to love. Vibrant and high energy, she took over every room she walked into, one of those people you can't help but notice. Also involved in the development of the mega-theatre Country Tonite next door, she played the greatest role in making our longtime dream transition to reality. In one of her regular weekly visits to Showplace Boulevard, Evelyn introduced me to a newcomer in the community who went by the name of *"Chuck"*, and let's just leave it at that - *"Chuck"*.

At the time of our initial meeting, he was involved in a few other corporate makeovers locally and had shown interest in helping us create a new ownership entity, formulate and expedite a buyout of the existing partners and attract the investors to take us to the next level. By way of Evelyn's endorsement and the credibility of those who had introduced *"Chuck"* to her, I gave no thought of any potential issues with his personal integrity.

FIRST MISTAKE.

We all tended to dismiss the glaring fact his appearance was stereotypically Mafia-like. Short in stature, an Italian from New York with jet black hair appropriately waxed back, shiny suits, a hard shell briefcase always at his side, incessantly rattling on about his most recent conquests in a very thick Empire State accent, rolling off his tongue at about five hundred words a minute. Robert De Niro would be cast to perfectly play this role in the movie. Looking back, it seems *"Chuck"* would have been the last guy anyone in East Tennessee would have trusted for any reason, let alone embrace as a business partner. For some now mystifying reason, everyone kept handing him the keys to the safe and their contracts, including me.

SECOND MISTAKE.

As it sometimes goes, people can become infatuated with a new angle or personality and *"Chuck"* just happened to be the latest and greatest playmaker in town. 'Dude was everywhere, with his hands into hotels, theaters, restaurants and timeshare condos. Again, because of the way he was introduced and the widespread approval he appeared to have among so many legitimate business owners in the county, I opened my business and my life to him, believing he had arrived right on time to help conquer the next objective.

THIRD MISTAKE!

The negotiations had begun to buy out the existing partners and establish a much broader base of financial support, the step needed to proceed with the major expansion of the Cafe into other markets. Concurrently, the little issue of greed had begun to rear its' hideous head. In fact, the initial round of this fight had occurred even previous to *"Chuck's"* arrival on the scene.

THE SHOWDOWN BEGINS.

Two of our partners, we'll refer to them as Mr. Laurel and Mr. Hardy, called a meeting of our entire cast while Nancy and I were away for a few days of relaxation with our kids. They did so without Evelyn's knowledge, knowing she always *"watched our backs"*. Upon our return, we received the blow-by-blow detail from several cast members as to the statements made by those partners. Here is the essence of their communication, corroborated by multiple people who loved and cared for my family, and who were personally in attendance at the compulsory meeting:

"There is too much d--- God and Jesus in this place. People don't need to hear all that when they come to have dinner. This has got to change!"

"Eddie will be removed as principal performer and be replaced by more of a classic country-style entertainer. We are assuming all executive decisions of the daily operations and in every aspect of the Cafe. We, of course, will be renaming the Cafe, as it will no longer be named Eddies'."

You can well understand how thoroughly devastating it was to hear this summary. Though the partners had certainly been bullheaded at times and driven only by profit and not principal, I never anticipated this degree of confrontation, having absolutely no idea how to handle this development. I did recognize an intense fighting spirit rising within me, a tenacious urge to violently reciprocate and blow them out of the water, all having to be constantly tempered by wisdom and Spirit-led judgment.

I called my Pastor and friend, Don Polston, now living in Indiana, to obtain his advice. We spoke on the phone for hours over a couple of days. In one of those crucially compelling conversations, Pastor spoke of how he had seen in his spirit the main character of hostility in my opposition, describing him physically and in character with nearly perfect detail, though he had never once seen nor met him in person.

He told me: *"By the end of the year, this man will no longer be in your life. In the meantime, carry on outwardly with your team and business associates as though nothing is wrong, wage war in the Spirit and not in the flesh, diligently praying for the anointing and Presence of God to be more tangible than ever. You will be surrounded by angelic protection and God's favor. No weapon formed against you will be able to prosper. It is unclear how it will happen, maybe a buyout of his interest, or possibly he will voluntarily relinquish his role in the Cafe operations, but very soon he will no longer pose a threat."*

I WAS VERY CAREFUL TO FOLLOW HIS INSTRUCTION.

The remainder of the year had its share of tension, but I did my best to respond without any flagrant demonstrations of bitterness. Skirmishes would break out like wildfires over issues such as my dogmatic insistence to tithe off the Cafe's weekly sales receipts. I believe to this day, our tithe was one of the distinct reasons for our steady growth in a market where we should and could have been effortlessly crushed by our competition.

For Nancy and me, tithing was non-negotiable.

For them, the idea of giving any portion of our income to ministry was sheer nonsense.

The most ruthless and heartless action forced upon me by the contentious partnership, was the firing of my parents, employed in our office to handle the Cafe accounting, payables and tax reports. It's a rough day when you have to relieve your own parents of their job. We all knew this was most likely their initial move toward a hostile take-over. At this juncture, the vulnerability of our thirty percent (30%) equity share in the ownership became brutally apparent. It must be added, the regular over-the-top defensive actions my mother directed toward the partners only served to shift the conflict into hyper-drive. Subtlety was in no way her strongest attribute. This greatly added to the call for their dismissal.

The uncertainty brought on by this constant opposition was tempting to embrace. Partnership meetings thru that fall season invariably set me in a defensive posture, having to stand firm on crucial issues, discern what was negotiable, and then have the courage to give up enough ground on inconsequential matters, so my partners garnered some feeling of accomplishment.

Standing toe-to-toe and eye-to-eye with the strongest of my rivals, at the culmination of one those impassioned daylong meetings, Mr. Hardy growled how his self worth and measure of success was in direct proportion to the contents of his wallet. I showed no sense of surprise or doubt in my expression as to the sincerity of his statement.

THERE WAS TO BE NO ARGUMENT FROM ME IN REGARDS TO THE OBVIOUS.

I routinely embarked on prayerful walks in the woods to pursue healing for my soul. Therapeutic drives thru the National Park listening for specific instruction from the Holy Spirit would occupy my early morning hours, seeking relief from the incessant pounding of war drums in my head. To give this battle over to God in submissive trust was all but impossible, but it was absolutely necessary. Otherwise, I ran the risk of lowering myself to the malevolent level of the barracudas guised as my partners. Remaining determined to rise above that underlying temptation, I knew my struggle was in the spiritual realm and only a supernatural solution would culminate the madness.

DECEMBER 18 – THE ANNIVERSARY OF OUR OPENING

Nancy took the incoming call at the Cafe. The news was staggering. Our business partner, Mr. Laurel, the same individual who had instigated the tasteless and profane meeting with our cast and crew announcing his intention for my removal, had died suddenly of a massive heart attack in the front seat of his car while on his way to the dentist office for an appointment.

An unnatural, otherworldly hush hovered within the atmosphere of the cafe.

In an instant, I thought back to my phone conversations with Pastor Polston. While having full confidence in his discernment and the prophetic words he had uttered concerning the future of my partner, I never dreamed Mr. Laurels' combative and petulant reign would end in this astounding manner.

Please understand - there was no rejoicing over the news of his passing.

NO VICTORY LAPS. NO GLOATING.

Though nearly impossible to articulate, a distinct and unusual consciousness was awakened in me, an unwieldy sense we had just moved into a measure of spiritual warfare we had never known heretofore. The most meticulous discernment on my part would be imperative, as the stakes had now become exceptionally higher.

In the thoughtful silence of the afternoon, Nancy and I sat by the fireplace in the Cafe, realizing everything had just changed forever.

Well…almost everything.

Our other business partner, Hardy, arrived nearly breathless, anxious to discuss the issue at hand.

Briefly acknowledging the tragedy of our associates' death, he promptly launched into full crisis mode. Aggressively dragging another chair to our table, he scribbled madly on a napkin the number of challenges the days' turn of events had instantly brought to bear. His ad-lib checklist quickly expanded with plans to protect his financial position and minimize exposure to any loss. The only mention made of Laurel's widow during his impromptu inventory, was a somewhat panicked declaration that should she fail to follow through with financial obligations to the partnership and our corporate business interests, there would be no hesitation to take her house, savings, retirement accounts and shares of stock to cover himself, all of which had been contractually pledged to him in personal guarantees she and her now late husband had signed when joining our ranks.

After nearly a full hour of rant, rhetoric and spewing, Hardy exited the building, jumped into his black Mercedes and drove away to further mull over how the death of his partner three hours earlier would possibly impact his investment portfolio.

By the way: Within minutes of Hardy's abrupt and alarmed departure, I re-implemented the practice of tithing off the sales receipts of the Café from that day forward.

CHAPTER 8

"and in the end...."

CLOSING THE DOORS BEHIND US @ THE HEART & SOUL CAFE

I n the months following the memorial service for Laurel, our remaining partners essentially left Nancy and me to manage the Cafe on our own. Just after the New Year, I made a very robust appeal for them to essentially become silent and distant, making the argument too many CEO's present in the building were mucking up the works. Even more crucial, our cast members found it unnerving and stressful, constantly trying to determine which talking head to follow.

While I make no assertion of God physically taking out my nemesis, it was amazing to watch how quickly the remaining partners complied with my demand for them to back away.

NO ONE EVEN HESITATED.

In somewhat of a concession, I assured Evelyn and the others, no requests would be forthcoming on my part for financial support or capital infusion of any kind should they be willing to honor my petition. Nancy and I desperately needed to assume full control of the Cafe to reestablish our original vision, as well as rejuvenate an environment of solidarity in daily operations. No matter the nature of a business, when partners are openly and systematically at odds over the future direction of a company, that quickly escalates into aggregate uncertainty.

In our scenario, the entire Cafe cast and crew knew my door was perpetually open for expressing creative ideas that could help make us leaner, faster and stronger. However, the crux of our ever-evolving partnership struggle was for the very heart of our corporate existence. I was steadfastly adamant we conduct the most trivial of daily business within the parameters of our established core principals for the Café. While revenue and cash flow are essential to maintain and expand any business model, Nancy and I had drawn a non-negotiable line in the sand from the very beginning declaring we would never sell our soul for the sake of profit.

The partners always seemed willing, if not fully determined, to sacrifice the concept, excellence, integrity, and even people - if it meant enriching themselves in the short term.

I WAS NOT!

We sought to surround ourselves with individuals wanting to be a part of something bigger than the sum total of our parts. There is power in agreement. The Bible teaches that one can put a thousand to flight, yet two can put ten thousand on their heels. To establish the Café as a world-class venue would require pristine clarity, laser focus, and resolute visionary leadership. We aspired to never flinch in a minor challenge or an extreme crisis. Nancy and I were fully devoted to maintaining the highest standard of integrity in every facet of the Café, as well as our personal lives. Anything beyond the parameters of that level of commitment would be considered illegal and out-of-bounds for us.

Integrity is never cheap. Excellence comes with a price, but it is worth it.

The impact of our renewed singularity in leadership was immediately productive. The cast and crew became more energized by the peaceful and amiable atmosphere. Happy servants resulted in happy guests. Our servers enjoyed one of the highest tip averages of any venue team in the Smoky Mountain region.

As we all know, the most powerful public relations tool is *"word of mouth"* advertising, a reality that can either be your best friend or the proverbial kiss of death. We quickly became the beneficiary of a renewed *"public buzz"* over the Cafe, as we pulled out all the stops and swung for the wall. The aforementioned awards and national recognition arrived on our doorstep during the next three-year segment of the Cafe's existence. Our trajectory routinely indicated we were on target for a bright future, resulting in an ever-expanding number of prominent business executives taking notice, including Disney. Our dream had come true.

AS DESIGNED, WE WERE IMPACTING THE LIVES OF PEOPLE.

The testimonies over the last twenty years of how our ministry through the Cafe profoundly impacted lives are more than I could have ever imagined. It is unquestionably what we had prayed would be the result of our existence. As we resurfaced online through Facebook and a new website, old friends and patrons of the Cafe reached out with narratives of how a casual visit to Eddie's Heart & Soul Cafe culminated in far more than just a satisfying meal and the enjoyment a few well-loved songs.

LINDSAY'S STORY

Toward the end of each performance set of music at the Cafe, I would most often share how God had intervened in our lives in some way, then close that set with a Gospel ballad of some kind, such as *"I Bowed On My Knees And Cried Holy"* or *"I Believe In A Hill Called Mt. Calvary"*.

The most enduring story was of our daughter Lindsay. At the time Nancy was carrying Lindsay, our son Jason was three years old. The pregnancy had been going well and everything appeared normal. During a routine exam, the doctors failed to find any indication of Lindsay's heartbeat. Upon their discovery, they felt strongly the baby had died in utero and needed to be extracted, therefore preventing any harm to Nancy.

During this visit to the doctor's office, I was immersed in a studio session and not present for the exam. Nancy explained to the clinical staff she would break the news at home of their diagnosis and we would notify them of our decision the following day. We dealt with this dreadful revelation the best we knew how. The decision had to be Nancy's to make. My singular task was to support her in whatever action she chose, that being to get a second opinion from another group of doctors.

In short, five different exams with three groups of doctors and once at the hospital - all arrived at the same prognosis. No heartbeat. The baby needed to be removed.

We cried and we prayed. Again, I trusted Nancy's discernment, believing she would know best what to do. I did so under some protest from the family who expressed their concern Nancy was simply in denial and that it was my role to intervene. My inclination was to trust a mother's heart and her reliance on that still small Voice to lead her.

Through these darkest of days, Nancy clung to the simple, yet powerful scripture verse:

> ***"Be still and know that I am God."***
> PSALM 46:10
> NIV – ZONDERVAN PUBLISHING

She requested one final test with the original group of doctors, explaining she had now given the process adequate time and a decision thoroughly bathed in prayer. If the exam failed to detect a heartbeat, the baby could then be removed.

At this point in relating the story from the stage, I would pause for a brief moment - then tell the audience, *"I have the privilege of introducing to you a living, breathing miracle, the possessor of the heartbeat discovered by a stunned group of doctors and nurses on that spring morning."*

As I began playing an instrumental version of one of our favorite songs, "A Dream Is A Wish Your Heart Makes", Lindsay stepped onto the stage, performing a beautifully choreographed jazz/ballet style dance. This endearingly stunning moment never failed to fill the room with tearful exuberance and joyful applause.

There were times of apprehension at the idea of sharing this story - cognizant of the fact someone might be present in the audience whose similar story ended with a painfully different and tragic outcome. That being said, I received steadfast encouragement from a myriad of people, in person and by mail, to never resign from telling Lindsay's story.

One such encourager returned to the Cafe with a busload of friends who were in town for a women's conference. After exiting the stage – this enthusiastic gaggle of female Presbyterians encircled me in the gift shop, buzzing and whirring like bumble bees drunk on Redbull.

My encourager friend told me of a trip to the doctors' office with her daughter, suffering pain and troubling symptoms during her pregnancy. After a time of testing and examination, the doctor encouraged an abortion to evade any unfavorable issues present in the development of the baby. Mother asked for a moment alone with her daughter.

She asked her daughter what she wanted to do. Her immediate tearful response; "Remember the story about Lindsay? I'm not quitting on my baby."

Now, two years later, here is a tearful grandmother reappearing at the Cafe accompanied by a busload of her friends, presenting photos of her grandchild, born perfectly healthy.

They had just adopted a puppy for the now toddler grandson, naming him Eddie in honor of me. To clarify, they named the puppy after me, not the baby.

THE WEEK OF VALENTINES WAS ALWAYS A SPECIAL TIME AT THE CAFÉ.

Wedding proposals took place, as well as anniversaries and special date nights. We turned the lights down, the fireplace was roaring and I kept the music geared toward a decidedly romantic vibe. Red Velvet cake was in abundance as well, a traditional Cafe favorite.

The final February of our existence was during the most challenging and brutal days I had faced with the partners. Though exhausted mentally, physically and emotionally, I did all I could to stay *"up"* for the formidable Valentines weekend upon us. Large crowds and wait times of up to two hours were gratifying and grueling all at once.

Late afternoon on Saturday of that weekend, I was visiting guest tables after finishing my performance set when I noticed a young couple sitting on the upper level near the fireplace. She was crying to the point of appearing nearly inconsolable, so I redirected my attention toward some other guests, not wanting to disturb what seemed to be a very private moment. After a bit, I glanced toward them again, as she beckoned me to their table with a wave of her hand.

Asking me to join them at their table – she whispered there was something I needed to hear.......

The young couple was from Birmingham, Alabama. Her father had been to the Cafe the preceding October. Along with two business associates, they had made the short trek to the mountains of Tennessee for a weekend of golf.

She described her family, all of whom had been faithful followers of Christ for as long as she could remember, with one exception, her Daddy. He was a loving father and devoted husband, providing for his family in every way. He was not hostile toward the church or Christianity by any means - he simply wanted no part of it. She believed this was due, in large part, to events in his childhood that had left him cold toward organized religion.

Upon his return home from the Smokies, her father called a family meeting for Monday evening, a puzzling surprise and something quite unusual for him. He sat before everyone and told of his visit to a remarkable place in Pigeon Forge called Eddie's Cafe. He described aspects of his encounter in detail, including hearing the story of Lindsay, followed by some song called *"I Bowed Down"*. He described how he was shaken to his core, sensing something uncommon from the moment he arrived in our parking lot.

On the drive to their hotel immediately following their experience at the Cafe, he announced to his golfing companions he was going home to Alabama and giving his life to God.

After this family meeting, her father made an appointment with their pastor, telling him of his experience and subsequent decision. They prayed for him to receive Christ into his life. He made a public profession of his newfound faith on Wednesday evening and was baptized the following Sunday.

Three days later, doctors discovered aggressive stage-four cancer. Eight weeks following, they had his memorial service.

His daughter now sat weeping in front of me and said in a barely audible voice, "I had to see for myself the place God used to reach my father when nothing else could. My Daddy is in Heaven tonight because of you and this Cafe and I came all the way from Alabama to thank you".

I WILL NEVER FORGET THAT MOMENT AND SO MANY OTHERS JUST LIKE IT.

Couples wrote to say their marriages had been healed and restored.

We heard from several people in ministry who were ready to give up and vacate their calling due to weariness and frustration, telling us how their resolve to keep serving was renewed thru their experience at the Cafe.

Something I have always believed: Placed within a cozy and non-threatening environment, being skillfully entertained and enjoying scrumptious food, people have a tendency to gradually lower their internal defense mechanisms. They become pliable and more vulnerable. In those moments, the simplest nugget of truth or encouragement can calm a fear, heal a wound, encourage a weary soul and in some cases, radically transform a life.

PREACHING AT FOLK IS NOT ALWAYS THE ANSWER............. SOMETIMES IT'S ALL ABOUT JUST "LOVING THE HELL OUT OF PEOPLE".

One local resident wrote to say she heard me on the radio during a morning talk show. Having been to the Cafe, the interviewer asked if I would share the story of my daughter, Lindsay. Listening to the account of our miracle baby, she pulled her car onto the shoulder of the busy highway, unable to continue driving due to a flood of tears impairing her vision.

Her mission that particular morning had been to successfully navigate her way through the Knoxville rush-hour traffic for her appointment at the Planned Parenthood Clinic on the west side of town, there to abort her pregnancy and destroy her baby. After nearly a full hour of heart-wrenching prayer, pleading with God to help her be the mother she needed to be, she dried her eyes and turned her car toward home.

Included in her letter of gratitude was a color photo of her three-month old baby girl.

NEWS LIKE THIS STILL HUMBLES ME TO THIS DAY.

The awards for food and excellence were awesome, yet the deepest gratification always came in hearing from the people whose lives had been eternally impacted. In the words of C.S.LEWIS, many of our guests found themselves *Surprised By Joy!*

NEW LEVELS – NEW DEVILS

When you become a legitimate threat to Darkness, the battles quickly escalate. To whom much is given, much is required. This is why I believe Jesus instructed those who followed Him to count the cost of their commitment before rushing headlong into the unseen.

You will see in the narrative that follows, how the tactics of my adversaries became more numerous, subversive and intentional. I was in new and precarious territory drawing on every ounce of instinct, anointing, experience and resource I could possibly tap into.

THIS IS WHERE WE GET BACK TO OUR FRIEND "CHUCK".

He was a daily presence at the Cafe by this point, putting together numerous scenarios, any of which could open the door to our expanded future, or so I thought. At the same time, my friend Malcolm graciously stepped in once again on my behalf, securing the services of Rich Levine, a brilliantly accomplished corporate attorney from Evergreen, Colorado. Rich and I became instant friends. In his wake were a history of achievements such as assisting in the formation of the World Cup Soccer League, the development of the World War II Memorial in Washington, DC and a host of other world-class projects. To have Rich in my corner was both a great personal joy and a magnificent professional addition to our team.

Our new legal counsel made multiple cross country flights in the months to follow, bringing to bear his unsurpassed knowledge of corporate law, structuring a solid proposal designed to put the existing partnership in my rear view mirror.

By mid-January of 2000, the long silent and formerly distant partners had once again been awakened in their cave. Out of necessity, Rich and I had poked the sleeping wolf with a stick in the form of an offer: Two Million, One Hundred Thousand Dollars ($ 2,100,000.00) to purchase their interest in the Cafe. *Consider this:* the combined capital investment of the three remaining partners in land and business totaled less than Sixty Thousand Dollars ($60,000.00). With those three individuals collectively representing sixty-six percent of our stock ownership, it was reasonable they be adequately rewarded for their assistance in getting us off the ground, then promptly dismissed.

My sincere speculation: The news of our offer would surely result in their giggling all the way to the bank. Having purchased the property years before for less than Two Thousand Dollars an acre, to now to realize a return on investment of more than Two Million Dollars for that same three acres would appear to be a fairly good day by anyone's estimation. Evidently, that proved to be a gross presumption on my part.

I NEVER IMAGINED THE WAR ABOUT TO ENSUE.

Prior to submitting our offer, we conferred with some of the best minds in the food service industry and by their assessment, our offer was confirmed to be on the top end of fair. Any purchase agreement north of our proposed figure, by everyone's determination, would create an insurmountable deficit. Even given our early successes, the Café was just a nose beyond the start-up phase. No question, more investment capital would be mandatory to shore up our position in the immediate future as well as the long-term expansion plans. Any effort by the partnership to extract more cash in our settlement could never be entertained as a reasonable consideration. The numbers would never work.

MY FIRST OFFER WAS THE BEST WE COULD DO – *and it was fair and equitable.*

Nancy and I had placed our offer into the ever-present hands of *"Chuck"*, delegating to him the task of spelling out the details to the partners. By all appearances, he played the role of the non-biased agent, acting for the benefit of all parties involved. In having *"Chuck"* to act as liaison, my desire was to keep the animosity to a minimum and conceivably expedite any further negotiations, moving us briskly toward signatures on a contract. Enough precious time and energy had already been wasted on personality conflicts and childish carping. The negative energy and angst quickly ramped up to Code Red levels whenever the partners were in a room together for any reason or length of time. Admittedly, I had become more and more reactionary, weary from the constant greedy nonsense and trivial yammer. Then, I stumbled headlong into yet another egregious blunder. Following months of staggering due diligence, I commissioned *"Chuck"* additionally, to serve as broker with all potential new investors in the Café.

In retrospect two decades later, that regal move was akin to trusting coyotes to guard the henhouse. It also proved to be the singular decision from which we would never recover.

AND THE HITS JUST KEEP ON COMIN'!
The Top Ten List

NUMBER TEN
"Chuck" Was Working For Our Partners - Against Us

Oh yea, this is unquestionably true. Meanwhile, down the street and through the woods, it seems *"Chuck"* had entered into a lease agreement with the widow partner *(referred to as Maleficent from this point forward)* on her former residence. She had moved into a smaller house next door and placed her former home on the market, only to rent it to *"Chuck"*. He now enjoyed opulent accommodations in seven thousand square feet of fabulous overlooking the Smokies from a wooded hillside, all credited to his notorious talent for making the cushy deal.

I would discover much later in the scheme, he regularly reported to Maleficent the specific details of our frequent conversations regarding the Café. Given their close residential proximity, covert communication was effortless. In addition, one of the newly hired servers at the Cafe took the sugar-daddy bait, moving into the big house with *"Chuck"*, kids in tow. This created a convenient avenue for he and Maleficent to feed disinformation amongst the other cast members, a conduit of which they enthusiastically took great advantage.

NUMBER NINE
The Rejection of Our Purchase Offer

The partnership laughed off our proposal of Two Million, One Hundred Thousand dollars for our purchase of their interest in the Cafe. Their counter-offer was swift and unsurprisingly arrogant. Unless I agreed to pay them a total of Five Million, Three Hundred Thousand dollars, they would essentially put their two-thirds voting power into full effect, ousting Nancy and me as officers of our Corporation, Anders Industries, Inc., as well as securing our immediate removal from the Limited Partnership. The primary issue spawning such a significant discrepancy between our two non-reconcilable figures was defined by the appraised value of the land beneath the Cafe, coming in at $750,000.00

per acre. Hardy, the principal land owning partner, was clear-cut in his demand for the full value of the real estate, or he would simply take over everything. Maleficent had no other choice but to comply with his lead, given everything she owned was legally pledged to him in personal guarantees, underwriting her position in the partnership and serving as additional financial security for Hardy should the Cafe fail.

In addition, even though I had sung during Laurel's funeral service at her request, three years after the fact, she then and to this day directly blames me for the death of her husband. Her personal vendetta toward me became more enraged and vicious on a daily basis. Maleficent was more than willing to sign onto any mission that carried with it the potential of making life difficult for me.

NUMBER EIGHT
The Great Impasse of 2000

I consulted with everyone, and I do mean everybody!

Beginning with my attorney Rich Levine, followed by long conversations with my family, Pastor Polston, Malcolm, the bank president and his senior commercial loan officers, Jerry Falwell, Truett Cathey and his sons at the Chick-fil-a corporation, members of Pat Robertson's legal counsel, various friends in ministry around the country, the CEO of one of the largest food service companies in the entire Southeast, and last but certainly not least, members of Billy Graham's family, as well as a couple of Dr. Graham's closest confidants.

I was surrounded by spectacular and loving people, rich with wisdom and integrity in business and legal matters, among the very best in the entire world. With a unison voice they delivered their professional opinion, acknowledging the only viable option was the first one I had placed upon the table. Without any alteration to the original offer, I should stand firm. With all the partners stood to gain financially, given their modest original investment, surely they would accept our deal rather than risk the ongoing success of the Cafe, or even the greater challenge, the vast undertaking before them should they follow through on their threats to remove me.

We informed Hardy and company we were resolute in our offer.

The response from the partners came back a resounding no. It was to be all or nothing – full price or no deal.

NUMBER SEVEN
Greed Versus Common Sense

The partners had witnessed the parade of personalities pass before them over the last five years, a continuous stream of high profile endorsements, glowing reviews in national publications, awards for our food and service, and the ever-increasing following among tourists as well as locals. Evidently, our work ethic, enthusiasm and sheer fortitude had not gone unnoticed, in addition to the recurrence of Supernatural provision.

Within the context of what would prove to be our final partnership meeting, without the least provocation, Hardy suddenly blurted out his best attempt at a compliment toward me: "*Never in my lifetime have I seen someone do so much with so little*".......

I trusted the sincerity of his statement. All the same, the cumulative effect of his observations resulted in some very skewed and erroneous thinking on his part. Hardy had long believed I would pay any price or climb any mountain to hold on to that for which we had worked so hard to achieve. He played his hand fully confident of my stubborn pigheadedness, to always find a way to "*make it work*".

HIS WAGER, HOWEVER, WAS FAR BEYOND ANY VOICE OF REASON.

I remained in full agreement it was reasonable for Hardy to negotiate for the best terms possible, given the appraised value of his prime real estate. However, with a long list of successful business ventures to his credit, it seemed logical to presume Hardy would have been among the first to know the Cafe could never survive under the amount of debt he was proposing, let alone flourish going forward. Beyond that obvious reality, common sense would also lead one to think the proposition of a two million, one hundred & forty thousand dollar return on investment, could be considered enough of a win to at least entertain the idea of a compromise.

It was simply not to be. GREED HAS A WAY OF MAKING PEOPLE RADICALLY DELUSIONAL.

Such was our reality, creating gridlock of the highest order. No one, even if they could, would pay the kind of money he was demanding, a fact borne out over the last sixteen years. Since our departure, in the spring of 2000, the building has remained empty the lion's share of that time period and perpetually on the Sevier County real estate listings. Granted, there would be a few runs at a variety of concepts, engaging unwitting new tenants with stringent lease agreements and significant down payments, only to fail within mere weeks of reopening.

One compelling observation - the listed negotiable asking price for the purchase of the Cafe has always been exceedingly less than my offer to the partnership in May of 2000. At one point, Hardy offered the building to a mutual friend for just under, One Million dollars.

NUMBER SIX
Locked Out

The partnership made good on their promises, as our battle intensified to an entirely new level. I arrived one morning to discover the locks of our business office had been changed, along with the safe combination updated. At the behest of the partners, Nancy or I were not granted access to any of the financials. We were figuratively and literally locked out of every facet of the daily operations, the exceptions being access to my dressing room, stage and role as featured performer. Bank accounts were changed as Maleficent assumed the role of General Manager, a title and responsibility bestowed on her by Hardy.

CONFUSION REIGNED SUPREME ON EVERY FRONT.

The wretched show being played out in front of me was equivalent to a comedy of errors starring a gimpy rendition of the Keystone Cops. Even more staggering was the pretentious display of arrogance executed flawlessly by my partners in thinking they remotely had a clue what they were doing. Most regrettably, my name still adorned the signage, brochures and magazine advertisements, though any semblance of control had suddenly vanished from my hands. The most detrimental impact of the new management procedures administered by Maleficent was displayed prominently in the quality of our food.

In her first shot out of the gate, our award-winning deserts were replaced with inferior products and reduced to half the size. Adding insult to injury, she correspondingly raised the prices. Rather than offer our famous homemade carrot cake and other scrumptious delicacies, Maleficent opted to make supply runs to Sam's Club in Knoxville, purchasing frozen cheesecakes and turtle pies in bulk, then in the tradition of Ebenezer Scrooge, doled them out to our guests in the most pathetic portions imaginable.

In her exact words: "People will like these just as well and we'll significantly lower our costs."

Like a flooding torrent laying waste to a Colorado canyon, devastation was imminent as Maleficent took direct aim at our celebrated menu. She wildly succeeded in diminishing the quality of the whole caboodle, savoring her trifling portrayal of a general manager and enforcing as much modification as possible. Unaware of the struggle behind the scenes, returning patrons constantly besieged our servers with complaints, as new guests openly wondered how we could have ever achieved award-winning success, given the potent mediocrity now encountered in our food offerings.

Meanwhile backstage, Hardy loved a competitive fight and was picking one with me, believing I would not stand by and watch them destroy my dream. It was pure extortion. He knew Maleficent was incapable of sustaining the standard of excellence we had achieved. To the complete contrary, she was a massive train wreck on her way to happen. He simply hoped to stun me into throwing an exorbitant amount of money at him, a sum far beyond reason. Hardy was fully persuaded I would do anything to see this through, never believing for a minute I could muster the courage to walk away. He hedged his bet on my refusal to fail.

He was in for a big surprise. For me, heartache lay just ahead.

NUMBER FIVE

The Taxman

In the now infamous terminal partnership meeting, I was introduced to yet another tool of extortion the partners were to implement, positioning me personally in the crosshairs of the IRS. Their announced intention, after locking me out of the office and excluding me from any business decisions, was to simply cease paying the Café quarterly payroll taxes. As the President of the operating entity, Anders Industries, I would be held liable for any payments missed, in addition to all accrued interest and penalties.

In Hardy's own words: *"We can and we will very easily hang the target for all the corporate taxes squarely on your back".*

At the time, I was not aware of the significant relationship he maintained with comrades deep within the IRS who were to make negotiation on my behalf completely futile, a particular reality confirmed by my attorney months later.

The partners followed through on their threat. With my inevitable resignation now firmly established on the foreseeable horizon, the filing of personal Chapter 7 bankruptcy would be accompanied by the obligation to Uncle Sam for more than seventy thousand dollars ($70,000.00) in unpaid payroll taxes.

Even at this point, Hardy and Maleficent remained convinced I would still find a way. The obvious was not lost on them, quitting was not a part of my DNA. We had so much invested - to surrender the Café could never be an option.

Pretense, lies, unethical maneuvering and the arrogant disregard for anything other than their bank accounts, they worked their cozy relationships within the vast *"good ole boy"* network to turn things to their advantage. East Tennessee has remained the gold standard for sleazy politics and blatant conflicts of interest within the legal community. Hardy's longstanding illicit connections with influential people within the courts and IRS, willing to do his bidding, ultimately led to our fraudulent tax liability.

Early on, I had been strongly cautioned to be wary of the business ethics, or lack thereof, in East Tennessee. My first impression was to believe this was simply an exaggerated warning originating from a nasty batch of sour grapes. That optimism, however, was misguided. Sixteen years later, I am still paying for the misstep of naively trusting subversive and unethical people. Numerous of my performance colleagues, once occupying theaters and commercial venues in Sevier County amid this same season, have comparably woeful stories as mine, some who weathered impassioned altercations with many of the same unsavory characters.

NUMBER FOUR
"Untouchable"

As gossip saturated the community of the Heart & Soul fracas, it was as though the entire population of Sevier County decided it was finally time I should know what they knew all along - *absolutely no one wanted to deal with my partners for any reason, nor from any distance.* Time and again I heard the words: "You should have talked to me prior to getting involved with those people."

While grateful for their consolation, late as it was in arriving, I was astounded to learn the degree to which Hardy and associates were regarded as diabolically untouchable.

Though investor interest in the Cafe had remained strong regarding our maturing potential, so too was the non-negotiable caveat requiring my existing partners be entirely off the radar before anyone would come close to discussing involvement in our future. Woefully, the lone resolution to satisfy that requirement would be the transfer of an overwhelmingly unreasonable amount of money. The gridlock was only to become even more incurable.

NUMBER THREE
One Last Appeal

Now obligated to the demanding performance schedule of a new tourist season, the telephone was my ever-present accomplice whenever I was not on stage. My vitality was being depleted by hours of agonizing arbitration, attempting to maneuver toward some sort of solution.

In one last conversation, I again made the appeal for common sense to prevail, pointing out to Mr. Hardy the financial legitimacy of our offer. I vigorously reminded him of the spectacular profit he stood to realize on a minimal real estate investment years earlier.

Beyond that, I encouraged him to consider the role he played in orchestrating a ministry touching the lives of thousands of people each year from across the entire country. Surely, that would count for something in his consideration.

As we stood nearly nose-to-nose in the lobby of a neighboring restaurant within sight of the Cafe, my nemesis slowly placed his hand on his wallet and without so much as a blink he quietly declared: *"There is only one thing that determines the way I feel about my life - it's all about how a decision impacts my hip pocket."*

AND WITH THAT, NEGOTIATIONS CLOSED ONCE AND FOR ALL.

As had been the case from day one, my partners loved to boast of their many exploits among the townspeople. As galling as that might be, their vain gushing proved to be a decisive advantage for me. I was repeatedly informed of their intentions, as well as the equipment and furnishings they were purchasing for the *"retooling"* of the Cafe, and contract negotiations with various entertainers in an effort to replace me.

Most of those people would call to let me know what was happening behind my back, declaring their allegiance to me, as well as their intention to have nothing to do with my partners.

Taking my parting shot - I reminded the partners Eddie's Heart & Soul Cafe had been a Divine mandate. We were there on purpose. As the Blues Brothers had declared, we were on a *"Mission From God"*. I assured them I would never pray against them, but as we left, all the favor and blessing assigned to our lives and mission would leave with us. They should expect a distinct and unexplainable shift in the atmosphere. Nothing would ever be the same again in the building once called our home. More than sixteen years later, the Cafe remains unoccupied and silent, crumbling in disrepair and depreciation. I candidly admit the mere thought of that bleak reality still generates moisture in my eyes and the need for a long deep breath.

NUMBER TWO
Chapter Seven Bankruptcy

Compassion is not something one readily associates with attorneys, and yet, our attorney John did all he could to lessen the pain of what we faced. As President of our corporation and operating entity, my fiscal exposure to the banks, food service companies, and various other vendors would stand to be significant, especially given the way my now former partners were conducting business. They simply walked away from companies with whom we had been associated for years, creating new contracts with other suppliers and conveniently laying all responsibility for existing agreements on my doorstep, knowing my signature was affixed to those business documents as guarantor.

In addition, it was critical the investors in our venture knew we were not simply bailing out with their money in our pockets, enriched and happy. Far from that scenario, every personal dime we could find and every line of credit I could make use of, had gone into the development of the Cafe and the proposed buyout of the partners.

My attorney was quick to point out our quagmire was the judicious reason bankruptcy had been created. Everyone realized I had given it my very best. My demise was not due to a lack of diligence or poor work ethic, nor was our departure caused by flagrant mismanagement or failure of our business plan.

In the end, this was indeed about greed and personal vendettas.

I understand from friends still employed at the Cafe following our departure, Maleficent displayed a great sense of gratification in seeing my name removed from the signage and the extensive collection of personal memorabilia removed from the walls, much of which was simply tossed into the dumpster. She personally destroyed a bible given to me by Dr. and Mrs. Billy Graham.

BREATHLESS IN COURT

One of the hardest days in my life was sitting before a judge in the Sevier County Courthouse, surrounded by the scrutinizing scowls of familiar faces, a couple of whom had invested in the Cafe. Consequently, they were somewhat peeved with the circumstances of the moment. 'Can't say that I blame them.

I was tormented with embarrassment, with no option but to face the music. In regards to the actual court proceedings, this was a relatively brief, unremarkable event. My attorney presented the required evidence and detail. The presiding judge directed a few questions in my direction to confirm my understanding and intentions. From start to finish, the entire matter took about forty-five minutes.

It felt more like three days.

I had already surrendered the keys of our home to the mortgage company, knowing we were moving out of the area. As an act of good faith, I delivered a portion of my musical gear and video production equipment to my banking friends who had financed its purchase along the way. We made every effort to be transparent about our situation, all the while wanting to just quietly disappear.

Several theatres and business owners reached out to me, offering a slot in their shows or a staging area in their dining establishments to perform as I had at the Cafe. It was just too painful to even contemplate staying in East Tennessee. The facts were rough enough, but now the rumor mill was ablaze. With the remnants of my long-held dream reduced to debris floating in the wake of a violently dismantled partnership, there was no shortage on speculation, opinion and judgment.

When the general public has no access to factual information, predictably, they enthusiastically fabricate their own version of the truth as they see it from a distance. I never ceased to be amazed at the outlandish theories people propagated as an accurate account of our departure.

NUMBER ONE
Striking The Rock

Even when you have witnessed the undeniable Hand of miraculous provision, in the heat of the battle it remains far too easy to get swamped by emotion. As days run together, we can have a tendency to operate on instruction meant for another time and place. Hearing the voice of God in the moment is crucial, especially during times of transition or warfare. There is purpose and provision to be found in His promptings and leadings.

Let's digress back in time to Old Testament days for an example of what I mean.

During the Exodus from Egypt, Moses had been instructed by the Lord to take his rod and strike a rock, from which God would provide water for Israel. This was specific direction given to Moses and Aaron, which The Lord honored as they obeyed. This story in found in Exodus 17, very early in their departure from the land of Egypt.

Later on, after God have given the Ten Commandments, as well as the detailed plans for the construction of the Tabernacle, the people of Israel once again found themselves in need of water. You can read for yourself the accounting of this found in the book of Numbers, Chapter 20. Very similar circumstances, but at another time and place.

The people rallied against Moses, complaining of their situation and accusing him of leading them to their demise. They quarreled with their leaders, declaring it would have been better to remain in Egypt than to die in the wilderness, an ever-present theme throughout their journey. I would say the people were close to full-on rebellion mode, at least a core group.

Moses goes into the Tent of Meeting, the very Presence of God, to inquire of The Lord what to do. Once again, he receives specific instruction to take his staff in hand and assemble the people. Before their eyesight, Moses is to now speak to the rock and God will cause the provision of water to abundantly flow from it to meet the needs of His people.

However, as the witnesses gathered at the instruction of their leaders, something happens which disrupts Moses in carrying out the plan exactly as he was told to do. I tend to believe as he moved thru the complaining crowd to do as he was told, the incessant whining and dissent finally got the best of him. By the time he gets in place at the rock, he's livid.

Not only does he fail to speak to the rock as God instructed, he strikes it twice with his staff. Probably, more like hammers it. I can see in my mind's eye Aaron taking a couple of very large steps backward. Moses just lost it.

I can hear it now -"You want water, I'll give you water!"

The water flowed in abundance, instantly meeting the needs of the people. God honored his anointed and appointed leader and blessed him with results, but Moses' disobedience and violent overreaction would come with a very high price.

As a direct result of his actions, Moses would not have the privilege to cross the Jordan River and enter the Promised Land. In allowing the loud spoken opinions from the people to generate an angry response, he stumbled over himself yet again. You may remember it was his inherent anger and rage, righteous as it may have been, that led him to kill an Egyptian some forty years earlier, resulting in his exile to the desert for four decades.

Similarly, here in my story is the trigger-point for the unraveling of my spirit and the onslaught of depression revealed.

Having the Cafe and all of her promised potential forcibly removed from my possession, triggered guilt and self-condemnation on a whole new level.

I blamed no one but myself for our dilemma. As Moses had done, I over-reacted to the people and circumstances surrounding me rather than responding properly to God. My rage toward the partners took over my spirit. I flailed against flesh and blood rather than battling principalities and powers, becoming unhinged and combative with the partners rather than warring in the spirit. Resentment and cynicism replaced peace and self-control, molding the cauldron of origin for my dark night of the soul yet to come.

Life issues can become a much greater challenge when your first response is to pick up the phone to fight before you get on your knees to pray.

I too stumbled all over myself. Obsessed and self-absorbed with loss and disappointment, in a moment, the enemy unleashes his devious ability to exploit our weaknesses and persuade us that failure surely disqualifies us from deliverance and blessing. The attitude and bent of our minds give way to the haunting ever-present question, *"What's the point?"* Here begins the slide down a lethally dangerous slippery slope.

It was never God who pounded me with condemnation and accusation, but a substantial evil presence savaged me at every level. There is an accuser in the spiritual realm employing a powerfully focused agenda, to kill, steal and destroy. He can and often does drive people to feeling abandoned, hopeless and completely alone.

I know better. I know the truth. I have led countless people to the truth.......

And yet, I bought in - hook, line and sinker.

I became an accomplished practitioner of muttering and mumbling self-condemnation and malediction. I cursed myself without pause. Moment by moment, I was complaining to God how I was *"so very tired of being me"*. Imagine how everyone else must feel. I constantly rehearsed the idea that I was a miserable disappointment, open to anything that reinforced the need to punish myself for my *"failure"*. The pattern now established in my head and heart would ultimately lead to my self-destruction six years later.

I let "them" finally get to me.

God's provision never ceased, but my focus was on my dilemma.

I empowered the questions in my life.

Why did this happen?

What did I do wrong?

Why did this not turn out differently?

I began focusing on what I wished God had done rather what He was doing, undermining the calling and anointing on my life.

I hadn't truly failed, not really. I had maintained my integrity in a very ugly war. Faith in God had been the cornerstone of our provision and success. I saw Him time and again do amazing things that can only be described as legitimate miracles. He provided a way when there was no way. Yet in the end, having actually taken residence in my personal Promised Land, I had now been brutality beaten and forcibly removed by the enemy.

For that, I would never forgive myself.

Upon our departure from the Café, various ministries and entertainment venues around the country extended invitations and offers. Disney, the House of Blues, beach resorts, churches in several locations, Christian television, had all extended offers with wonderful potential. While grateful for the intervention of friends to provide a place to land and a reliable source of income, Nancy and I were so burned-out and weary from the struggles of recent years the idea of taking on another major role immediately was too overwhelming.

We made the decision to accept the invitation of an old friend to join his church staff for a while as a place to heal and refocus. It seemed the most benign, undemanding situation and a safe haven to get my legs back under me. I would soon discover just how drastic that recovery would be.

One year following my departure from the Café, I suffered ruptured diverticulitis, gallstones and appendicitis. For seven days I was hospitalized with infection and a sustained fever of 105 degrees, receiving constant doses of high-powered antibiotics. Once the infection and accompanying fever had been sufficiently dealt with, major surgery was embarked upon, resulting in the removal of my appendix, gall bladder and more than twelve inches of my colon.

Essentially, my insides had exploded from the years warring with my accursed partners in East Tennessee. I had internalized the conflict, nearly paying for the wretched struggle with my very life.

With a heart of gratitude, I am humbled to say God came to my rescue yet again. Though the tedious recovery would require several months, the surgery was successful and free of any ongoing complications. Following another post-surgical week in the hospital, I was then discharged to heal at home.

There were a few rather distressing moments while still in the hospital:

- My first 12 hours out of major abdominal surgery was without pain medication due to a failing morphine pump. I reportedly sweat like a bull in August during this time.

- The accidental overdose of pain meds as a result of a shift change - the nurses lost track of the morphine administering times and ran the doses too close together. I became a mess in a hurry.

- Just prior to my discharge, the removal of the drainage tube that had been placed in my side was breathtaking agony. The words of the very large attending male nurse: *"Focus on something across the room because this is gonna hurt like a son of a -----!"* That lovely moment is never to be forgotten.

Through the fall of 2001, as a result of the surgery and weariness derived from the previous decade of living as an unyielding workaholic, I had collapsed into an exhausted mess. The attacks of 9/11 occurred during the time of this post-Café rehabilitation. I recall the very morning, lying on the bed and watching the reports with Nancy throughout the day.

Due to the fact I had trained myself to function with a minimum of sleep throughout the 90's, my medical team collectively determined the need to place me on heavy rounds of Ambien, helping me to acquire the rest needed to properly heal in a timely fashion.

This was the beginning of my relationship with the powerful narcotic. Knowing what we know now, the Ambien was to become a major contributor of intensifying the development of depression.

COMEBACK 2003

Being known as a veteran and resilient performer, people waited for me to make the proverbial comeback. I gave it the best shot I had.

IN MONTHS TO FOLLOW:

I would write songs that would go to Number One nationally on Christian Country radio....

I would be blessed with the honor of performing at the historic Ryman Auditorium in Nashville and broadcast on worldwide live television.

I would release a new cd of original material entitled "POSTCARDS FROM HEAVEN."

I became music director for the JAMES BURTON INTERNATIONAL GUITAR FESTIVAL.

Then - the door opened for me to return to Iowa as worship leader for a congregation that would become the fastest growing church in the Midwest over the next two years.

In conversation with a longtime friend just before my returning to Iowa, she made the comment: *"Edward, you always seem to land in clover".* Life did have the appearance of taking off once again. No one looking in on my world could fathom the volcanic rage I felt for myself deep within. It was during these days one of my best friends declared: "You have nothing to complain about, everybody wants to be you."

Therein lies the reason the news of my suicide attempt would rock the minds of my peers and elicit such a volatile response. No one saw it coming. I was not entertaining some childish tantrum of *"feeling sorry for myself"*. Rather than heal, my emotional wounds would gradually turn toxic and gravely lethal.

WELCOME BACK TO THE 6TH OF JULY 2006.

CHAPTER 9

REWIRED

IT'S A BRAND NEW DAY

Imagine, if you will, a small box with assorted push buttons, each wired to initiate specific motion and activity in the areas of life tormenting you most. These buttons are designed to activate brief or sustained encounters with the world's most irritating people, those inglorious intruders of your vital personal space who are elaborately equipped with voices designed by Hell itself to grate you down to your very last nerve, like sand-paper on an apple.

This miniature magical box appears to have an other-worldly direct connection to mail originating at the IRS, mechanical issues with your car, irritating nasty leaks in the bathroom plumbing or sewer backing up into the tub, traffic issues on your daily commute, luggage failing to arrive at baggage claim, luggage arriving at baggage claim in pieces, those little wild hairs growing from your ears and other weird places, zits, incorrect items placed in your take-out bag of greasy food discovered upon your late arrival at home, the people behind the counter of any Division of Motor Vehicles in any town of any county in any state, and the tediously redundant day-long *"somebody please kill me now"* staff meetings where the blame for everything wrong is eventually and conveniently laid squarely on your doorstep. Those moments when it seems as though your sweat-soaked skin is going to fall from your bones as blood begins to spurt from your eyes.

ARE YOU FEELING ME HERE?

Now, place the menacing box in the hands of your worst enemy and abdicate control of said box to that individual. He has the prerogative to activate any of the buttons specifically designed to goad you at any time of the day or night and without warning. Even more amazing, this horrid little toggle box not only seems capable of inciting endless combinations of irritants and interruptions, it also appears to be linked to your most personal internal response center.

The signals generated from this remote control, send shock waves through the emotional channels and the deepest regions of your soul violating your inner peace. Before long, mild intolerance and frustration evolves into bursts of fiery overreaction, a hair trigger temper and the eventual meltdown of your soul's innermost core.

We quickly become something like that little toy many of us used to play with as children, a small cartoonish figurine held together with elastic string. Once you push the buttons on the base of the figurine, he collapses into pieces. Remove your finger from the button and the figure immediately comes back together.

The minions of Satan, our accuser of the soul, have a particular knack of securing access to those push-button boxes of our lives. They know the joy of the Lord is our strength, and if they can subdue your joy, they will diminish your strength. They want you to fall apart.

Once your resistance begins to erode, then the mere daily rhythms of life begin to wear on you like the Malibu surf. Circumstances and outside forces begin to regulate the condition of your heart, soul and mind, as your vulnerabilities are gradually exposed allowing the full-on assault to begin in earnest.

This is how humans can be systematically programmed to become perpetual victims.

Satan takes great joy in *"pushing your buttons"*. He and his pernicious crew know your weakest points, what brings you down or blows you up. Manipulation of your emotions and resolve is among his greatest skills. There is no denying it, once you are fully wired for volatility the combinations for chaos and calamity are endless.

What are the buttons igniting your life, those pressure points setting your head ablaze and your pulse racing? Take personal inventory right now of the triggers consistently setting off internal explosions, knee jerk reactions and the spontaneous elevation of your blood pressure.

This had been the conditioning thru my darkest days, remaining in a continual state of overreaction, intolerance and cynicism. Conversely, reactions were not limited to barbaric anger and rage, even though I did slam my share of phones into splinters. The double pane exterior glass door of my office at the Café fell victim to an airborne cell phone following a brutally heated four-hour conversation with one of my partners. I was blowing off enough steam at times to power a riverboat.

Once my adrenal glands had been obliterated by the years of unyielding bombardment, my reactions slowly evolved from fight to flight. Every prompting now began to drive me further into myself. As depression coiled its' way around my spirit like some hellish python, the urge to escape intensified. With every day lived and each breath drawn, the grip of darkness grew more foreboding.

Now on the other side of my rescue, there was a *"rewiring"* process God intended to put me through in order to effectively sustain the restoration. My mind had to be renewed and reprogramming had to occur if my passion for life was to ever be rekindled.

He was disconnecting the diabolical box and setting me free from the old responses.

As I speak to audiences of various descriptions around the country concerning what the Lord has done in my heart and life, people silently wonder how they can experience this transformation for themselves minus the trauma of venturing down the extreme path of potential self-destruction. In conversation after conversation following those presentations, I hear their doubts of how God might do the same for them. I exhort them to simply believe!

Please consider and understand, each and every day, many times a day, we all have opportunities to act on what we know is the established Truth, or conversely, to react to every other impulse and trigger point under the sun. With each new morning arrives the choice of our will as to how we shall respond to the day.

Thank God His mercies are new every morning, but what of our response?

The cornerstone and foundation of my new journey and life is simply this:

This is the day the lord has made - I will rejoice and be glad in it!
PSALM 118:24

A FOUR LETTER WORD IN THAT VERSE HOLDS THE KEY TO SUCCESS - WILL.............

It is an active choice of our will each and every day to determine what happens to opportunity laid before us, opportunities to respond to challenges with negativity and cynicism or according to the hopeful instruction presented in the Word of God.

As Gary McSpadden always used to say, *"Life is just so daily"*.

God has a way of transforming our perspective of the daily grind, in quite the same way eye glasses do not actually alter the physical aspects of the world around you, yet prescribed corrective lens radically change the way you see everything in that same world.

I am fully cognizant some will be quick to assert I am oversimplifying the intense issues bringing people to depression and potentially self-destructive behavior. To the contrary, I acknowledge how brutal and devastating life can become in an instant. I do not presume to downplay or trivialize the harsh realities of a life lived in our modern culture. In fact, herein lies the reason I believe Scripture addresses what is referred to as Spiritual warfare.

We are in a very real and savage war for the lives of people. Your soul hangs in the balance. This struggle is in no way trivial, yet we do have the privilege of engaging the enemy from a position of complete domination as a result of what Christ accomplished in His mission of Salvation and Restoration. Through envoys of His choosing such as the Apostle Peter, Paul and John the Revelator, He dictated His insight and instruction for us to successfully navigate life on earth. The greatest problems seem to be our bent for losing focus, not referencing the manual and failing to carry out orders.

On a battlefield, that sort of blatant disregard for protocol will get you killed.

Like some of you, I too have rolled my eyes and huffed in frustration with the *positive thinking* crowd and their shameless rehashing of trite clichés and worn-out platitudes. I used to belch sarcastically how John Maxwell and Zig Ziglar were just circus clowns spinning their tripe like cotton candy at the State Fair. Their winner-winner chicken-dinner quasi-spiritual concoctions were sweet and fluffy, but could never satisfy the real hunger of the soul longing for peace and contentment. Many dispel and cast-off Joel Osteen in much the same way.

Now healed of cynicism and free from corrosiveness, I get it.

In the noisy complications of modern living however, we have completely lost the concept of being still and de-cluttering our hearts. Human beings have been poisoned by the pace of modern-day living, leaving no margin in which to detox and simplify daily life back down to the basics and fundamentals.

Simple must never be confused with trivial. The fundamentals are most often uncomplicated.

Knute Rockne, legendary football coach at Notre Dame University, will always be remembered for saying it best when addressing his players concerning their over-complication of the game by holding up the pigskin and declaring, *"Gentlemen, this is a football"*.

We require regular reintroduction to the basics of life and faith.

It is not oversimplification wanting to clear the deck of an aircraft carrier of any and all clutter so pilots aloft can safely land their planes. The function of a strategic vessel must be defined by the purpose and focus of the mission.

The Navy could choose to use aircraft carriers as supply ships, loading the flight deck with tons of food and medicine. They could create tent cities on those same decks to house homeless refugees of war. While those are meaningful operations, the Navy must choose to keep the carrier flight deck and the crew assigned to maintain its integrity, pure in their mission and function.

We must keep the main thing – the main thing.

Relentless focus is non-negotiable and rehearsal of procedure is a routine requirement. Detailed checklists must be gone over with the launch and/or landing of every flight. Only in strict adherence to mission and function will the flight crew and those on the carrier be ready when called upon in crisis and combat. This uncompromised level of intense focus and discipline for the most routine detail is the key to ongoing victorious missions.

THE URGENT HAS A WAY OF BECOMING THE PRIMARY ENEMY OF THE VITAL.

The slightest overreaction in the pressure and urgency of a moment has the potential to kill you and others around you.

Airline personnel will always instruct passengers that in the event of the loss of cabin pressure and as the oxygen apparatus is deployed from above the seats - always put your mask on prior to attempting to help your child or any other individual. Otherwise, you will put yourself and those you are hoping to assist at even greater risk.

Spiritually, I allowed myself to slowly suffocate while passing out lifelines to others. Many well-meaning people teach us to be outrageously self-sacrificing for the benefit of the wounded and lost among us. Burn yourself out for God! Leave nothing on the field! While that sounds noble, at issue was the fact I was so depleted of life and hope that I could no longer genuinely assist others. The stark reality is that very few people ever perish by sacrificing life for another human being. Most casualties are a result of inattention, overreaction, distraction or being haphazard in preparation.

Now, as God was reinventing me, his constant gentle reminder was on the most simple of life-sustaining fundamentals, the basics I had lost sight of in my tormented self-complication of life.

"THE PURE IN HEART WILL SEE GOD".

Unless you become like a little child, you will never fully realize abundant living.

I WAS WILDLY SUCCESSFUL AT MAKING EVERYTHING COMPLICATED.

Analyzing. Dissecting. Criticizing. Doubting. Overreacting. Over-reaching.

THE ONLY THING THAT SEEMED TO ROLL OFF MY BACK WAS PEACE.

There were days when a simple visit to Walmart for groceries could dissolve my joy like teabags in a tsunami.

Day to day and moment by moment, I turned the life-giving Truth of God into a powerless cliché by my own decisions to be consistently miserable and brooding. Out of my mouth flowed endless verbal torrents of discontent. Piece by piece, I assembled an elaborate prison of misery and proceeded to lock myself away.

Once I realized the miraculous nature of what God had done for me in Minneapolis, it was as though He whispered into my now attentive ear of how He had graciously made all things new within. The task would now be to work in concert with Him solidifying those changes and transitioning into a permanently renewed and upgraded lifestyle.

If I did not proceed with the meticulous rewiring process of my heart, mind and soul, everything would quickly snap back to the old ways of thinking in just a matter of days, if not hours.

Moving from the effect of years spent verbalizing hopelessness and frustration, success going forward would be found in the energetic habit of declaring the Word of God over my life. The new practice would now be to say what God says about me, in place of the world's opinion or my own disappointment. Realigning myself mentally and verbally with what the Bible says I can be in my daily life and in relationship with God was of extreme importance.

The same is absolutely true for you. It is an act of your will, empowered by the Spirit of God, to revolutionize your mind, will and emotions. You have exactly the same opportunity I did then and continue to have daily.

I love the way T.D Jakes articulates this: *"You may not be able to change your job just now, you might be unable to increase your talent, acquire great wealth, or even trade in your old junky car for a better ride. There may be very little you can do to affect a major makeover in your personal appearance or wardrobe. However, YOU CAN CHANGE YOUR MIND!"*

The exact & immediate need of my life was contained in his simple spot-on statement.

I HAD TO CHANGE MY MIND.

Paying close attention to this is critical. Even though I had been teaching this sort of thing for years, it was as though I had been spiritually lulled to sleep. The war in which we are engaged is close range combat. We wrestle with principalities and powers in tight proximity. Held in a suffocating sleeper hold, the whispers and suggestion of our enemy combatants play a significant role in our disqualification and demise.

Should I ever return to my old patterns of defeat and discontent, before long the symptoms of discouragement and despair would once again take up residence in my spirit. As the power and influence demonic forces we battle are broken and removed, if we fail to fill the void with Light, virtue, the Word and the Spirit of God, those elements and influences of darkness will return with a vengeance seven times stronger than before.

Come to a place of gut-wrenching honesty with yourself and God, before life thoroughly unravels. If you should say to yourself, *"this could never happen to me"*, that very thought is the quintessential mistake, the classic first warning marker and deadly sign of initial spiritual dishonesty. My personal meltdown required a full-on miracle to rescue me from self-inflicted annihilation.

It was only then God captured my complete and undivided attention, finally allowing Him to rewire my head, heart, and emotions. It was a process of refocusing on the most basic truth and once again coming to terms with the paramount issues of life.

GOD WAS REWIRING THE BOX AND RENEWING A CHILD-LIKE SPIRIT WITHIN ME.

He was leading me back to a simple faith lost long ago in the forests of complication.

Although my enemy maintained access to *'the box'*, he quickly discovered his pushbutton mayhem had been deactivated. He could still trigger events and send in all the various deviant clowns to wreck my day, but I was no longer blowing fuses in my central nervous system by my overreaction. There was a distinct disconnect to my former internal response system. My *"wiring"* was rerouted, new hardware installed, and a complete system upgrade downloaded as my new self came online.

Old things passed away and all things became new. I finally knew first-hand what that meant.

Peace that passes understanding was becoming a tangible attribute in my life. New alignment in my thought processes had arrested the avalanche of cynicism. I was evolving into a person who could actually live in the moment and experience joy.

My kids would tell you they experienced a miracle firsthand as witnesses to my transformation.

IT IS THE LORD WHO RIEGNS!

In Him we live and move and have our being. In Him everything has beginning and conclusion. The new life within is not of my own doing, rather it is a practice of His Presence – His Presence makes all the difference.

Walking thru this process, I have relearned to guard my heart from the suggestions and accusations of the enemy, regardless of the source he chooses to introduce them into my path. There is discipline involved in learning to hear the voice of our Shepherd and not the voice of a stranger.

"Pay attention to what I say, listen closely to my words. Do not let them out of your sight, keep them within your heart; for they are life to those who find them and health to a man's whole body. Above all else, guard your heart for it is the wellspring of life."
PROVERBS 4:20-25

AS HUMANS WE TEND TO LOOK FOR LIFE OUTSIDE OURSELVES.......

People look to outside resources to discover satisfaction and contentment – however....... YOU WILL NEVER FIND LIFE UNTIL YOU HAVE LIFE....

Life must be lived from the INSIDE OUT. We have to deal with the spirit man within. Most people spend their days looking for happiness and significance in something acquired externally, be it monetary gain, business success or athletic achievement. Current culture is wired to believe fulfillment can be ordered from the Home Shopping Network and delivered to our front door by the FedEx driver, yet people continue to discover the acquisition of toys, baubles and doodads only leaves us aching for more. Proverbs tells us the satisfaction we are so desperately searching for, must originate in our hearts.

YOU MUST GUARD YOUR HEART – IT IS THE SOURCE OF WELLBEING.

If you choose to ignore this life-giving Biblical fact, things will most likely not go well for you over time. You will be controlled by something other than the Spirit of God. Allow God to disconnect the sinister little box in your life and rewire your spirit according to a new schematic, His Word.

The tragic reality - if you believe the cause of your futility is completely external, you will never be healed and whole internally until you can fix everything around you.

Therein lies an acute problem. I was always trying to fix everything to get to a place of contentment. That is the misconception used of Satan to render us dysfunctional and broken, and yes, even suicidal. The most agonizing thing in my life was trying to *"fix"* the way everyone felt about me or responded to me. When things would go bad and projects would be less than brilliantly successful, I would be the first to take the blame, believing I had failed to do enough to make the outcome good for everyone.

And please listen very closely, when people around you feel certain you will take the blame, they will be more than happy to post the guilt into your column without delay.

Taking the blame is an orientation I established early on in life, mushrooming into a cutthroat monster. I defined my own life as faulty and inadequate on so many levels, there developed an innate tendency to apologize for things really having nothing to do with me. I presumed myself to be guilty for everything.

Completely losing touch with the idea of the dual existence of my being hidden in Christ and who He was in me, my heart and mind became open game for the accuser and any assault leveled against me. It is the power of Christ within enabling us to overcome the external ravages of life, not our own resolution. That is precisely why Scripture has a great deal to say about the heart and why we are to live in the Spirit. We must practice the Presence of Christ. It is in that place called the heart, our core - that the Life of God can flow out from to every part of our being.

'There is now therefore, no condemnation to those who are in Christ Jesus!"
ROMANS 8:1

Early one morning as I was reading in the Psalms and reflecting on the benefits we have as children of God, I began writing down various thoughts resulting in what has become a daily confession over my life for the entire year. You might want to consider making this a reular part of your devotional time:

TODAY IS THE DAY THE LORD HAS MADE!

I do now and will continue to rejoice until my eyes close in peaceful sleep tonight. Because of the finished work of Jesus on the cross and thru the power of His resurrection, I have now been set free from the law of sin and death. The power of sin has been broken. I will not submit myself to the accusation of Satan and his cohorts ever again. There is now no condemnation to those who are in Christ.

I will listen closely to the voice of the Spirit - be quick to repent and slow to react. I will seek to remain in a constant awareness of the presence of God, praying without ceasing and focused on the eternal. Today - there is and there will be peace within in each moment and thru each challenge - both great and small - for I dwell in the House of the Lord God now and for of all Eternity. There is a calm and abiding trust that I am exactly where I am meant to be.

There is trust and confidence in my soul, that as I follow the prompting of the Holy Spirit, goodness and mercy will follow me all the days of my life. All of my needs shall be met and every good thing my Heavenly Father has for me shall overtake me. He will provide as I have chosen to seek His face and not just his hand of blessing.

I will not forget the infinite possibilities that are born of faith in God. The Word of God shall be my authority over every perceived limitation. My imagination is under the control of the Spirit and is empowered by the same.

Angels assigned to my family and myself shall guard our every step. No weapon, known or unknown can come close to causing us harm. Possessions and the opinion of others have no control over my joy, peace or confidence. Only You, Lord God of my heart, have control over me.

I will use the gifts that I have received to their complete capacity. Then I will discover a whole new realm of creative thought I have never known before. There can and will be Divine joy in every moment of this day - no matter the circumstances surrounding me - for Your Joy - Jehovah-Jireh - is the soul source and origin of my strength. I will operate in that joy and as a result - I will be able to walk and not faint. I will now be able to run and never grow weary.

BY THE WAY – the scripture says those who wait upon the Lord shall renew their strength and will mount up with wings like eagles. Many people think waiting on the Lord is to sit on the couch and complacently dawdle about until God chooses to do something on our behalf. Even as we wait – it is imperative we invest our faith through training and preparation. Many times the reason God delays the blessing we have solicited of Him, is plainly because we are not equipped to handle it. We fail to prepare ourselves to receive the answer to the very prayers we have prayed.

For example, church congregations will pray and fast for a solid month for God to send revival and bring a great increase of people into their fellowship. However, they have made no practical preparation to receive that for which they prayed. Facilities require expansion to provide the room needed for the anticipated growth while teachers and leaders must be trained ahead of time to accommodate the inbound young believers who will stand in need of instruction. God would tend to ask: "What are you going to do with the increase should I bless you in direct response to your request? You must get ready in anticipation of the answer."

Faith in motion means taking action on things yet unseen.

HOWEVER, IN REALITY, WE ARE NOT WIRED TO THINK LIKE THAT.

We must have our minds renewed or rewired by the Spirit and Word of God.

Let's continue now with the Biblical confession over life:

I have the mind of Christ and every choice I make shall be determined by the clarity He gives. I am and I will continually be content, at peace and without anxiety or frustration. My soul has been given divine freedom to sing, dance, praise and love. The Divine Love which has been imparted to me, I will pass along to every person I encounter everyday regardless of their attitude or response to my offering toward them. In all I set my hand to do today … I am blessed. For you, oh Lord, have given me new life and I will not squander it on the worthless and the temporary. Your anointing has broken every yoke and crushed every weapon of the enemy.

All the old patterns, reactionary ways, and curses on my old life have been redeemed. All the chains of self-condemnation and depression have been broken. The power of the Blood and the word of my testimony will cause me to be victorious in

every endeavor - and all that I say, think and accomplish shall result in the Name of
Jesus Christ being glorified.

Anyone in my family, as well as many of my friends, would be quick to
tell you this sort of attitude in no way resembled my countenance before my
supernatural encounter with God, ten years ago.

I AM THE LIVING BREATHING TEXTBOOK DEFINITION OF A
NEW CREATION.

A KNOCK @ THE DOOR FROM THE COACH

My personal transformation was not confined to the spiritual realm.
Everything changed. Besides, the nurse on Monday morning of my hospital
stay in Minneapolis had declared me to be a well-conditioned athlete. It would
soon become my goal to turn that particular proclamation over my life into an
emphatic reality.

About two weeks into my recovery time at home, the doorbell rang.

Nancy had remained very intentional about shielding me from phone calls
and personal contact from visitors during this vitally important time. I had been
hibernating within the safe confines of my man cave on the lower level of our
townhome, reading, praying, resting, and just learning to breath again. We wanted
to keep my exposure to the opinions and commentary of the gallery essentially
non-existent, and rest assured, boundless opinions and infinite commentary
flourished just beyond the safe insulation of my underground cocoon.

She came downstairs after a few minutes, saying I might want to hear what
this friend had to say. Ascending the steps and turning the corner into our living
room, there stood my longtime friend, Jim. After a bit of introductory chatter,
he described his ordeal during the previous hour at the steering wheel of his
car. By his account, he had been anxiously driving through our neighborhood
attempting to muster the courage to ring our doorbell, endeavoring to do so on
two occasions, both times retreating to his Toyota to drive around yet again. The
third attempt being the charmed and now seated on our couch, Jim proceeded to
tell us why he had been confronted with such intense apprehension.

"I am not in the habit of saying things like this, which is why it took three shots at it to even ring the doorbell. I hope you will not think me to be some sort of lunatic, but I believe God wants me to train you and lead you through a rigorous conditioning program. Weight training, cardio, I'm supposed to put you through the paces like a marine drill sergeant. God says He wants me to be your coach and training partner for the next few months to help get you healthy."

My response, *"Well. If that is what He wants, then what are we waiting for?"*

In recent years, Jim had continued to win multiple gold medals competing at the Senior Olympics in Las Vegas. He certainly knew what he was doing and was determined to push me beyond the limits of my couch-ridden, Cheetos devouring past. We implemented a training schedule of four days each week, running, lifting, throwing tractor tires around, more running with weights tied to my waist, push-ups, pull-ups, rowing, dragging a sled, everything imaginable.

Then following a water break, more running.

The first time I ran the steps of the football stadium at the University of Northern Iowa, I threw up for about an hour and then slept the reminder of the day. The overdose of Ambien had not been successful in taking me out, but I was convinced in my mind, running at this pace was sure to kill me. Over the weeks to come, the extra weight I had carried for so long began to fall away and the metamorphosis was becoming apparent to my family. I will always remember the day Lindsay loudly declared, *"Wow, I have never seen my Diddy with arms like these!"*

That was a very cool and satisfying moment, I must admit!

Ironically, the thing I most embraced from the intense training regimen was a devotion to running the steps of not only the stadium, but parking garages and office buildings as well. Soon, I was sprinting the equivalent of 80 floors, four times a week. As I would sprint up four floors and then jog down, repeating the process until I met my goal. By the way, I did not count the descending steps, so I actually traveled 160 floors entirely in this training routine.

It was at this point, Jim gave me my native-American name: *"Man Who Runs Many Steps".*

At fifty years of age, I once again got to a thirty-inch waist, losing 45 pounds and being in much better physical condition than at in point in my entire life.

The results only encouraged me to accomplish more. This fierce physical training also became closely tied to a concentrated spiritual regimen as well. As I sprinted up the steps, I would make Biblical declarations over myself, as well as my family, aligning my mind and spirit with what God's Word has to say about me.

I have the mind of Christ.

No weapon formed against me shall in any way or by any means, be able to prosper.

I've been seated with Christ in heavenly places.

I declare the Holy Spirit has control over my mind and body. The Spirit rules my flesh.

Any and all generational curses have been broken by the power of the Blood of Christ.

I no longer live, but Christ lives within me.

Satan has been made an open spectacle and rendered powerlessly defeated by the finished work of Jesus and has absolutely no access to or power over me, or my family, in any way.

I can do all things through Christ who gives me the strength, strength like I have never known before. My spirit shall rule my mind and flesh. I am an overcomer and more than a conqueror. I will break thru all the former limits and restrictions of my mind.

On the way down the steps, I would receive and welcome all the things God wanted to become a part of my new and improved nature. The old passing away and all was becoming new. These are just a small sampling of my declarations.

I receive your wisdom – even faith itself is a gift from you, Lord.

Thank you for peace that passes understanding.

Thank you that my Nancy and our children are healed and blessed even as I am. Thank you for full recovery and a revived spirit within all of us.

Thank you for favor with everyone with whom I come into contact.

Thank you that your blessing, goodness and mercy overtake us.

Thank you that your mercies are new every morning.

EVERYTHING CHANGED.

My diet was radically altered. Dr. Pepper had been my constant companion for years, sometimes consuming as much as 32 ounces in a single evening. Since my rescue and healing ten years ago, the only beverage to pass over my lips has been water, not a drop of anything else. That alone has resulted in greatly improved health.

While physical training should not become another maniacal obsession drawing our focus from the priority of spiritual conditioning, it is imperative we assume responsibility for the temple we have been given. God had rescued me. I was obligated to take better care of myself. This attention to physical discipline directly results in a much greater reservoir of strength and vitality, impacting your spiritual life. The gains in physical stamina, clarity of mind, energy and enthusiasm I unearthed were remarkable.

I did not realize how bad I had felt until I discovered how amazing I could feel.

The culture I grew up in would religiously and routinely drag their bodies ridden with diabetes and heart disease to the church altar for prayers of healing, some even at risk of losing eyesight or the amputation of a leg. As the prayer time would end and the service would conclude, those self-same people for whom we had all prayed in earnest, would immediately exit the sanctuary, drive a couple of miles down the street in the Studebaker, pile into the back-booth of the local Shoney's and proceed to devour massive amounts of all-you-can-eat fried chicken, deep fried okra, green beans cooked in salted fat, buttered rolls, gallons of sweet tea awash with sugar, then finishing the feast off with a gigantic slice of double-stacked hot fudge cake, extra fudge on the side.

What is wrong with this picture?

This was normal, not occasional. In fact, the religious minions I grew up around spent far more time at the table than they did at the altar. Fried chicken has become so much a part of regular church functions, it's been affectionately dubbed, *"The Gospel Bird."*

You know it's true.

We conduct funerals on a regular basis for people who have committed recreational suicide using cigarettes and Big Macs as their weapons of choice. Respiratory issues and pneumonia claim the lives of countless hundreds every day of people who refused to get off the couch or even think of choosing the stairs over the elevator, let alone any sort of disciplined cardio exercise. Please do not blow smoke in my face declaring my cowardice for attempting suicide, when you are habitually doing the exact same thing by way of those little tobacco filled rolls of paper, alit between your nicotine stained fingers. I have friends suffering from bouts of congestive heart failure, dealing with anxiety over their condition by smoking one cigarette after another. My own father suffered from lung cancer due to that very habit.

My Pawpaw I told you about in LET IT BE, smoked two to three packs a day since the time he was a teenager. In one of those long rocking chair conversations, he told me as he was driving home along the interstate earlier in the day, he suddenly felt a strong sense of God's Presence. He pulled the car over to the shoulder of the road, took the pack of cigarettes from his shirt pocket, crumpling it in his fisted hand, and tossed it ceremoniously out the window. He then prayed, *"Lord, at your command and by your strength, never again will I be a slave to this disgusting habit."* He told me to be careful to never so much as pick up a cigarette, let alone light one. I never saw him smoke or use tobacco in any form ever again. No nicotine gum, no agitation, no habit replacement therapy – after 50 years he just stopped, cold turkey. When God calls on you to do something, He'll give you what it takes to make it happen.

God wants to revolutionize every aspect of our lives. He wants to make us entirely whole.

I pray as you read of my personal transformation, you will recognize the life of which I speak is available to you and to anyone who will believe. If joy and peace are not the primary attributes of your life, you are living far beneath your privilege as a child of the Most High.

His Name is above every name and we have been established and seated with Him in heavenly places. We are empowered to live life in a much loftier place than most of us have ever known, a secret place very few are even aware exists. Do not misunderstand what I am saying here. We are not promised a life free of challenges, difficulties or hardship, but we have the promise of peace that passes understanding when we keep our hearts and minds stayed on Him as we pioneer through life.

We have been given authority and dominion in the earth by the power in the Name of our God. We have the mind of Christ and are fully equipped to operate in it. As a result, even in the most challenging of circumstances, we have the potential to live free from anxiety. The Word says the Lord gives sweet sleep to His children, a direct benefit of the calm assurance we have knowing Jesus is Lord of every detail of life.

HIS NAME IS HIGHER AND STRONGER THAN DEPRESSION AND DESPAIR.

Prior to my outright meltdown, every dinky push-button skirmish in life would readily pilfer away the surety of who I am in Christ, and who He is in me. No more and never again will I forget or doubt the preeminent reality of that dual relationship. Nothing can separate me from the Love of God found in Christ Jesus, which is alive in me, for I no longer live but Christ lives within me and the life I now live, I live by the faith of the Son of God who loved me and gave Himself for me.

Neither height or depth, principalities or powers, nagging carnal deacons, frustrated preachers or their wives, unethical business partners, bankers or even attorneys, especially attorneys, can ever separate me again from the peace of God in my heart.

I no longer need anyone to appreciate me to be at peace with myself. I am loved and mentored by the actual Creator of the Universe. His life and Joy sustain me! He is my source, my refuge and deliverer, and the One who completes me. When I lay down at night, I relinquish to Him all that happened throughout the day and will rest in absolute peace, for when I rise in the morning, His mercies will always be new and living fully alive in the present moment is, without question, the will of my Heavenly Father.

So yesterday is in the books for being just what it was and tomorrow may never come, so I will celebrate and make the most of every moment. For the name of the God I serve and love is *"I AM"*. There is no sense of distance and time with Him, for it is always the eternal now. Wherever I happen to be, there He is, for He lives and abides within me. This is the day the Lord has made, I will rejoice and be glad in Him. Let it be!

God has made it distinctly clear, the choice is mine each minute of every day to declare and receive the blessing of God over my life and reject the lies and accusation of the enemy.

I must choose between the blessing and the curse.

He has fully rewired my thinking. Acceptance by Him is not conditional on my performance. His love is unfailing and His mercies are new every morning. That assurance never serves as a license for sin or permission to live any way I desire. Rather, it is healing for me. I am now a new creation. I have truly been born again. I wholeheartedly welcome the reality of those words into my life for the first time. Allow God to rewire your mind and reprogram your thoughts with the Word and what it has to say about you and who you are as His child. For as Biblical revelation becomes a part of your DNA, it will radically transform everything in your life, just as it has for me.

I wrote the following while sitting on my deck overlooking the Teton Mountain range in Jackson Hole, Wyoming. I refuse to ever abandon or allow my renewed childlike faith to be stolen away again by the push-button antics of the enemy or the daily grind of life. It is a choice we have been empowered to make.

THERE ARE WORLDS OF MUSIC TO BE COMPOSED AND PLAYED.
SOUNDS, LYRICS, AND ART TO BE CREATED...
LAUGHTER AND LOVE TO BE ENJOYED...
LIFE TO BE DISCOVERED AND LIVED TO THE FULLEST

TAKE IN THOSE TENDER PRECIOUS MOMENTS TO BE
CHERISHED LIKE TREASURE

DON'T WASTE A DAY IN REGRET OR WORRY
MAKE THE MOST OF NOW

YOU ONLY HAVE ONE SHOT AT TODAY - THEN IT'S GONE
TREASURE EVERY SUNRISE

DRINK IN THE MOONLIGHT OF A CRYSTAL CLEAR NIGHT

ENJOY THE SOUNDS & MOVEMENT OF THE MAJESTIC CREATION
AS IT ENDLESSLY PERFORMS FOR HER CREATOR

THE DANCE OF A MILLION STARS
ACROSS AN ENDLESS CANOPY OF SPACE
AND THE MUSIC OF THE HOLY SPIRIT RIDING
ON THE GENTLE WINDS OF HOPE
CAN ONLY BE EXPERIENCED BY THE ONES
WHO ARE QUIET ENOUGH TO TAKE NOTICE

- BE AT PEACE -
- LISTEN WITH YOUR HEART -
- LET IT SETTLE IN YOUR SOUL -
- BE STILL AND KNOW -
- THERE IS INDEED SO MUCH MORE -

CHAPTER 10

FILL ME UP

REPROGRAMMING OUR THOUGHTS, WORDS & ACTIONS

I've always loved this thought by Wilbur Rees:

I would like to buy $3 worth of God, please. Not enough to explode my soul or disturb my sleep, but just enough to equal a cup of warm milk or a snooze in the sunshine. I don't want enough of God to make me love a black man or pick beets with a migrant worker. I want ecstasy, not transformation. I want the warmth of the womb, not the pain of a new birth. I want a pound of the Eternal in a paper sack. I would like to buy $3 worth of God, please.
-WILBUR REES

"THREE DOLLARS WORTH OF GOD" - JUDSON PRESS 1971

According to the Bible, for us to maintain a lukewarm condition of the soul is sickening to God. Unfortunately, that seems to be the very place a great majority of people camp out, not really against the idea of a personal relationship with God, but playing it cool enough to avoid being deemed the proverbial wacked-out Jesus freak. As a result, the radical spiritual transformation of a life is an idea long left by the wayside. The Post Modern church has, for the most part, relegated itself to twelve step programs and culturally acceptable self-help methodologies to assist humans in navigating life.

My former staff mates at Hipster Cathedral refused to speak of anything *"radically spiritual."* Rather, they chose to refer to people as eventually stepping across *"the faith-line"*. Pastor Hipster and his Lemmings in tow, maintained a nocuous obsession with appearing in the *"now"* when it came to communication of Biblical truth. Let's approach this *"faith-thing"* in a way that is reasonable and acceptable in our culture, lest we appear unhinged, out of touch or just plain loony. We can represent God while maintaining a distinct coolness factor. Only then can we have a shot at capturing the attention of the Gen X'ers and Millennials.

Welcome to Lukewarmville!

What is needed in the lives of most people is a full-on transfusion, a flushing out of the old and interjection of the new. It's an all or nothing proposition. By Jesus' own definition, you must first lose your life if you want to find it. There is no reference to *"stepping across a faith-line."* There is plenty of talk however about being crucified with Christ.

I purpose life be lived as it was designed to be lived by the Creator of life.

Humanity needs to be reawakened to the power of the Gospel and the authority found in the Word of God as the definitive method of reconditioning a mind and spirit crushed under the weight of depression. I believe the idea of aligning the way we think, the words we say and the actions we take with what the Bible says about us, is the one thing that can and will revolutionize our lives, if we apply it.

As T.D. Jakes often says: *"The Word will work if you work it."*

FOR ME, THAT IS NOT AN UNTESTED THEORY - IT IS FACT!

We are daily bombarded with images of violence, corruption and blatant evil. Even more so are the relentless voices reinforcing doubt, fear and the implied foolishness of anyone who chooses to literally believe in God. The vast majority of public schools, university campuses, office complexes and world marketplaces have become devoid of anything remotely resembling faith in the God of the

Bible. People quickly affirm personal interest in benign spirituality yet reject the practice of authentic faith.

By and large, the mass of humanity wants little or nothing to do with the idea of traditional Christianity. However, that is not what I am proposing here. In fact, it was my personal religious practice of traditional denominational Christian legalism that nearly killed me. What transpires in the vast majority of the twenty-first century congregations has little to do with the overcoming power of the Blood of Christ and the words of testimony we speak. It is more of a superficial form of Godliness, proving powerless to authentically change a life.

My goal here is to challenge you in ways you may have never experienced before. Every effort will be made to shy away from the use of religious guilt, while we focus on the Words of life spoken by Jesus and the instructions He left for us to follow. Remember, the road leading to life is narrow and few there will be who will find it. Count the cost. There is a price to pay, but the results are worth it. Again - salvation is free via redemption by the Blood of Christ, yet spiritual maturity comes with a price of devotion and discipline.

THE THOUGHTS WE THINK

"As a man thinks in his heart - so is he".
PROVERBS 23:7
THE NIV BIBLE - ZONDERVAN PUBLISHING - 2005

It is the meditation or the thoughts of our heart at the creative core of who we are. The focal point of our imagination most often becomes reality.

Watch your thoughts - they become words.
Watch your words - they become actions.
Watch your actions - they become habits.
Watch your habits - they become character.
Watch your character - it becomes your destiny.
- FRANK OUTLAW

We improve our lives or destroy the same by our thoughts. Most of the worst things in life that happened to me were in some way actually created by me. The power of our thought life is far beyond what most people understand or are willing to acknowledge, yet God repeatedly addresses the significance of our daily meditation throughout His Word. Thoughts are like seeds and whatever you plant in the field of your mind will indeed produce a harvest. Your thoughts are never neutral. We are consistently creating some sort of reality.

I love the way Vance Havner said it: *"Whatever gets thrown into the well, eventually comes up in the bucket".*

IMAGINATION IS CREATIVE ENERGY

We determine how it gets channeled. Imagination can be the crucible for life, peace and a heart for God, or it can be the birthplace of darkness, depression and defeat. Recently I posted a quote from Mark Twain on my Facebook wall: *"I am an old man and have known a great many troubles, but most of them never happened."*

How true is that? We spend enormous amounts of energy in worry over things nowhere to be found on our radar screens. Consider what happens when you have watched a horror movie prior to bedtime, terrifying you to the core. With every creak, crack and snap heard in the darkness, your imagination runs wild with the fear of your impending demise.

Fearful thoughts and a jaundiced imagination simply cannot coexist with faith. They are oil and water - elements never intended to mix. The outcome of any given situation has less to do with circumstances than it does with our thinking. If you think you can accomplish something, you have a shot. If you choose to think you can't, you are finished before you even begin.

> **"We demolish arguments and every pretension that sets itself up against the knowledge of God, and we take captive every thought to make it obedient to Christ."**
> 2 CORINTHIANS 10:5
> THE NIV BIBLE 2005 ZONDERVAN PUBLISHING

"Do not conform any longer to the pattern of this world, but be transformed by the renewing of your mind. Then you will be able to test and approve what God's will is - his good, pleasing and perfect will."
ROMANS 12:2
THE NIV BIBLE 2005 ZONDERVAN PUBLISHING - USED BY PERMISSION

When you are blessed with a vigorous imagination, it can also become a source of faith-obliterating, self-defeating thinking. The thoughts I had established toward myself were nowhere close to being held captive in obedience to Christ. I had to reprogram my mind. Depression, anger, anxiety, self-pity, bitterness and selfishness had taken up residence in my spirit due to the fact I relentlessly meditated on those things day and night for years.

Much of your thought life is composed of those words and phrases mentally rehearsed over and over again that no one but you can hear. We must continuously take inventory of those inner conversations to determine the type of seeds we are planting in the soil of our souls. It is impossible to continually sow seeds of despair, fear and cynicism, expecting to reap a harvest of joy, peace and blessing.

"The most influential person who will talk to you all day is you - so you should be careful what you say to you."
- ZIG ZIGLAR

Our minds - that is our thinking, can be revolutionized by the power of God and His Word. Trusting our own willpower to break down these strongholds that have taken years to assemble is most often futile and frustrating. We overcome by the power of the Blood of Christ and His resurrection. At issue with most of the church today is the choice to live by resolution and not by supernatural restoration. There is a resource available to the people of God that remains relatively untapped.

Faith is not a cheap gimmick, neither is it a mentality of entitlement. Faith will always seem like foolishness to people who are perishing, but the fact is - faith can revolutionize a moment or a lifetime. David stood before Goliath in faith as the remainder of Israel cowered in fear. He knew God was far greater than the giant he faced, even though logic and reason would declare otherwise. His courage was strong and sure, bolstered by the seeds of faith he had sown along the way as a shepherd boy. The slaying of the giant not only won the moment - it changed the course of David's life and the future for the entire nation of Israel.

Never discount the power and significance of a single moment of faith.

"You were taught, with regard to your former way of life, to put off your old self, which is being corrupted by its deceitful desires; to be made new in the attitude of your mind; and to put on the new self, created to be like God in true righteousness and holiness."
EPHESIANS 4:22-24

THE NIV BIBLE - 2005 ZONDERVAN PUBLISHING - USED BY PERMISSION

THE WORDS WE SPEAK

"The word is near you; it is in your mouth and in your heart, that is, the word of faith we are proclaiming. That is you confess with you mouth, 'Jesus is Lord' and believe in your heart that God has raised him from the dead you will be saved. For it is with your heart that you believe and are justified, and it is with your mouth that you confess and are saved".
ROMANS 10:9-10

NIV BIBLE - 2005 ZONDERVAN PUBLISHING GROUP

Most people occupying houses of worship have no idea the power contained in the words they speak over themselves, their children and their lives everyday.

"If you could find someone whose speech was perfectly true, you'd have a perfect person, in perfect control of life. A bit in the mouth of a horse controls the whole horse. A small rudder on a huge ship in the hands of a skilled captain sets a course in the face of the strongest

winds. A word out of your mouth may seem of no account, but it can accomplish nearly anything - or destroy it!

It only takes a spark, remember, to set off a forest fire. A careless or wrongly placed word out of your mouth can do that. By our speech we can ruin the world, turn harmony into chaos, throw mud on a reputation, send the whole world up in smoke and go up with it, smoke right from the pit of hell. This is scary: You can tame a tiger, but you can't tame a tongue - it's never been done. The tongue runs wild, a wanton killer. With our tongues we bless God our Father; with the same tongues we curse the very men and women He made in His image. Curses and blessings out of the same mouth!"

JAMES 3: 2-10

THE MESSAGE BIBLE - 2002 EUGENE H. PETERSON - NAVPRESS PUBLISHING GROUP)

"Jesus called the crowd to him and said; 'Listen and understand. What goes into a man's mouth does not make him unclean, but what comes out of his mouth, that is what makes him unclean'."

MATTHEW 15:-10-11

THE NIV BIBLE 2005 ZONDERVAN PUBLISHING - USED BY PERMISSION

In "WAR OF WORDS", John David Tripp wrote the following: *"We think that words are not that important because we think of words as little utilitarian tools for making our life easier and more efficient, when they are actually a powerful gift given by a communicating God for His divine purpose.*

You have never spoken a neutral word in your life. Your words have direction to them. If your words are moving you in the life direction, they will be words of encouragement, hope, love, peace, unity, instruction, wisdom and correction. But if your words are moving you in a death direction, they will be words of anger, malice,

slander, jealousy, division, contempt, racism, violence, judgment and
condemnation. "
JOHN DAVID TRIPP
"THE POWER OF WORDS AND THE WONDER OF GOD - 2009 CROSSWAY PUBLISHING

CREATION

When God created the heavens and the earth, He did not do so with His hands. He created all there is by simply speaking it into existence, with the power of His Word. Given we are created in His image, the fact is, there is creative power on the words we speak.

"Words kill, words give life; they're either poison or fruit - you choose.
"

PROVERBS 18:21

THE MESSAGE BIBLE - 2002 EUGENE H. PETERSON - NAVPRESS PUBLISHING GROUP --
USED BY PERMISSION

In the same way positive faith results in positive results, negative words and proclamation can and will produce very negative results. I spent several years practicing the habitual cursing of my own life, constantly mumbling under my breath how worthless I was and deliberately pleading with God to kill me. I believed any ability I once possessed to be successful had evaporated into the mists of distant memory.

My disgruntled internal speech was riddled with intolerance aimed mostly toward myself, believing I was a miserable waste of breath. I had *"talked myself into it."* And once you reveal to the enemy the portals of vulnerability through which he can gain access, the onslaught begins. He will bring every available weapon against you to reinforce the destructive confessions you make over your life.

Refuse to allow yourself to trivialize this fact: The creative force in your negatively charged words opens your life to more darkness that you could ever begin to imagine.

"He (Jesus) touched their eyes and said, 'Become what you believe.'
It happened."
MATTHEW 9:29

THE MESSAGE BIBLE - 2002 EUGENE H. PETERSON - NAVPRESS PUBLISHING GROUP - USED BY PERMISSION

"You have been trapped by what you said; ensnared by the
words of your mouth."
PROVERBS 6:2

THE NIV BIBLE - 2005 ZONDERVAN PUBLISHING - USED BY PERMISSION

What we say with our mouth gives evidence of what we believe in our heart. Only God is Omniscient. Only He knows the thoughts of our inner most being. How we react to challenge is the only way our souls' enemy can determine our strengths and weaknesses. Words and speech give us away.

The primary reason God prevented a generation of Israelites from entering into the Land of Promise, was due in large part to their incessant grumbling and complaining. They declared multiple times over, it would have been better to live as a slave of Egypt than to die free in the desert.

"The Lord said to Moses and Aaron: How long will this wicked
community grumble against me? I have heard the complaints of these
grumbling Israelites. So tell them, 'As surely as I live, declares the Lord,
I will give you the very things I heard you say: In this desert your bodies
will fall - every one of you twenty years old or more who was counted in
the census and who has grumbled against me. Not one of you will enter
the land I swore with uplifted hand to make your home'."
NUMBERS 14: 26-30

THE NIV BIBLE - 2005 ZONDERVAN

Hopefully you are beginning to see how strategically important our words are. The Bible clearly states we will be judged by every idle word we speak. In retrospect, I have come to see with twenty-twenty vision the degree to which I cursed my own life. During the first couple months of recovery, I took detailed daily inventory on the words of my mouth, stunned by the amount of thoughtless chatter uttered from my lips in direct contradiction to the Word of God.

Reprogramming our heart's content is imperative if restoration is to be complete and lasting, for it bears repeating; out of the abundance of the heart our mouths speak. We must speak what God has spoken, as opposed to doubt, fear, cynicism and intolerance.

There must be a dramatic shift from the constant drone of, "I'm a disgusting failure who will never amount to anything" to the proclamation found in Philippians 4:13 which declares, *"I can do all things through Christ who strengthens me."*

Another important part of this reprogramming process is to not only embrace the Word of God in your heart or meditate upon it in your mind, but to actually speak it out loud. Romans 10:17 states clearly: "Faith comes by hearing and hearing by the Word of God."...

In Joshua 1:8, God spoke to Joshua this instruction: *"Don't let my Word depart from your mouth; meditate on it day and night, so that you may be careful to do everything written in it. Then you will be prosperous and successful. Have I not commanded you? Be strong and courageous. Do not be terrified; do not be discouraged, for the Lord your God will be with you wherever you go."*

Remember we are engaged in spiritual battles with unseen forces, both for and against us. Everything we say is heard by God and His angels who watch over us, along with the minions of Satan who are seeking to exploit your weaknesses and enslave you in any way possible.

Here's a question you might ponder for a moment: How do you think the angels who are dispatched to watch over your life...might respond to the things they hear you say?

I happen to believe the angelic guardians assigned to protect us might become slightly dazed and bewildered at times when they hear the things uttered by the people of God. Remember, we are told, *"God inhabits the praise of His people"* – therefore, that singular uncomplicated truth should be motivation enough for us to trade in thoughtless chatter in exchange for a sacrifice of praise! Even on days when we feel lousy, we have the authority to impact and most often, even create the environment we inhabit. That is categorically true!

Replacing the old habitual lifestyle of constant negative muttering and whining with verbal declarations of God's Word, the atmosphere around me drastically changed. Total strangers began to treat me differently. Restaurant servers seemed to attend to my needs in greater detail. I even began to find favor with people at the DMV. The people, places, problems and pressures being encountered in the normal daily ebb and flow of my life remained unchanged for the most part, however, my internal perspective was being radically transformed.

My vision was being corrected. I was in training to respond to life in a whole new way.

When I first began hitting the gym early in recovery, to lie down on a bench and pull seventy-five pounds of free weights over my head from off the floor behind me was a literal impossibility. Now, it is part of my normal weekly routine. The weights did not change. Their mass and substance remain fixed. The bench is identical. The Earth's gravitational pull has not been altered in the least. What changed is that my body and mind have now been retrained to practice that which was once far beyond my ability.

The same is true in the spiritual realm. The realities of life remain. Goliath still stands on the hill and bellows insults. The Red Sea lies before you with an army closing in from the rear. The walls of Jericho appear to be impenetrable. The bills continue to arrive in the mailbox and that insufferable dweeb at work still grates on your very last nerve. Your response, however, can be radically altered. That internal alteration will prove to change the outcome of every challenge you face.

I can tell you this, when your life is bathed in the Presence of the living God and His anointing is tangible, it will revolutionize the way people respond to you. Jesus referred to it as being salt and light in the world.

I WILL ALWAYS CONTEND FOR THIS IDEA
THE BEST TESTIMONY FOR THE EXISTENCE OF GOD
IS THE POWER OF A RADICALLY TRANSFORMED LIFE.

This is not about stepping over some *"faith-line"* into an ankle-deep, tepid dishwater version of *"I'll try it and see what happens"* religion. A caterpillar does not weave a cocoon in some half-baked attempt to test the water and see how he feels about being a butterfly. There is no turning back. This is about total transformation of form, substance, and function. Everything is new and the old is gone forever. There remains not the slightest indication of the former.

THE ACTIONS WE TAKE

The problem is not that we don't know what to do - the issue is we don't do what we know.

> *"Be careful obey all the law my servant Moses gave you; do not turn from it to the right or to the left, that you may be successful wherever you go. Do not let this Book of the Law depart from your mouth; meditate on it day and night, so that you may be careful to do everything written in it. Then you will be prosperous and successful."*
> JOSHUA 1:7-8 THE NIV BIBLE

> *"With God, nothing shall be impossible."*
> LUKE 1:37 THE NIV BIBLE

> *"But do you want to know, oh foolish man, that faith without works is dead."*
> JAMES 2:20 NIV

Eventually, it all comes down to put up or shut up. David could have made all the proclamations he could think of, sat up all night and meditated on all the victory scriptures he knew, and yet the proof of his faith was in the moment he picked up five smooth stones and approached the towering giant. Even in the face of Goliath's intimidation, snarling threats and mocking laughter, David knew in his heart God was going to deliver this Philistine into his hands, taking definitive action on that knowledge. As the direct result, Goliath fell dead into his own shadow, defeated by the faith of a shepherd boy who decided to take action on the truth he owned in his heart.

Conversely, as the disciples gathered for the Last Supper, Peter pledged to Jesus his loyalty declaring he would never abandon Him no matter the challenge. And yet, the Lord knowing the approaching confrontation that would soon result in his arrest, prophesied the disciple would publicly deny Him three times before the sun came up the next morning.

Our actions of obedience to the truth we know…are crucial.

THIS IS A VERY TEDIOUS AND DIFFICULT PATH TO EXPLORE, IN THAT WE RUN THE RISK OF ESTABLISHING ANOTHER LINE OF GUILT AND INSUFFICIENCY. This is not about performance, rather, this is about the appropriation of God's provision.

Be very careful here.

I became my own worst enemy. No matter how much affirmation I received, relentless self-analysis always erroneously concluded I failed to make the grade. In my head, I would never be adequately holy for acceptance, always holding myself up against the pristine poster-boy image of what a successful Christian should look like. It's all I had ever been taught to do.

I was trained to work hard in order to be spared God's displeasure & punishment. It was all about achieving just enough to stay out of God's detention hall.

Contrary to rituals of the religious kind, the true Gospel is fully about the finished work of Jesus Christ. C.S. Lewis described the difference between the Gospel and religious legalism: *"Legalism declares that God will love us if we are good enough, while the Gospel tells us God will make us good because He loves us."*

That, ladies and gentlemen, is a gigantic difference.

Focusing on what we do or achieve leads directly to being placed in laborious chains again, while focusing on what Christ has done brings us into a world of joyful freedom. The foundation of a new life must be rooted in the understanding of Christ in us, the Hope of Glory. That is not some cheap trumped-up religious jargon. Within the finished work of Jesus Christ and His impartation of new life within us, are found the keys to our freedom.

WE ARE NOT REQUIRED TO MEASURE UP ON OUR OWN. WE DIE IN HIM SO HE CAN NOW LIVE IN US! I NO LONGER LIVE - HE LIVES THRU ME!

I recently heard a significant Christian leader declare on television: *"The secret to living a success Christian life is strict adherence and obedience to the Scripture."* While sounding correct at first blush, I categorically disagree with that particular statement. I believe the idea of that being the goal has led multiplied thousands of seekers to a frustration and failure.

I rather believe the *"secret"* is found in the truth of Galatians 2:20.

" I have been crucified with Christ. It is no longer I who lives but Christ lives within me. The life that I now live in the flesh, I live by faith in the Son of God who loved me and gave Himself for me. I do not nullify the grace of God, for if righteousness were through the law, then Christ died for no purpose."

THE ESV BIBLE

2011 CROSSWAY PUBLISHING USED BY PERMISSION)

Jesus did not come to provide instruction on how to improve our lives. He came to show us how to die so that we might live again in Him. Our old nature could never be renovated. It had to be crucified. We cannot identify with Christ in His resurrection power until we have identified with Him in His death. This is the prerequisite to old things passing away and all things becoming new.

Herein lies the definition of the statement, *"We love Him because He first loved us"*. Devotion is not to be born out of obligation to Orthodoxy, but with passionate thankfulness toward our Savior who made a way where there was no way. He did for us what we could never do for ourselves. Jesus restored us. He has made us whole. His completed work makes us Holy. We are the righteousness of God in Christ. In Him we live and move and have our being. We have been established in Him. He has adopted us and we now have the privilege to cry out Abba - Father. We are part of the elect, His chosen people.

It is out of this truth a genuine transformation begins. It is rooted in Truth. Grounded in the relationship, we then align ourselves with Word of God. We learn via the scripture to engage life from a position secured by the finished work of Jesus, not in order to acquire status or position in His sight. Religious activity may help people feel better about them-selves for a moment, but it ultimately achieves nothing of eternal value.

"I have come that they might have life and have it to the full.
JOHN 10:10
THE NIV BIBLE - 2005 ZONDERVAN PUBLISHING   USED BY PERMISSION)

Far beyond religion, we are in intimate relationship with the King of the Universe.

Religion is like standing outside the gate of a magnificent palace and being in knowledgeable possession of regal facts and pertinent history of the King dwelling just beyond the fortressed walls. You might be his faithful servant living in compliance to his dictates with loyal honor and dignity, declaring your allegiance and gratitude daily in public. You can live under his majesty's lordship for an entire lifetime, and yet never be in personal relationship with the King. You know about him in great detail, and yet, you do not know him personally.

You can quote his words, teach others for him, sing for him and be involved in the work of his kingdom throughout various cities and lands, and yet, never even so much as meet the King. To actually know the king would take your passion for his service to a whole new place. The privilege of personal access to the king would radically elevate your demeanor and attitude. To have audience with the king on a regular basis would most certainly change everything.

However, consider a step even further in that relationship; suppose you were to be legally adopted by the King into His actual family, to have the privilege of placing your feet under His table at dinner with access to all that is His, would be a remarkably different proposition.

To know the King gave His only Son in battle to acquire you as His heir would most likely impact how you see the everything in the world around you. It would, indeed, create a whole new reality for you and within you. To be given the use of His Name and all of the authority behind it would radically alter the way you measure any threat from any enemy or weapon positioned against you.

Fear and anxiety would greatly diminish, as courage thrived in the security of your newfound habitat.

Devotion, peace and comfort grounded in that relationship would rule your heart. To be a child of the Monarch, to know Him as a Father who loves with a perfect love that casts out all fear, would change the course of your life and impact every decision you ever had to make from that moment on.

So it is in our relationship with God.

FILL ME UP

When combating the enemy of depression, diet is important. Exercise is critical. Proper rest plays a very strategic role. Since my meltdown, I have read book after book over the years about the prevention and treatment of depression. Herbs and fruit seem to help. Sunlight and interaction with positive-minded people will assist in your improvement. There are Twelve Steps and Thirty-Day Plans. There is meditation, Yoga and breathing exercises. Vitamin supplements and nutrients can aid in the support of mental health. Counseling is always a valid consideration. Tips and techniques abound in print and online to help overcome debilitating depression. And yes - it could be your thyroid.

HERE'S WHAT I KNOW FROM MY JOURNEY:

- *Depression is not trivial. It can be deadly.*
- *I lived my life strung-out on the opinions and approval of other people.*
- *I became very bitter. Bitterness impairs judgment & distorts our memories.*
- *My soul and mind were polluted with the noise of this cruel and fallen world.*
- *My focus became all about me.*

This is not about being positive - this is war. I must be strategic, constantly referring to the manual.

- *What I truly believe in my heart will be reflected in the actions I take.*
- *Faith and cursing cannot come from the same lips.*
- *Faith and unbelief cannot co-exist. They are oil and water.*

- *I need to constantly develop a child-like faith while having the heart of a warrior.*
- *Be as sly as a serpent and innocent as a dove.*
- *My words are creative and powerful.*
- *My imagination is a formidable weapon - either for me or against me.*
- *I overcome this world by the power of the Blood and the word of my testimony.*
- *There is not enough room in my soul for both Eternity and the clamor of this world.*
- *I must keep Truth before me - morning - noon and night.*
- *My spirit must have dominion over my mind and body.*
- *God is speaking - I need only to develop the habit of listening.*
- *Purge the system - cleanse the soul. Make room only for the Holy.*
- *Be still and know that He is God.*
- *I have nothing to prove - I no longer live. Christ lives within me.*
- *I have been seated with Christ in heavenly places and all things have been placed under His Dominion. I have the weapons of warfare at my disposal and the authority of the Name of Heaven's King, which supersedes any other name or power on earth or throughout the universe.*
- *No weapon formed against me can prosper in any way.*
- *The Joy of the Lord Himself is my strength.*
- *This is the day the Lord has made and I will rejoice!*
- *We can choose this day who we are going to serve. You gotta' serve somebody!*
- *If I draw close to Him - He will draw close to me.*
- *Where the Spirit of the Lord is - there is peace.*
- *The anointing of the Lord - His Presence - breaks the yokes of bondage.*
- *The Presence of God in me can and will change the atmosphere of any room I enter.*
- *Goodness and mercy follow me and shall do so for the remainder of my life.*
- *His Word is unchanging and will never pass away.*
- *He is a friend, who is closer than a brother.*
- *I have hidden His Word in my heart that I might not sin against Him.*
- *My words are never neutral. They are creating some sort of reality in my environment.*

This all comes down to deciding how you and I want to live. The invitation has been extended and the provisions we need to thrive are abundant, we simply need to appropriate that supply. It is not enough for an infection to be diagnosed by the doctor, a prescription issued and the medication purchased. You may believe in the properties of the medication for your healing as you have it in your possession, but you must act to believe on the medication by actually consuming it into your body. That, in essence, is appropriating the supply.

Make the choice. Appropriate the Word. Choose you this day!

"Wide is the gate and broad is the road that leads to destruction, and many enter through it. But small is the gate and narrow the road that leads to life, and only a few find it."
MATTTHEW 7:13

Without question, there is a quality of abundant life and communion with God available that only a handful of people ever discover. Most assuredly, breathing this rarified air requires venturing off the beaten path. While the masses climb over one another to discover their fortune on Broadway where the lights are bright, fame is regal and the party never ends, there remains the proverbial road less traveled leading to the Highlands, a place in stark contrast to the chaotic swarm of Mardi Gras or Vegas.

The Highlands of God are calling - and I must go. There is adventure to be discovered. The higher we climb, the more spectacular the view. The atmosphere is clean and refreshing. As our journey continues, you will discover the significance of where this Trail has led, as you look back below to the lowlands where once you struggled to even breath.

God's Word instructs us that we are in this world, but are not to be of it. By our very nature, we are to be of another place and dimension. That would seem to indicate we should be somewhat abnormal or perhaps even *"peculiar"*. As the people of God, we are collectively living far beneath our privilege as His children, hindered by complications of Lowland living.

As I began my recovery, there was a lifetime of toxic habits and attitudes to be dealt with. Forgive the analogy, but I was bloated and impacted with spiritual sepsis, constipated with the opinions, theories and judgments of others, and blocked up from my own gluttony of joyless self-condemnation. There was little to no room for anything else.

There had to be purging and cleansing before I could move forward.

KEEP THIS IN MIND: I'm not implying a focus on improving our performance. This is where the appropriation takes place. We must change our reference points. It is the recognition of supernatural intervention on our behalf and then submitting to the process.

I love the way Gary Clarke, pastor of Hillsong London, recently stated this:

> *"We must learn how to live FROM God's love - not FOR God's love.*
> *We live FROM God's acceptance - not FOR God's acceptance.*
> *We live FROM God's forgiveness - not FOR God's forgiveness."*
> GARY CLARKE
> FROM THE MESSAGE: - "THE LOVE OF GOD / PART ONE" - 2015 HILLSONG LONDON

Again - the difference is in understanding everything has its' origin and completion in Him. This is what Jesus described when he declared, "I am the Vine and you are the branches." Our very existence flows from Him. Cutoff from Him, life ceases. Once you fully grasp this Truth, everything changes.

Take inventory. Determine what is keeping you from seeing God for Who He really is and all He wants for your life. What are the pollutants, needing to be expunged from your soul, preventing Him from filling you with His Presence? Most people experience the minimal black and white television - rabbit ears wrapped in aluminum foil life-view of God, where the least little storm can interrupt the signal. Be assured - there is a HIGH-DEF full - color plasma screen, quadriphonic audio world He has waiting for you.

It is time for an up-grade!

GAZING INTO ETERNITY

Standing in the wilderness of western Wyoming on a clear winter night, you can see forever. Even on the valley floor, you are standing at over seven thousand feet in elevation. For anyone visiting from urban areas, it is amazing to watch their faces the first time they experience the Wyoming night sky. From horizon to horizon, there are more stars than they ever dreamed of seeing or could possibly begin to imagine. There seems to be no end as to what is visible. I often felt as though I had a window into eternity. In addition to the astonishing view, the peace and quiet of the wilderness defies description, even more so when several feet of snow cover the ground.

I know what it is to actually be able to hear the quiet.

Regarding Wyoming's window to the universe, that identical sky and multitude of shimmering stars also stretches out high above city dwellers gazing upward in their back yards of Houston, Atlanta or Chicago. The problem is humidity, pollution, and nasty atmosphere, in combination with the massive amount of artificial light from the city, obstructs the view of what lies before them.

It's all there, right in front of them. They just cannot see it.

The object of our observation is identical, yet our perception of its' reality is radically altered by the simple repositioning of our viewpoint. In other words, you have to get above the pollution and obstructions to see what was really there all along. Just because you cannot see it, does not mean its' existence is in question. I hear people say all the time, "I'll be glad when the sun comes out."

The truth is, the sun is always out, yet is often obscured by storm clouds. Your perception of sunlight could be impaired when hiking a cave, being submerged in a submarine, traversing the East River via the Holland Tunnel, or by simply being in the dark of night as a result of the earth's regular rotation. Remember however, the reality of the sun's existence never changes due to a place in which you may find yourself.

In a very similar way spiritually, it is all about our 'world-view'. Many people believe themselves to be brilliant in declaring since they "just can't see it", it simply doesn't exist. There is a trend, especially in the West, toward secularism and the complete dismissal of the idea of the existence of God. More and more people are embracing the now 'chic' atheistic world-view. Well-read, highly educated Hipsters really have a hard time bowing their knee to the Lordship of an unseen God. For them, the Lordship of Jesus Christ is an ignorant and antiquated mythology dismissed as irrelevant folklore and trivial nonsense. Our current post-modern culture has become far too sophisticated to embrace the idea of a personal supernatural relationship with a Triune God.

They just cannot see it.

With the explosion of information, entertainment and technology, the distractions leading humans away from any authentic encounter with Jehovah are becoming more powerful and persuasive. Just the overload of daily news from around the globe has desensitized us to any subtleties. To hear the still small voice of God has become more of a challenge than ever. It is absolutely no surprise people are unable to see Eternity. Why should we ever expect anyone to hear the still small Voice of God in this age of perpetual noise in which we live?

> *The Bible says: "Be still and know that I am God."*
> PSALMS 46:10
> THE NIV BIBLE

I love technology. I have made use of it in the writing of this book, traveling to tell my story, and recording the music contained on the companion cd to this text. I love cell phones and the joy of being in touch with my kids across several time zones with the press of a button. The networking and communication with friends and business partners around the globe via Facebook and Twitter is magnificent! However, the same technology blessing us also curses us. Communication in today's youth culture is almost exclusively electronic. The idea of looking at one another eye to eye is nearly laughable.

Is it any wonder the premise of developing a non-electronic gadget-free innate ability to communicate with something as abstract sounding as God has become a completely outdated notion? At best, current society catalogues such ideas under fantasy roles and relegates their relevancy to the context of films such as Star Wars, Harry Potter and The Hobbit.

There is most assuredly a 'disturbance in the Force'.

Our greatest challenge is to lay aside the entanglements of an appallingly polluted world, and begin our ascent to the uncommon Highlands where the atmosphere is clean and clear, and man-made distractions cease to exist. Only there we can peer into a world beyond our most vivid imagination or elaborate dream, to witness the vast expanse of the Glory of God - what He desires to be in our lives – and where old things fall away and the new begins.

For several generations, mankind has fascinated himself with the glare of artificial light. It's bright and entertaining, originating from movie screens, city streets and concert stages. You can hold it your hand or display it on your desktop.

iPads - iPhones – iWatches – the Disney Illumination Celebration - the Vegas Strip - Hollywood - New Year's Eve in Times Square and New York, New York!

THE CITY THAT NEVER SLEEPS!

As amazing as it all proves to be for humanity, the fact remains that the lights of this world are manufactured and temporary. Simple failure of the power grid or a terrorist EMP attack, and the party pretty much shuts down in a hurry. By comparison, God Himself is Light and in Him there is no darkness at all. Regardless of the condition of the power grid, our access to communication satellites or the duration of my cell phone battery, I am always online with the Voice of God and even when I am fast asleep, He is watching over me, and my family.

The same North Star helping Columbus to navigate the oceans centuries ago - shines bright in the Wyoming sky tonight. The One, who actually created that reality by speaking it into existence, is the Voice I hear and to which I respond. He Himself is Light and in Him resides no darkness at all. It is He who has promised to never leave or forsake me.

Should you ever discover that reality - you'll never find satisfaction in the artificial again.

CHAPTER 11

BLESS THE BROKEN ROAD

THE PATHWAY TO HEALING AND WHOLENESS

"There are only two ways to live your life. One is as if nothing is a miracle. The other is as if everything is."
– ALBERT EINSTEIN

The day God reached into a hotel room in Minneapolis rescuing me from myself, He knew a complete renovation of my heart and soul was the only solution. The day of reckoning had arrived. I could no longer smooth it over, suck it down or simply get over it. No matter what it took, I was far beyond giving any thought to what people might think.

Metamorphosis begins with coming to the end of your-self, as the self-improvement train grinds to a tortuous halt. Our personal best is no longer the goal. Genuine transformation involves risk and amplified discomfort. It takes humility to begin again and the winds of public opposition will most often blow strong against you. God is not interested in simply ramping up your performance.

He wants to radically regenerate you from your soul's core outward. His joy is to see us evolve from marginally managing life to living as over-comers. Our eyes can be opened to realize the extraordinary eternal value veiled within ordinary life. It is indeed an exchanged life, ours for His.

We can become the people God intended us to be. That is where hope is born.

"THE POSSIBILITY OF TRANSFORMATION IS THE ESSENCE OF HOPE".
JOHN ORTBERG

FROM: THE LIFE YOU'VE ALWAYS WANTED - 1997 ZONDERVAN PUBLISHING

Jesus identified Himself as actually being the Way. He discussed the idea of choosing between a narrow road leading to life or the surpassingly broad thoroughfare leading to eventual destruction. Pathways, journeys, destinations and pilgrimage are familiar words in describing our adventures of life and spirituality.

"BLESS THE BROKEN ROAD", written in 1994 by Jeff Hanna *(from the Nitty Gritty Dirt Band)* and Marcus Hummon, is a song I first heard on the "ACOUSTIC" project by the Nitty Gritty Dirt Band, loving it in an instant. And yet, it would be ten years later the song would actually become a number one hit, recorded by Rascal Flatts in 2004, and winning the Grammy Award for Best Country Song.

In describing the process of writing **BLESS THE BROKEN ROAD,** Jeff had this to say:

"The circuitous route you take in life and how sometimes you think things are horrible and are never going to get better, often they lead you to something that ultimately is a lot better, whether it's a relationship, spiritual path, business or whatever."

I believe most every human being knows the reality of brokenness to some degree. Everyone has a story. No one gets thru life without scars and bruises. Consider this; even Jesus Himself, the Son of the Living God, was described as a *"man of sorrows"*. In His lifetime, he had to deal with rejection, slander, false accusation, betrayal and profound physical pain. Jesus was even thought to be crazy by some of his family and close associates. He suffered heartache over the death of his friend Lazarus, weeping at the news. To have been a distant bystander in the time Jesus walked the earth, you might have had the impression His life was broken and in great turmoil. Let alone growing up *"in the hood"*, even His birth was seen by most friends and neighbors in Nazareth as illegitimate. Could anything good possibly ever come out of Nazareth? He seemed to be an accident from the bad side of town.

It appeared to many the road Jesus traveled was broken from the very beginning.

Dare I say it, there had to be numerous times Jesus must have been tempted by depression. The Bible says He was challenged in every way as we are, yet without sin. He taught us to *"be angry and sin not,"* to *"not let the sun go down on our anger"*. These emotions, in and of them selves are not the issue. Jesus showed us He could be angry as He ran the moneychangers from the Temple, turning over tables and declared them thieves in His Father's house. He cursed a fig tree, causing it to die on the spot. He went on a public rant against the religious leaders and declared them to be no better than decaying filth found in tombs of the dead.

I can just imagine the disciples huddled around the campfire later that evening, discussing how badly Jesus had lost it in the Temple. If He expected the public to vote Him in as the Messiah, He was going to have to back it down a notch. Flipping out like that was surely not considered to be politically correct behavior. This helps us to understand why God chose to join our ranks on earth in the form of a man named Jesus - so we would know he went through it all just like us - yet without sin. The Lord of the universe understands even the depressed and downtrodden.

He lived it. He felt it. He got it. Without sinning. Best of all - he conquered it.

He was loved and heralded as Messiah in a joyous parade thru the streets of Jerusalem, only hours later Jesus found Himself spit on, criticized, beaten, whipped and crucified by many of the very same people who had earlier sang His praises.

The Via Dolorosa was the definitive broken road of all time.

He was scared and broken so that we might live and be whole, and out of His brokenness would come our redemption. Salvation would be made available for all humanity. Out of what appeared to be utter defeat and suffocating darkness, the Light of Eternity would ultimately radiate across the span of infinity and His Name would be exalted to the highest place. The broken road of Christ would become the promised pathway leading to life as He created it to be, abundant and eternal.

BROKENNESS AND STRUGGLE ARE NORMAL IN HUMANITY.

"It is a myth that faith is always smiling."
EDWARD T. WELCH
DEPRESSION: A STUBBORN DARKNESS - NEW GROWTH PRESS 2004

Because we live in a fallen world of conflict and hardship, the remarkable secret to survival is found in how we process pain and disappointment. Jesus always maintained His focus on the big picture, the will of His Heavenly Father, living on purpose and mission. The Son of God humbled himself to the point of becoming a servant, even death on a cross.

As He walked His road, Jesus revealed faith was far more than fulfilling religious duty and discipline – rather it was about relationship with His Father. Success would be born out of hearing His Father's voice and knowing it distinctly from the voice of any stranger. Retreating to prayerful solitude with His Father was a highly common priority, not out of some duty-bound obligation, but as the very source of strength and resolve. Apart from that vital connection, the implication seems to be that even Jesus Himself might have failed. He knew the determination and courage to complete His mission would only be cultivated in relationship with His heavenly Father. During the hours just prior to his arrest, Jesus prayed over what he was facing with such agony, blood oozed from the pores of his skin. And yet, even then, he would remain resolute.

What he accomplished was directly connected to who He was at His core. Though he was the Son of God in flesh, Jesus did not turn to or rely upon the unlimited resource of His own Divinity. This was exemplified in how He dealt with the temptations and compromising propositions offered up by His adversary, Satan, in the wilderness experience just prior to launching His ministry. Jesus would draw upon intimate relationship with His Heavenly Father and the ascendancy of scripture to resist compromise and disqualification. He modeled for all would follow how common man can overcome the strongest of temptation in the weakest of moments.

While it is true tortured artistic souls searching for the ever-elusive utopian state of being are rarely satisfied with the hand they are dealt, I always knew there was a fulfilling relationship with God that could be realized. The core issue in my missing the point completely - I always made it about me, not God in me. At the root of my meltdown was an unrelenting drive for perfection and the resulting torment of simply being me.

Without realizing it - my aim had become to please God more than know God.

This was the major fault-line in the bedrock of my core being, built upon from early childhood, then patched and paved over for decades. By most observers' estimation, I appeared to be strong and vibrant. There appeared no alarming warning signs of fragility apart from the normal wear and tear of life, so I was encouraged to continue reaching, growing and expanding. Success would be found in my resilient spirit and fortitude.

As losses mounted and disappointments grew with time, the fractures would become more pronounced and eventually make their way to the surface. When I was forced to walk away from the Cafe in what I could only perceive as abject failure, it seemed the pavement beneath my feet cracked open and a million voices of accusation emanated from the darkness, screaming at me with barbaric savagery day and night.

My road crumbled.

Any attempt at movement, either forward or backward, seemed useless. I could no longer pretend everything was fine. It wasn't.

Such was the condition of the deepest regions of my soul on the 6th of July 2006.

A CHANGE OF ACTION ALWAYS PRECEDES A CHANGE IN SITUATION.

You may have been on your journey of faith for years. Your marriage is strong while you have remained active in church and faithful in the giving of your time and resources, living in such a way to win the respect of your peers as a person of integrity and authenticity.

Your core strength and resolve have withstood the many challenges life has flung in your direction with great ferocity. You have been strong for a very long time, navigating the road ahead with as much wisdom and insight as one could hope for. The career, the home, the kids, the bank account and mortgage, along with a little retirement nest egg, are all in relatively satisfactory shape. However, in the quiet solitude of the night when introspection seems to be most pronounced, you find yourself more weary and frayed around the edges than you are willing to admit to anyone. Thoughts of suicide may not be hovering in your mental spaces, but there is a sense of dying a very slow death in your soul. Joy has dissipated and now as you war on to be your resilient best, something is missing.

Surviving the journey, or even flourishing to great acclaim, have not delivered the satisfaction you had anticipated. Your road is broken and you are far more vulnerable than it may appear from the outside.

Depression can creep into a life like rainwater flowing into a creek. Unnoticeable at first, then suddenly flash flood conditions have developed while you slept, turning a gentle stream into a raging torrent and threatening everything in its path.

Homeowners in Iowa can tell you about the most secure of homes and workplaces, experiencing the ravaging effects of relentless rains in the *"flood-month"* of June. Rising water from the deluge of late spring storms upstream can and will find it's way into places no one ever dreamed possible. In addition, a flood of several feet is not required to wreck havoc on a structure. A few inches of rainwater and moisture, concentrated in certain undetectable places, can render great foundational damage over time.

This happened to our home in Pigeon Forge. Built in a well-established neighborhood on a steep wooded hillside just north of town, we were centrally located with other homes above and below us on the landscape amidst hundreds of trees and thick forest vegetation. The paved streets and drainage infrastructure had been in place and functional for years. Even so, the consistent flow of water from above our property over time undermined the structural foundation of our attached garage, resulting in the floor cracking and the walls bowing out to the point that everything had to be torn out and built again.

Life can often be like that. The Bible defines it like this: *"Catch for us the foxes, the little foxes that ruin the vineyards, our vineyards that are in bloom"* (SONG OF SONGS 2:15)

Most often, it is not the obvious but the unseen posing the largest threat. Day after day, year after year, the *"little foxes"* slowly diminish our resolve and strength.

Performing outside on the piers and resort beaches along the east coast in recent years, on brilliant sunny days you would have no idea great damage is actually being done to my sound equipment and even the cases I carry it in. Though set up on stages or performance areas underneath canopies and other coverings, the moisture and salt of the ocean air, in addition to the southern humidity, slowly begins to destroy everything, sight unseen.

After a few months of consistent exposure thru the summer and fall performance season, inspection of my gear revealed a significant amount of rust and corrosion of microphones, connectors, stands and instruments. The daily assault was not something you could visibly see occurring, but the damage is undeniable. In addition, the effects of this corrosion are not limited to just the surfaces of the equipment, it permeates the casings to the innermost areas of every piece of gear that has been exposed.

LIVING LIFE IN A FALLEN WORLD – A VERY CORROSIVE ENVIRONMENT

There are many accounts of automobile passengers and truck drivers suddenly plunging into the depths of a frigid watery grave as the bridge beneath them gives way, this following years of corrosion to the road surface and structural supports. This is exactly what happens to so many human beings. We all know of people who woke up one day in a place of personal crisis in which they never dreamed they would find themselves. One too many snaps, crackles or pops and the catastrophic unthinkable 3am phone call delivers the message no one remotely saw coming in the distance.

Just last evening, while taking a break from writing this text to lead worship and share my story at a conference, I engaged in conversation with a young woman who had recently lost her best friend to suicide. Weeping almost uncontrollably, she attempted to tell me of the tragedy in broken bits and pieces. A mother of a four-year old little girl, without warning of any kind, fell victim to a self-inflicted gunshot wound to the head. There had been no apparent indication her friend was anywhere near the point of violent self-destruction. Now only days later, standing in the parking lot following the conference, we were dealing with the painful aftermath and the gut wrenching blame she was heaping upon herself for not realizing the crisis her friend was in and as a result, not being able to do anything to help.

On average, thirty thousand people kill themselves each year in the United States. Every thirty seconds, the loss of a person to suicide shatters the lives of family and friends. Annually, seven hundred and fifty thousand people make some attempt to take their own life, the number one reason being untreated depression. Even with violent crime a major issue in our nation, more individuals die by their own hand than by homicide.

Depression is without question a major worldwide epidemic. If someone near to you, be it a friend or family member, seems to be wrestling with depression, never assume they are just going through a temporary phase that will soon pass. What appear to be moderate symptoms on the surface can be the definitive warnings of something ominous raging deep within.

YELLOWSTONE – Warning Signs of Things To Come

Millions of tourists from around the globe travel to Yellowstone each year to marvel at the sight of Old Faithful, as well as the other countless wonders of America's first national park. There are precautions to be taken and warnings to be heeded when visiting Yellowstone. The magnificent wildlife roaming freely across the open range can pose an extreme danger if not observed from a safe distance. Hiking among the famous geysers must be done within the confines of the trails and bridges placed there for the safety of the guests. Venturing off these paths could quickly result in in any number of injuries.

Yet the greatest threat posed by Yellowstone lies in the fact it is the world's largest super volcano. Beneath the surface of this popular destination is a four hundred mile cauldron of churning lava and magma boiling it's way toward what geologists say will someday be a catastrophic eruption. Such an event would destroy every living thing within a one hundred mile radius within minutes and alter life on the entire planet within hours.

Since 2004, seismologists monitoring the Yellowstone region have recorded an average of two thousand tremors and quakes per year, while the ground throughout the geyser region has risen and fallen as much as three inches a year. Tourists, breathlessly capturing cellphone selfies with Old Faithful and roaming grizzlies, dining at the Lodge and purchasing t-shirts at the various gift shops, have no idea of the lethal forces conspiring against them just a short distance beneath their feet.

Chances are nearly one hundred percent, one of the next four people you encounter is battling depression at some level and several of those could very well could be nearing the point of eruption where the choice is made to bring life's struggle to an end.

If you should happen to be that one in four, it is my belief one of the reasons God rescued me was to assist you in seeking healing for your soul. The very fact you hold this book in your hands is no mere coincidence. He is reaching out to rescue you from yourself at this moment just as personally as He did for me in a Minneapolis hotel room. Believe that. This is not just a coincidence.

YOU NEED ONLY TO TRUST HIM.

Your broken road does not have to dead-end at the intersection of misery, depression and tragedy. Though this highway of life almost always weaves it's way through disappointment, heartache and the unrelenting temptation to feel abandoned and alone, there is a living God who cares for you in ways far beyond your most fertile ability to understand. This is where Faith begins.

HOPE IS ESTABLISHED IN THE MOMENT YOU SIMPLY TURN AROUND.

For a very long time I aimlessly stumbled about, disoriented within the mental deserts and emotional battlefields of my own making. I endlessly mumbled through the litany of reasons why I hated myself and then assumed everyone else must be just as disgusted with me as I was.

I had fallen wounded and broken behind enemy lines, captive to the opinions of critics and the folly of my own misplaced wisdom.

The amazing thing about God, He is always waiting nearby for us to finally come to the end of ourselves and give up trying to do life on our own. Attempting to somehow get our stuff together to the point of gaining His approval is not what He requires. No matter how far off course you have wandered, the moment you turn around to head back to that place where you ventured from the pathway, God is right there. There is no clawing your way back thru some dirge of purgatory or perfunctory religious activity to prove your sincerity.

He meets us exactly at the point of our need. This is repentance defined. A simple turning away from the noise, distraction and fatal fascination with a temporary world, and turning toward the outstretched arms of a loving Savior Who has already secured your freedom.

This is where you and I cease trying to prove our worthiness. We will never be worthy, but God Himself believed we were worth it, that is, the price of redemption. You are of such great value to God that Jesus died a brutal death to fully absorb the entire penalty for all of your sin and foolish stumbling.

Stand up in the midst of your mess and simply turn toward Him. He is here in this moment, ready and willing to embrace you. He has made provision for all the selfish, silly and ugly things we have ever taken up with. You will have to lay aside your pride, but the rewards far exceed whatever momentary embarrassment you may feel.

ACCEPT YOUR FORGIVENESS.

EMBRACE YOUR FREEDOM.

WRAP YOURSELF IN THE PEACE OF GOD.

FIND THE LIFE THAT FLOWS FROM ETERNITY.

On July 8, 2006 - everything began to change within me and for me. God walked onto the scene and began to pick up the splintered fragments of my life. In the days to follow, He continually showed me how He wanted bless the Broken Road I had traveled and turn it into a trail of Grace others could follow to find healing and peace in His Presence.

It is my prayer you may be one of those very people.

CHAPTER 12

WHOLE AGAIN

WHOLENESS AND THE DWELLING PLACE OF GOD

It has often been said the majority of people view peace as life free from conflict or turmoil, thus begins the unrelenting struggle to rid our lives of troublesome confrontations and pesky people. However, a genuinely peaceful life is not simply void of conflict but rather one occupied by the Presence and reality of God. He is, by definition and title, the Prince of Peace and Light of the world. He promises peace the majority of the world will never comprehend, a peace surpassing human understanding. The Bible declares all the Fullness of God dwells in Christ, and as our lives are fully hidden in Jesus, He dwells within us via the indwelling presence of Holy Spirit. We have been made complete or whole in Him.

The idea is that of a dual relationship: I am in Him and He abides in me.

Through my ever-present attempt to gain the approval of people, I seemed to develop some sort of inability to actually enjoy the Presence of God. I was committed, in my head, to believing He loved me and could quickly spout off all the various scriptures declaring it to be so, yet in my heart burned the frustration of being convinced I would never measure up.

Describing his similar struggles, former Yale religion professor Henry Nouwen had this to say: *"I kept running around looking for someone or something that could convince me that I was indeed loved by God. I was much more eager to listen to the other voices saying: 'Prove that you are worth something; do something relevant, spectacular or powerful, and then you will earn the love you so desire'. Meanwhile, the gentle Voice that speaks in the silence and solitude of my heart remained unheard or, at least, unconvincing."*

I had been indoctrinated with layers of condemnation theology and the fundamental idea human beings were essentially wretched, wicked and worthless. We were told God loved us - but also made to feel He had to hold His nose to do so.

To believe God thought of me as being of great value and worth the price of redemption was a foreign concept. Fear and guilt in the hands of misguided clergy have proven to be powerful tools for manipulating the religious.

In a book entitled "Codependency", the author Pat Springle expresses his take on this subject matter: *"Motivation by guilt is usually associated with the desire to avoid condemnation and the desire to perform, or measure up to standards set by someone else or ourselves."*

This sort of relentless pressure to perform for others breaks us down. It has been a significant part of my modus operandi through my entire life. At the behest of my family, I rode horses as a kid in various shows, even though I was terrified to my core of the extremely large beasts. On several occasions, my face was violently introduced to the ground as I was rejected as a worthy passenger by the feisty equines. One particular event, I sustained severe injuries by being thrown headfirst into the rustic wall of the stable. Splinters were carefully being extracted from the left side of my face for days. Without question, the horses sensed my fear.

As you might have already suspicioned, however, the air around me was filled with chatter about getting back on the horse, all for my own good of course.

Even in school, I graduated as a B+ student, deemed significantly less than stellar within the circles I occupied. Somehow it always seemed I never quite made the grade or qualified as a starter on the team. My most spectacular efforts came up a step too slow or a yard shy.

When I did begin to make great strides, becoming proficient in something such as my love for classical music and the development of performance on the French horn, I would sabotage those achievements by suddenly trading in my valuable horn at the local music store for an acoustic guitar. I would then disappear down the highway and over the horizon with a group of singing Jesus people, armed with my suitcase, new guitar and a thirty-five dollar a week income.

Friends thought I had lost my mind and joined a cult.

As I would make gains within that particular genre and culture, in time I would change instruments and roles once again. Years of piano and keyboard study, rehearsal and concert performance, would arbitrarily be traded in for returning to play bass guitar. In the next dispensation I would be a vocalist, then back to keyboards, moving from southern gospel, to rock and roll and back to a more classical regiment. I would be in the recording studio for several months as a session musician and leader, then suddenly off to rejoin some itinerant road ensemble fulltime yet again - ultimately accepting the role as a minister of music in the local church in the Midwest. Sure enough, just as things were taking off and growing at a rapid pace of success in the church, former band-mates and their customized bus would roll into town. Within hours, I would be climbing back on, overtaken by the aroma of diesel fuel and the romance of an elaborately intriguing tour schedule.

Without realizing it at the time - I was fragmenting my own life.

I became known as the quintessential utility person, able to fill vacant positions in urgent need of attention. I was the guy most often called upon to bridge gaps in personnel within a music group or organization, gaining a sterling reputation for a strong work ethic and energetic stage presence.

To be eclectic and adventurous was exhilarating and fun, yet simultaneously detrimental. Personal strengths also became significant weakness. My penchant for shifting focus from one shiny object to another diluted my potential to excel in one specific area. It was as though I minored in many subjects and majored in none.

The blessings of the life I have lived are innumerable and the amazing diversity has enriched my soul beyond description. However, you may have already arrived at the core of the issue. Because I never fully belonged to a community or became wholly associated within a certain genre and culture of music or ministry, my life became exponentially more splintered.

It is something of a vagabond existence, with no place to call home. Admittedly, this was of my own design and life choices. My desire had always been to find a place to inhabit long-term, and yet that tier of appointment always seemed to circumvent me for a colorfully expansive assortment of reasons, some we have reviewed throughout this book.

While personally long established in my theology, the opportunities to serve on the pastoral and music staff of various churches, represents a broad denominational range including Southern Baptist, General Baptist, American Baptist, Wesleyan, Charismatic and Community Churches. Again, moving among the various camps has been a gratifying experience and yet eventually left me without any *"roots"* or sense of belonging.

When finally arriving back in Iowa as worship leader & teaching pastor, this following my recovery period from the demise of the Café, as well as my radical surgery in 2001, I believed this to be a place I could settle in for the long run. We were back in community with friends who had long been a part of our lives and it did indeed feel like home.

Little, did I know - my age was soon to become the elephant in the room.

The remarkably goofy thing about age being an issue in my career, one of the descriptions repeatedly assigned to me as I pushed people to stretch out and embrace new things: *"You've always been thirty years ahead of your time."* Suddenly I was being labeled as genetically unqualified due to the simple duration of my existence. While several of the *"youngsters"* with whom I served had not a single *"hip"* gene in their DNA, sporting wardrobes of retired golfers and preppy insurance salesmen, it would be the birthdate printed on my drivers license used to discredit any further usefulness to the church. By their accumulative definition, I was now genetically disqualified from being *"hip"* enough to serve among them....

When my pastor and ministry peers in Iowa officially declared me too old to be relevant, it served as a powerfully destructive blow to the psyche of someone wired his entire life to be hypersensitive to criticism. Additionally, the glue had barely dried from *"Humpty-Dumpty Edward"* being put back together again by the doctors, friends and family following the Café wars in Pigeon Forge years earlier.

When the *"youngsters"* on staff began their assault, it smashed me like a dime store light bulb. Gathered around the long table in our conference room, the Senior Pastor launched into his in-depth assessment with those oft repeated words I always dreaded to hear: ***"Don't take this personal, but …"***.

Those words always seemed to be the precursor of yet another mind numbing, *"Here we go, again"* opinion as to why I would be found less than what was required. I had *"amazing potential, yet was not a proper fit for this particular staff."*

The final dig from *"Pastor Hipster"* directed toward me prior to dismissing the meeting: *"Besides, if you are so good at what you do, why in the name of heaven are you in Iowa?"* In a second, my breath was gone and my heart was broken, stunned beyond description. The sound of his office door closing behind me was perfectly choreographed to the snapping of the proverbial last straw in my head.

Three days later I would make the determined attempt to take my life.

YOU'LL NEVER BE GOOD ENOUGH

Once upon a time, there existed a saying: *"God is less concerned with your ability than He is your availability"*. Not so much anymore.

I was fifty years old and available, with a lifetime of experience and a heart for the people of our community in Iowa. I believed He had brought me to serve this particular congregation at a strategic time leading them into the future. The growth of the church following my arrival bore out that belief. However, as it turned out, I was the singular staff member who obviously did not fit the mold called for by their corporate image guru. My personal oddity therefore posed an ominous threat to the world they sought to create.

The stark reality, I was nowhere close to being a failure in my role on staff at *"Hipster Cathedral"*. Yet given my wiring as a melancholy and the broodingly sensitive creative type, the rejection of the young athletic lemmings *"felt"* as though I had been deemed a veritable waste of breath and space. Being twenty years their senior meant that nothing I had to contribute would ever be considered remotely relevant or worthy of their consideration.

They readily took advantage of my suicide attempt as the golden opportunity to dismiss me with "righteous cause and justification."

Once again, I was summarily dismissed as the singular ugly duckling.

An unquenchable desire for perfection coupled with the nasty habit of not being able to measure up - has a way of setting the stage for long-term heartburn. In other words, those sorts of battles rip us to pieces from the inside out perpetuating a false sense of failure that almost always proves to be inaccurate. In much the same way humans burn valuable energy needlessly fearing things that never happen, we become stressful and panicked over reviews leveled by critics who are, at best, skewed by their own personal bias and prejudices.

The gatekeepers calibrate requirements for inclusion based on their own interests. Just because you may fall short of achieving acceptance by a few nefarious talking heads presiding over their own myopic version of reality, in no way discredits your value, calling or mission.

WHO CARES WHAT THEY THINK!
I guess I did – and far too much.

When we become exhausted and broken by the madness, our response is most often guilt and a congenital impulse to push even harder. We are coaxed in countless different directions by ambition, guilt, success, failure, weariness, more guilt, money, fear, adrenaline, urgency, deadlines, panic and stress. Life in the twenty-first century has become a frenzied race of appearances. Most people work harder on framing façades of success than they do at becoming authentically successful. Others began life's journey with a sincere desire to be centered and together, never imagining they will one day arrive at a place where everything falls apart.

Then storms roll in – wars break out – friendships are forsaken and hearts are broken. In an instant, life can blindside anyone. As John Bevere so perfectly described twenty years ago, in these moments, the bait of Satan becomes offence. Take inventory on any given day, how easily people in our culture are extraordinarily offended at the slightest altercation. Don't believe it? Just take a casual ride thru snarled traffic of any moderately sized city in America and witness the rage. The enemy of our souls uses offence to lure us into his web. It is then bitterness, cynicism, and an unforgiving spirit all begin to take root, initiating the process of spiritual imprisonment that, remaining unchecked, systematically removes all the joy, faith, vitality and freedom from our lives without us even noticing. We slowly become captive to hopelessness and depression, wondering all the while how we got there.

Sometimes - you simply have to be rescued, most often - from yourself.

IT'S A BRAND NEW DAY

"And I pray the Father, and He will give you another Helper, that He may abide with you forever."
JOHN 14:16
THE NIV BIBLE - 2005 ZONDERVAN PUBLISHING - USED BY PERMISSION

"Do you not know that you are the temple of God and that the Spirit of God dwells in you? Set your minds on things that are above, not on things that are on earth. For you have died, and your life is hidden with Christ in God."
COLOSSIANS 3:2-3
THE NIV BIBLE - 2005 ZONDERVAN PUBLISHING - USED BY PERMISSION

"I have been crucified with Christ. It is no longer I who live, but Christ who lives in me. And the life I now live in the flesh I live by faith in the Son of God, who loved me and gave himself for me."
GALATIANS 2:20
THE NIV BIBLE - 2005 ZONDERVAN PUBLISHING -

He saved them from their distress. He sent forth his word and healed
them, and delivered them from their destruction."
PSALM 107:19-20

THE NIV BIBLE - 2005 ZONDERVAN PUBLISHING - USED BY PERMISSION

HIS PRESENCE CHANGES EVERYTHING.

During our staff retreats and vision-casting times, Pastor Polston always loved to paint the picture of undiscovered ideas adrift in the limitless atmosphere of the universe, leftover bits and pieces of creative energy from the moments God spoke everything into existence. Pastors' encouragement was for us to *"put up our spiritual receivers"* and *"tune in"* to the voice and creative nature of God. He believed the cure for cancer or the next strategic plan for successful world evangelism might very well be out there and available within the airwaves, and if we were in-tune and paying attention, we might be the ones to make the discovery.

This would seem foolish talk to 'normal' people, but we have been upgraded and have the ability to hear on a different level – the voice of our Shepherd Lord.

"Now we have received, not the spirit of the world, but the Spirit
who is from God, that we might know the things that have been freely
given to us by God. But the natural man does not receive the things
of the Spirit of God, for they are foolishness to him; nor can he know
them, because they are spiritually discerned."
I CORINTHIANS 2: 12, 14

THE NIV BIBLE - 2005 ZONDERVAN PUBLISHING - USED BY PERMISSION

Remember with me again the wonderful movie, **FIELD OF DREAMS**, where the character played by Kevin Costner hears a voice in his spirit instructing him: *"If you build it - they will come."* Though startled by it on several occasions, no one else nearby could hear the voice. He then follows that instruction to the dismay of family members and friends, creating a full-size baseball diamond where once he planted lucrative crops of corn. Baseball players of a bi-gone era came from another dimension to enjoy the simplicity of playing the game they so deeply loved on this new pristine field. Only those who were *"tuned in"* could actually see the players on the field. Skeptics abounded, but for those who could *"see it"*, the games were a joyous reality. It may have been a converted cornfield in Iowa, but to the baseball heroes who came to play, it was Heaven.

Likewise, so many people around us have no concept of communicating with God. For them, hearing the *"voice"* of God is as radically unnatural and silly as staring at an empty baseball field hoping to see Babe Ruth or Ty Cobb once again run the bases. The very idea is childish and ridiculous. Even more, some label us as mentally unstable. Peculiar even.

And yet, what they deem as foolishness can and should be our reality. The mass of humanity declaring, *"I just can't see it"*, most often keeps us from living supernaturally. We seem to be so easily discouraged when those around us *"don't get it"*. As a result, most Christians quickly lower their expectations of the life they can experience in relationship with our living Lord simply because they do not want to appear foolish among their peers. The question remains, why would we ever expect those on the *"outside"* to embrace the Word of God on any level, let alone the idea of a vibrant interaction with the Author Himself.

Authentic daily communion with God and living life on another wave-link opens unveils the realities of being a new creation. The world around us doesn't change, but our perspective and responses are radically altered as we begin to see life from a new reality. Again, the lens prescribed for me by my optician, have no bearing on anyone else's surroundings. However, the clarity of my focus redefines everything I view.

I WAS BLIND, BUT NOW I SEE. I HAVE BEEN MADE WHOLE.

And you were dead in the trespasses and sins in which you once walked, following the course of this world, following the prince of the power of the air, the spirit that is now at work in the sons of disobedience - among whom we all once lived in the passions of our flesh, carrying out the desires of the body and the mind, and were by nature children of the wrath, like the rest of mankind. But God, being rich in mercy,

because of the great love with which He loved us, even when we were
dead in our trespasses, made us alive together with Christ.
EPHESIANS 2:1-5

Hope is now alive within me. It cannot be said enough - His Presence changes everything. This is where we discover real life. Religion is a searching and attempting to claw our way to God. Grace is God reaching down and rescuing us. It all begins and ends with Him. He is the pebble thrown into the pond. All the rippling effects created from that point begin with Him.

"I entreat you, give no place to despondency. This is a dangerous
temptation - a refined, not a gross temptation of the adversary.
Melancholy contracts and withers the heart, and renders it unfit to
receive the impressions of grace. It magnifies and gives a false coloring
to objects, and thus renders your burdens too heavy to bear. God's
designs regarding you, and His methods of bringing these designs, are
infinitely wise."
MADAME GUYON
STREAMS IN THE DESERT - ZONDERVAN PUBLISHING - GRAND RAPIDS, MICHIGAN 1996

"It is essential that we respond with trust in the mercy and goodness
of God. No bitterness or rebellion must be permitted to cloud your
vision of Him even when He seems not to answer. Otherwise the pain
designed to enrich and deepen your relationship with Him night have
the opposite effect as you allow yourself the luxuries of self-pity and
doubt."
JOHN WHITE
DARING TO DRAW NEAR - INTERVARSITY PRESS - DOWNERS GROVE, ILLINOIS - 1977

Let us fix our eyes on Jesus, the author and perfecter of our faith, who for the joy set before Him endured the cross.

HEBREWS 12:2

THE NEW INTERNATIONAL VERSION - ZONDERVAN PUBLISHING - GRAND RAPIDS, MICHIGAN - 2005

"The more we get what we now call "ourselves" out of the way and let Him take us over, the more truly ourselves we become.

C.S. LEWIS

The more I resist Him and try to live on my own, the more I become dominated by my own heredity and upbringing and surroundings and natural desires. But there must be a real giving up of the self... Lose your life and you will save it.

MATTHEW 10:39

THE NEW INTERNATIONAL VERSION - ZONDERVAN PUBLISHING - GRAND RAPIDS, MICHIGAN - 2005

"Submit to death, death of your ambitions and favorite wishes every day. Submit with every fiber of your being. Keep back nothing. Nothing in you that has not died will ever be raised from the dead. Look for yourself, and you will find in the long run only hatred, loneliness, despair, rage, ruin and decay. But look for Christ and you will find Him, and with Him, everything else thrown in."

C.S. LEWIS

MERE CHRISTIANITY - HARPER PRESS - SAN FRANCISCO, CALIFORNIA 2001

"We please Him most, not by frantically trying to make ourselves good,
but by throwing ourselves into His arms with all our imperfections,
and believing that He understands everything and loves us still."
BEST OF A.W. TOZER
BAKER BOOK HOUSE - GRAND RAPIDS, MICHIGAN 1978

Weaving the significance of those scriptural realities into my daily life has made all the difference in the battle against depression.

"God made Him who knew no sin to be sin for us, so that in Him, we
might become the righteousness of God."
2 CORINTHIANS 5:21
THE NIV BIBLE - 2005 ZONDERVAN PUBLISHING

My longtime friend, Marty Magahee of the vocal group 4HIM, had composed a song I believed to be very close to the message of my newfound life. I asked his permission to collaborate with him for a bit of reconstruction and additional lyric.

The following lyrics of **WHOLE AGAIN** are the result of that collaboration.

I remember the days as it happened, my soul being lulled to sleep
How I'd all but forgotten – who I was
My heart had been broken in pieces – struggling on the way down
'Down to the bottom – I was torn apart
My life and my heart – were torn apart

CHORUS
Now up from the place I had fallen
I'm raised to a new place in Christ
and though my soul had broken apart
From the depths of his love – I am whole again

VERSE TWO

For years I had roamed with the wounded
Treading thru pity and shame
all because I'd forgotten – who I was
Now I'm learning the art of forgiveness
Seeing things clearer with time
Just as long as I'm resting – in God's arms
Now I'm resting - in his arms

CHORUS

Now up from the place I had fallen
I'm raised to a new place in Christ
and though my soul had broken apart
From the depths of his love – I am whole again

BRIDGE

And now that I live in a different light
It feels like the first time I've opened my eyes
Here in surrender – his love lifts me high
His grace has given me wings to fly

CHORUS

Now up from the place I had fallen
I'm raised to a new place in Christ
and though my soul had broken apart
From the depths of his love – I am whole again
From the depths of his love – to the depths of my heart
I'm whole again - i am whole again - i've been made whole again

Whole Again / music & lyrics by Marty Magahee & D. Edward Anders
2016 Eddie's Heart & Soul Communications / All Rights Reserved...

THE TRAILS WE LEAVE BEHIND

A HERITAGE OF FAITH

*Let the heavens rejoice and let the earth be glad! Let the sea resound
and all that is in it; Let the fields be jubilant and everything in them.
Then all the trees of the forest will sing for joy; they will sing before
the Lord!*

FROM PSALM 96

THE NIV BIBLE – ZONDERVAN PUBLISHING – USED BY PERMISSION

I have always treasured long hikes thru the mountains, along streams, waterfalls, and into the innermost parts of a massive forest. Anyone who knows me at all can tell you of my love of the Rocky Mountain region of Colorado and Wyoming. For me, that area will always be home. I am best suited for the climate of the Northern Rockies where the air is crisp and clean and the humidity is rarely considered an issue. Cool and clear. I come alive somewhere around 50 degrees and 12% humidity. The days are wonderfully pleasant at an altitude where the sun seems to warm your soul.

This is why I also love verses such as the ones above from the Psalms, describing exactly what I sense taking in the wonder of the wilderness areas of Yellowstone and the Tetons. The Glory of God is all around you, untainted by the clutter and noise of humanity. In the evening, you are treated to the splendor of the heavens above as you gaze across the span of the universe. Creation finds joy in its Creator and I love being a small part of that celebration.

The joy of the Lord Himself is our strength. Additionally, He is the object of our joy reflected in nature and His people. (PSALM 43:4 - PSALM 21:6) Joy is not only within our reach as an intricate part of our lives, it is a mandate. We are challenged to choose joy.

> *This is the day the Lord has made, let us rejoice and be glad in it!*
> PSALM 118:24

Those who constructed the Westminster Shorter Catechism stated it this way; "What is the chief end *(aim)* of man? To glorify God and enjoy Him forever." He is the God

> *"Who richly provides us everything for our enjoyment."*
> 1 TIMOTHY 6:17

It was 18TH century Congregationalist Protestant theologian, Jonathan Edwards, who penned these words:

> *"Joy...consists in the sweet entertainment their minds have in the view or contemplation of the divine and holy beauty of these things, as they are in themselves. And this is the main difference between the joy of the hypocrite and the joy of the true saint. The former rejoices in himself, while the latter rejoices in God. The happiness of the creature consists in rejoicing in God, by which also God is magnified*

and exalted. Resolution One: I will live for God. Resolution Two: If no one else does, I still will."
JONATHAN EDWARDS
RELIGIOUS AFFECTIONS – NEW HAVEN, YALE UNIVERSITY - 1959

No question about it, for you and I to live joyfully is a daily determination. Joy is possible and we must make it a daily practice if it is to become integrated into our lives as a natural response to distressing challenge. This is the practical application of the old nature passing away and all things becoming new. For several years, joyful was not a description anyone would ascribe to my life.

The truly amazing thing, God Himself takes great joy in relationship with us.

"The Lord your God is with you, He is mighty to save. He will take great delight in you, He will quiet you with His love, He will rejoice over you with singing."
ZEPHANIAH 3:17

How cool is that?

So what happens to a room when you arrive on the scene? Does joy suddenly show up and life become invigorated? Or are you the blight on the leaves of life?

We all deposit some sort of evidence of our existence and passage on planet Earth. There is a heritage and legacy you are in the process of creating. For someone who had spent the majority of his life proclaiming the Gospel as truth and the source of personal peace and joy, by example I had slowly become indisputable evidence to the contrary.

I was off course and leaving a trail of contradiction.

I still believed the joy of the Lord was my strength, but had long since surrendered that joy, resulting in my strength being totally decimated. I was vulnerable and open game for every weapon formed against me. Any minor nuisance was blown out of proportion and the customary molehills appeared as fortified mountains, freezing me in my tracks. Once arriving at that point, the enemies of my soul rushed in with overwhelming accusation preoccupying my wearied mind and gnawing away at what little resolve I had left.

I WAS BLAZING A TRAIL TO DESTRUCTION, INEVITABLY LEAVING HEARTACHE AND PAIN IN MY WAKE, ALL OF WHICH MY WIFE, CHILDREN AND FRIENDS WOULD HAVE TO DEAL WITH.

God Himself intervened and rescued me from myself. The question of why He did that for me and not for others is nearly impossible to answer. For a while through my healing process, dealing with that issue created a hesitation within me to ever share my story. There always seems to be people in every gathering to which I speak who did not have the joy of seeing their loved one rescued from self-destruction. However, I believe God has reinvented my life and restored my joy to open trails of light, hope, and freedom for others to follow. There is a way out of the darkness of depression. I believe the journey to recovery is not as difficult as it is often made to appear, by those whose career choices tempt them to perpetually medicate us thru the landscapes of life.

THE TRAIL I DESIRE TO BLAZE – A PATH FOR OTHERS TO FOLLOW.

First – the pebble tossed into the pond, that is the genesis of everything else, is a personal relationship with God made available to each and every human through the finished work of Jesus Christ, His life, substitutionary crucifixion and resurrection from the dead.

Second – acknowledging His Word as our constitution, instruction and authority in this world, living and active – sharper than any two-edged sword and providing for us a map and compass to successfully traverse and conquer the wilderness of life before us. The validation of this Truth was accomplished when God reached out to mankind through the offering of His Son, Jesus. In Him, we now have our identity and hope. Name above every name. Lord of all that is or ever will be. I no longer live, but Christ lives within me. GALATIANS 2:20

Third – choosing to be led and controlled by the Holy Spirit – God with us – Emmanuel, dwelling in the soul of each one who surrenders to His Lordship, living as a fully devoted follower of Christ.

Fourth – Choosing joy, hope and peace. Practicing the Presence of Jesus Christ in my life daily. Knowing that greater is He that is within me, than he that is within the world. Knowing that it is Satan who comes to kill, steal and destroy life, but Jesus has come that we might have life and have it in abundance. I will choose the eternal over the temporary. I will face the day knowing no weapon formed against me can prosper. I pledge and devote myself to honor the One who sacrificed Himself for me in the choices I make and the words I speak. Life and death is in the power of the tongue, it is the rudder of our vessel. Each day from this moment forward, I shall choose to declare blessing over cursing, faith over fear, joy over depression and peace over panic. My greatest responsibility is acknowledging everything I need to live life with eternal purpose, has been provided by God Himself. I am accountable to make the daily choice to access that provision.

REGARDLESS OF CIRCUMSTANCES, EACH MAN LIVES IN A WORLD OF HIS OWN MAKING.
JOSEPHA MURRAY EMMS

Jesus talked about our greatest and most challenging dysfunctions are brought on by how we think and behave:

Then Jesus called to the crowd to come and hear. "All of you listen," he said, "and try to understand. You are not defiled by what you eat; you are defiled by what you say and do! It is your thought-life that defiles you."
MARK 7

"Words can never adequately convey the incredible impact of our attitude toward life. The longer I live the more convinced I become that life is 10 percent what happens to us and 90 percent how we respond to it."
CHARLES SWINDOLL

"Our best friends and our worst enemies are our thoughts. A thought can do us more good than a doctor, a banker, or a faithful friend. It can also do us more harm than a brick"
FRANK CRANE

Overcoming depression begins with how we choose to respond to the challenges of life with our thoughts and words. Thoughts are powerful, yet those thoughts become multiplied in intensity many times over when your spirit hears yourself verbalizing them. Case in point, I mumbled defeat and death over my life constantly for years and it took me down. I now choose to confess what the Word of God says about me. I am more than a conqueror and seated in heavenly places with Christ Jesus. I can and will be strong and very courageous. I will not be afraid or discouraged, for the Lord God of Heaven, Creator of the universe, is with me. He will never leave me or forsake me.

We must no longer separate our spiritual lives and our mental health. Those two issues are, in fact, tied together with a very short string. The Bible says we have been given the mind of Christ and according to all I have seen, if I have the same mind that envisioned and created the Tetons, the Milky Way, gravity and the amazing miracle of a newborn baby, then why would I ever dismiss the importance of who and what God says I am and can do with regard to my daily life and the challenges it may bring.

When David faced the giant Goliath, he displayed the courage and confidence the armies of Israel had totally abandoned. They cowered in fear in the shadow of the giant, mumbling only of their imminent defeat, enslavement or even death. What made the difference was David's mental and verbal approach. He knew the God he served had protected him in times past from danger and in life-threatening situations, He had every confidence this moment would be no different and even declared it to be so in the very presence and face of his adversary.

Moments later, the laughter and dismissive rant of David's arrogant foe, was followed by the earth-shaking thud of Goliath's lifeless frame falling in defeat before him, one smooth stone strategically implanted in the giant's forehead. His choice to believe God in a moment of intense challenge, and his subsequent actions rooted in that belief - forever altered the history and destiny of Israel. It was the defining moment for a shepherd boy anointed to be king.

The trail David left for us to follow has been retraced millions of times over thousands of years, bolstering courage in the hearts and minds of people of faith. In that moment, he had no idea the path he chose would impact the journey of so many people thru centuries to come.

> *"One ought never to turn one's back on a threatened danger and try to run away from it. If you do that, you will double the danger. But if you meet it promptly and without flinching, you will reduce the danger by half. Never run away from anything! Never!"*
> WINSTON CHURCHILL

I ran away. Without question, that is an embarrassingly difficult thing to admit.

I allowed the enemy of my soul to lull me to sleep, defeated and curled up in the trenches. I forgot who I was and to whom I belonged. One minute I was a witness to miracles, the next I was hiding in a cave from my partners. I was, however, in very good company. Becoming a victim of battle fatigue can render a mountain lion as useless as a burnt cat.

The mass of humanity will surrender freedom long before arrows take flight or the first shot is fired. People live in bondage, captive to their own fear and weariness. Emotionally and spiritually broken, we come to a standstill, no longer to be engaged in battle or opening adventurous trails. When Goliath stands before us shouting obscenities, many will cower in the shadows of the hillside. Running away from the challenge causes us to become the very things we most feared, useless and irrelevant.

It is as Winston Churchill so distinctly stated; *"To run away doubles the danger."*

I came as close as possible to leaving a legacy of self-destruction for my kids to have to deal with for the remainder of their lives, wondering why their Dad would ever choose a path that would abandon them to unresolvable pain. Words are futile in describing my gratitude for their forgiveness and healing love. I am the recipient of a very great grace of a God who reached into my mess and rescued me, answering the faithful prayers of my precious wife and soul mate, Nancy. Her prayers are the reason I am able to sit at this computer tonight.

I love the writings of Erwin Raphael McManus, leader of the Mosaic Community of Faith in Los Angeles. Check this out:

> *"God uses the challenges we face to shape the character within us. Power without humility is a bad combination. Wealth without generosity is equally dangerous. Freedom without faith and faithfulness will lead only to corruption and death. We are our own worst enemies when our hearts are left unattended. The fragmentation of everyday people has moved us to a point of devastation. The belief that people can actually live healthy and whole lives has almost lost its merit. Even churches are over-whelmed by the pain and brokenness they face in their communities. From clergy to psychotherapists, we are a society struggling to discover how to help people get better."*

ERWIN RAPHAEL MCMANUS

SEIZING YOUR DIVINE MOMENT – THOMAS NELSON, INC. NASHVILLE, TENNESSEE - 2002

What trails are you blazing? What will you leave behind impacting all those who follow in your footsteps? The choices are many in a wilderness that lies vast before you. There is a popular, well-worn route that is broad and leads to ultimate destruction. The Bible clearly decries many there will be continually choosing the path of the masses. Without question, the siren call of popular culture continues to move victims onto the road of least resistance.

There remains a distinct alternative. The promise of the road less traveled, a narrow path leading to abundant adventure and freedom. Few there will be who find it. For those who do, the benefits will prove to be worth the risk. Follow the ultimate Trailblazer who has successfully opened the passage to eternal hope and freedom.

IN 2006, I WOKE UP...

Dead to the old me and alive to the life of Christ breathed into me anew. I will never go back, anymore than a butterfly returns to the cocoon to reemerge a caterpillar. I am the living breathing textbook definition of a new creation. The old has past and all things have become new. I pray this text has been an encouragement in your personal journey, or may help in assisting someone near you suffering the torment of depression.

I will leave you with this – the lyrics of yet another song I composed for a production slated for the stage in Jackson Hole. Jedediah Smith was a mountain man and explorer of the Rocky Mountains and the North American West. He left the legacy of strong character, immense courage and a great conviction of faith. As a trailblazer, Smith is known as the American whose explorations led to the use of the 20-mile wide South Pass as the dominant point of crossing the Continental Divide for pioneers on the Oregon Trail.

His life...and my personal journey...are combined within the lyric of this song.

THE TRAILS WE LEAVE BEHIND

MUSIC & LYRICS BY EDDIE ANDERS – EDDIE'S HEART & SOUL COMMUNICATIONS - LOS ANGELES, CALIFORNIA 2016 - ALL RIGHTS RESERVED

All my life – I've been looking for
Whatever lies beyond the next horizon
That perfect place - eludes me still
But in my heart I just know someday I'll find it
The way is sometimes clear - it can be hard
Winding thru the hills to meadows green
Sometimes it's thru the deserts bleak and dry
Before we find the valley of our dreams

Every man leaves a trail behind
It reveals the path of life he chose to follow
May the tracks I leave lead all who follow me
To a life that's more than what mere eyes can see
As I blaze a trail across this hallowed ground
May I discover all of life that can be found

Every man leaves a trail
May I leave a path that's true for those who follow
I want to help them find their way thru the dangers to their dreams
To that brand new world that seems just out of reach
But it's just a prayer away
A simple prayer away

All my life – I've been looking for
Whatever lies beyond the next horizon
Now i I've learned it's not in the perfect place I'll find
But it's the life I lead and the trails I leave behind
Heaven touch the lives of the pilgrims who will find
The trails I leave behind.

Heaven bless the lives of pilgrims who find
The trails I leave behind

May God, grant you great favor and grace on your journey of faith. Peace and countless blessings.

Eddie Anders
SUMMER 2016

Morgan James
Speakers Group

↗ www.TheMorganJamesSpeakersGroup.com

We connect Morgan James published authors with live and online events and audiences whom will benefit from their expertise.

Morgan James makes all of our titles available
through the Library for All Charity Organization.

www.LibraryForAll.org

Printed in the USA
CPSIA information can be obtained
at www.ICGtesting.com
JSHW022219140824
68134JS00018B/1152